Business Administration

Third Edition

ARLENE DOUGLAS

GILL & MACMILLAN

Gill & Macmillan Ltd
Hume Avenue
Park West
Dublin 12
with associated companies throughout the world
www.gillmacmillan.ie

© Arlene Douglas 1999, 2003, 2008

978 07171 4194 4

Print origination in Ireland by Carole Lynch

*The paper used in this book is made from the wood pulp of managed forests.
For every tree felled, at least one tree is planted, thereby
renewing natural resources.*

A CIP catalogue record is available for this book
from the British Library

This book is dedicated to my parents Sheila and Oliver, to my husband Jim, to my sons Ciarán, Séamus and Colm and to my twin girls Dearbhla and Róisín.

I wish to sincerely thank all the organisations and individuals that contributed information to this book, in particular the Independent Newspaper Group and the Sunday Tribune.

Contents

Preface

What is Business Administration?

Business administration involves managing the performance of an organisation and adapting to change. Organisations nowadays emphasise the importance of 'Lateral Co-ordination'. This means that managers need to know how their organisation works and many elements across the whole organisation are integrated, for example in marketing, finance and people (i.e. staff). This understanding, as well as a willingness to compromise, will help managers manage teams, projects and departments.

Business Administration includes the effective and efficient handling of challenges: managers and administrators are now required to respond quickly and flexibly to rapidly changing markets and environments.

What is Retail Administration?

Retail Administration equally emphasises 'Lateral Co-ordination', but specifically in the context of the retail environment.

Retailing is defined as the means by which goods and services are provided to consumers in exchange for payment. Retailing thus excludes wholesaling and business-to-business selling. Retailing can be segmented into three distinct categories:
* predominantly food stores
* predominantly non-food stores
* non-store retailing.

Chapter 7 of this book will focus on current trends in retailing and the retail sector in Ireland.

* This book is designed to help students studying FETAC (formally NCVA) Business & Retail Administration.

* Chapter 1 focuses on the organisation and different organisational structures. Actual company organisational profiles and charts are included in order to back up the detail in the chapter as well as sample questionnaires and examples of SWOT and PEST analyses that will help students research information on organisations of their choice.

- Chapter 2 incorporates details on business controls, calculations of costs and selling prices, breakeven charts and cash flow forecasts.

- Chapter 3 focuses on banking, including online banking methods and ICT technologies in the finance and banking environment, display of business information, currency conversion, information on the euro and insurance analysis.

- Chapter 4 contains details on human resource management and manpower/workforce planning, as well as legal features affecting the employee, and the roles of the Ombudsman.

- Chapter 5 explains how meetings are planned, the protocol connected with them, reasons for them and the usual terminology connected with meetings.

- Chapter 6 details procedures regarding business documentation, checking and matching dockets and documents, spotting overcharges or undercharges, pricing, dealing with queries, preparing documents for dispatch and payments procedures.

- Chapter 7 introduces the reader to features of different types and sizes of retail outlets, legal aspects of retailing with information on RGDATA, the Sale of Goods and Supply of Services Act, aspects of consumer rights, the Consumer Association of Ireland, Consumer Choice and the role of the Director of Consumer Affairs.

NOTE:

- Sample assignments are located at the end of each chapter.
- Practice questions appear at the end of every sub-section within the chapters.
- Student assignments, as appropriate, are given at the end of some chapters.
- Two sample FETAC examination papers for Business Administration and one for Retail Administration appear near the end of the book.

1. The Organisation

Organisational Change and Strategic Decision-making

Forfás, the Irish national policy and advisory board for enterprise, trade, science, technology and innovation, says in its 2006 report on 'The Changing Nature of Manufacturing and Services' that Ireland is now the world's thirteenth largest exporter of services. Employment in services has increased by 21 per cent since 2000 in Ireland, compared with the average international rise of 6 per cent. Now seven out of every ten people work in this expanding sector. Computer services are the most significant export service sector (35 per cent) and others include insurance and financial services (25 per cent of total services exports). Overall the services figure rose from 21 per cent to 34 per cent of Irish exports. International trade has been the key factor in the success of the Irish economy.

Organisations are also relocating some of their activities abroad (referred to as outsourcing), thus benefiting from lower wages and other cost benefits and at the same time gaining access to new markets in Asia, for example. Areas such as research and development (R&D), sales, marketing, product management and technical support remain in Ireland and are developing into the future in Ireland.

Productivity (output produced per person) in manufacturing has become concentrated in only a small number of sectors such as medical devices and chemicals, but the number of jobs in textiles and electrical machinery has fallen. Manufacturing itself has remained strong, bringing in high levels of corporation tax to the exchequer (government), but employment in this sector has fallen, due mainly to the global ICT (Information and Communications Technologies) downturn. Job losses have occurred in the more traditional labour-intensive sectors such as textiles and leather.

Improvements in productivity often mean job losses and now organisations are more focused on supporting the workforce, with managers highlighting the importance of human capital, and providing training in higher-skilled and higher-value activities such as R&D.

Organisational Change Linked to Changes in the Economic Landscape

The rise in services activities is in part a reflection of rising incomes in developed economies, in which consumers tend to spend an increasing proportion of income on services (according to the OECD (the Organisation for Economic Co-operation and Development). We can see how the phenomenal growth of retail parks and the accompanying consumer spending has occurred in Ireland in recent years.

'Towards 2016' is a social partnership agreement (agreed in 2006) between the government, trade unions, employers, farming organisations and the community and voluntary sector, aimed at achieving 'a dynamic internationalised and participatory society and economy, founded on a commitment to social justice and economic development that is both environmentally sustainable and internationally competitive'.

The aim is to implement a life cycle approach to change, dealing with:

- The economy, the environment, infrastructure and social policy.
- Pay, the workplace and employment rights.

This agreement is an attempt to address changes in our work methods, public services and changing work practices. It is also aimed at the greater recognition and the better integration of the non-Irish nationals who are making an important contribution to our economy. The agreement is pivitol to the changing Irish and international economic and organisational landscape of our time. According to IBEC (Irish Business and Employers Confederation), 'we have it in our hand to take the practical measures to win back our competitive edge'. For further information on these issues look at **www.citizensinformation.ie**, **www.forfas.ie** and **www.ibec.ie**.

Organisations in Ireland – Citizens' Information

Organisations that matter to the business community, i.e. large organisations and small and medium enterprises (SMEs), are listed on the Internet. Some examples of state and semi-state organisations that business people look to are the Chambers of Commerce of Ireland, IDA Ireland (Industrial Development Authority), Enterprise Ireland, Shannon Development, Company Registrations Office (the CRO) and the Central Statistics Office (the CSO). Since Ireland became a member of the European Union and changed its currency to the euro, it is of paramount importance that Irish citizens and businesses are familiar with the workings of European organisations. Some of these organisations have a say in or can impact on the operations of businesses within the Irish economy. Examples of such organisations include the European Central Bank, the European Commission, the European Parliament, the European Agency for Safety and Health at Work and the European Ombudsman. A comprehensive listing of European organisations and their Irish connections can be found at the Euro Info Centres website –
www.eic.ie/links.html.

Types of Business Organisation

The main types of business organisation that exist today are:

1. *SOLE PROPRIETOR*: This is an unincorporated (does not have company status) business organisation owned by one person who receives the profits and incurs the liabilities personally.

2. *PARTNERSHIP*: In Ireland, the partnership form tends to be used for professional practice, such as solicitors or accountants. Partnerships are normally formed by a partnership deed setting out the agreement and conditions of the partnership. A less common form is the limited partnership, which allows one or more general partners who manage the daily affairs of the business and one or more limited partners who provide a fixed capital investment with financial liability limited to the capital investment.

3. *COMPANIES*: These fall into two categories:

PUBLIC LIMITED COMPANY

This is the main form of incorporation for firms issuing stocks or bonds, having stockholders, and directors that manage the company. The company is incorporated under a Memorandum of Association and Articles of Incorporation, providing the name, share capital, and commercial objectives. There must be seven or more stockholders. There must be a minimum of two directors who manage the daily affairs of the firm and who are usually selected by the shareholders. Annual meetings are required with 21 days advance notice provided. It is also necessary to disclose financial statements and meet statutory requirements for reporting.

PRIVATE LIMITED COMPANIES

The requirements for formation and reporting of private limited companies are generally the same as for the public limited companies. This form is the most popular type of commercial organisation in Ireland – a head office might be located abroad. There must be between two and fifty shareholders, no debentures or shares should be issued to the general public, and there is no minimum level of share capital.

4. *FRIENDLY SOCIETIES*: These are organisations registered with the Financial Regulator (IFSRA) since 2003: before 2003 they were listed with the Registrar of Friendly Societies. They include credit unions, some co-operatives, some water schemes, etc.

5. *STATE BODIES* – trading and non-trading

6. *SEMI-STATE BODIES* – trading and non-trading

7. *CHARITIES*

8. *CARING GROUPS*

Virtual organisations and SMEs fit into one of the types of business organisation listed above – usually private companies or partnerships.

- Virtual organisations such as virtual business schools, online tour operators, and Internet marketing companies, are some of the organisations that predominantly rely on Internet business and are called 'e-businesses'.

- SMEs are small and medium-sized enterprises that entrepreneurs develop when they find a niche in the market (where sufficient market demand exists) and with some state or semi-state help (e.g. IDA grants, funding from City and County Enterprise Boards, or through Business Expansion Schemes, which are offered by financial institutions to help small businesses get up and running or expand). SMEs' interests are represented by the SFA (Small Firms Association), by ISME (Irish Small and Medium Enterprises Association), and by IBEC (Irish Business Employers Confederation) in some cases.
  Note: The organisations mentioned here will be discussed in greater detail later.

What is an Organisation?

Chester Irving Barnard (1886–1961), author of *Functions of the Executive*, an influential book on management, in which Barnard presented a theory of organisation and the functions of executives in organisations. Baranard described an organisation as a 'system of co-operative human activities'. Organising involves the dividing up of tasks, the suitable allocation of these tasks to specialised personnel and the co-ordination and monitoring of the work in hand, to achieve agreed aims and objectives. According to Barnard:

- Everyone should know of the channels of communication.
- Everyone should have access to the formal channels of communication.
- Lines of communication should be as short and direct as possible.

What is the Safety, Health and Welfare at Work Act 2005?

This Act provides for the health and safety of people in the workplace. It is an update on the 1989 Act. It applies to all organisations' employers and employees (including fixed-term and temporary employees) and self-employed people in their workplaces. The Act sets out the rights and obligations of both employers and employees and provides for substantial fines and penalties for breaches of the health and safety legislation.

It contains a list of the following areas for which legal requirements are laid down by the Act:

- Employer's duties.
- Employees' duties.
- Risk assessment and safety statement.
- Protective equipment measures (e.g. for display screen equipment (VDUs)).
- Reporting accidents.

- Health and safety leave (Maternity Protection Act 1994).
- Health and safety and young people.
- Violence in the workplace.
- Bullying (employer and employee code of practice/prevention and resolution of bullying at work).
- Harassment (Employment Equality Acts 1998 and 2004).
- Victimisation.

The Health and Safety Authority (HSA) is responsible for enforcing health and safety at work in Ireland. It provides information to employers, employees and self-employed people on workplace health and safety.

Sole Trader

- This business person is the only owner of the business. Pubs, newsagents, hairdressers, restaurants, painters and decorators, bookshop owners, etc. can all trade as sole traders.
- If he/she wishes to trade under a trade name other than his/her personal name, he/she must register in Dublin Castle under the Registration of Business Names Act 1963 (See **www.irishstatutebook.ie**).
- The Safety, Health and Welfare at Work Act 2005 places responsibilities on all traders including the sole trader to ensure the health and safety of people at work and of the public affected by work activities. He/she must put into place appropriate safety measures, having carried out a safety evaluation of the risks involved and potential hazards to health and safety. A safety programme must be written down in the form of a Safety Statement.
- He/she must keep the books of the business in order and submit monthly and end of year tax returns and must only register for VAT if certain annual limits are exceeded.
- **Advantages of being a sole trader**
  (a) Speedy decision-making: no consultation required.
  (b) No profit-sharing.
  (c) Flexible hours.
  (d) No industrial relations problems.
  (e) Customer-friendly personal service ensures consumer loyalty.
  (f) Suits family-run business.
- **Disadvantages of being a sole trader**
  (a) Unlimited liability: he/she is liable personally for all debts of the business. The business is not a separate legal entity.
  (b) Higher trade prices: since a small business does not buy in bulk as much as a larger one, not as many trade discounts can be gained. This causes a sole

trader's costs to be higher and he/she passes on the cost to the consumer in the form of higher selling prices. Higher prices can cause decreased competitiveness and a loss of sales.
(c) A larger capital requirement is necessary, funded only by the sole trader.
(d) The business dies with the sole trader.
(e) Complete competence in all areas of expertise is required, i.e. versatility, otherwise the business will not survive.
(f) Administration overload can cause tax liabilities (owing money because books of the business are not in order).
- Sources of finance for the sole trader towards start-up:
  (a) Loans from banks and financial institutions.
  (b) Personal savings.
  (c) Hire purchase – getting assets like office equipment on loan.
  (d) Good credit terms – being allowed time by suppliers before purchases must be paid for. (Sources of finance are discussed in detail in Chapter 2.)

Many sole traders evolve into Partnerships or Limited Companies. However, many sole traders prefer to remain with this structure because of full profit-taking and control. It is advisable to have a good accountant to look after finances, tax returns and to implement changes in tax, VAT and employment legislation.

PRACTICE QUESTIONS

1. Briefly explain how the changing nature of manufacturing and services has affected the Irish economy.
2. Summarise the Safety, Health and Welfare at Work Act 2005.
3. Outline *three* advantages of the Sole Trader/Proprietor.
4. Outline *three* disadvantages of the Sole Trader/Proprietor.
5. How does the Registration of Business Names Act 1963 apply to the Sole Trader?
6. Why are Sole Traders' selling prices often higher than those of a larger trader?

Partnership

- This business operates on the basis of a minimum of two persons and a maximum of between twenty and fifty persons, depending on the business concerned.
- The partnership must register under the Registration of Business Names Act 1963 if the partners do not wish to trade under their own personal names.
- The Safety, Health and Welfare at Work Act 2005 applies also to the partnership (as it does to the sole trader).

- The books of the business must be kept in order. (VAT and other taxes must be paid regularly.)
- The partners usually draw up a Deed of Partnership to underpin the conditions of the agreement. Legally, if no written agreement like this is drawn up, the partners are covered under the Partnership Act 1890. Where the agreement is written up by the deed, the contents of the deed will overrule the conditions laid down by the Act.
- The Partnership Act 1890 states in general that profits and losses are to be shared equally. No new admissions are allowed without all the partners' consent. Disputes are settled by majority. Each partner can inspect the books and profits must be calculated before interest is paid to quasi-partners (partners who leave money in the business as a loan – explained below).
- There are four types of partner.
  (a) Active partner: one who participates fully in the running of the business.
  (b) Sleeping partner: one who contributes capital but does not take an active part in the running of the business.
  (c) Quasi-partner: one who retires and leaves his/her money in the business as a loan and is paid interest on the loan once profits have been calculated.
  (d) Limited partner: one whose liability or duty to pay debts is limited to the amount of capital which the partner invested – underpinned by the Limited Partnership Act 1907. With this type of partnership, one general partner with unlimited liability must exist. The Investment Limited Partnership Act 1994 was designed to encourage collective investment in businesses, and was aimed at attracting American investors to the Financial Services Centre in Dublin by providing them with a certain degree of financial protection.
- Unlimited liability means the partner/s, i.e. general partners, would have to cover their business debts by dipping into their own private funds if company monies could not meet the debt. One general partner might have to cover another general partner's debt because the partners are jointly and severally liable. The business is not a separate legal entity from the persons who own it and the partners are not protected by limited liability in a general partnership. Unlimited partnerships are risky and require a high level of trust to operate efficiently and survive.
- On the dissolution of a partnership due to the death, bankruptcy or retirement of a partner, or due to the partnership's completion (job finished), expiry time (which would be outlined in the deed), or court order to dissolve due to illegal activities, the procedure to dissolve is as follows:
  (a) All assets are re-valued and sold (i.e. the realisation of the assets – liquidated – converted to cash).
  (b) Creditors are paid off.
  (c) Quasi-partners' loans are paid off.
  (d) Capital is repaid to the partners.
  (e) If there is any profit left over on the sale of the assets, it is divided according

to profit-sharing ratios of partners. The dead partner's beneficiaries receive his portion.

(f) Beneficiaries have the option of becoming sleeping partners (leaving the money in the business, allowing it to continue to operate) or quasi-partners (leaving the money in the business as a loan where interest will be paid to them).

- **Advantages of a partnership:**
  (a) Greater capital: greater possibility of expansion.
  (b) Greater specialisation – range of talents and expertise leads to improved productivity, speed and efficiency.
  (c) Division of liability (sharing the debts).
  (d) Consultation regarding decision-making.
  (e) Accounts not published, so privacy maintained regarding transactions.
  (f) Smaller-scale partnership arrangements benefit from the ability to give personal service and gain consumer loyalty as a result, e.g. hairdressers, window companies.

- **Disadvantages of a partnership:**
  (a) Unlimited liability (except in the case of limited partners): debts of company may have to be covered by dipping into personal funds.
  (b) The business is not a separate legal entity from the owners: owners can be sued personally for non-payment of debts.
  (c) Differences of opinion can cause inefficiencies.
  (d) Sharing of profits.
  (e) The death of a partner means the automatic dissolution of the partnership.
  (f) New partners cannot join without full agreement of all partners. This could deprive the business of new capital input.

- Examples of partnerships:
  Doctors, solicitors, accountants, dentists, architects and many other regular businesses that trade either under their personal names or a trade name (in which case they must register under the Registration of Business Names Act 1963 in Dublin Castle).

- An example of limited partnerships that have grown is the amalgamation of the two largest accountancy bodies in the world, Coopers and Lybrand and Price Waterhouse, thus making a group of very powerful accountants.

PRACTICE QUESTIONS

1. Explain the differences between Active, Sleeping, and Quasi-partners.
2. What is the purpose of the Partnership Act 1890?
3. What is Unlimited Liability?
4. What is meant by 'The business is not a separate legal entity'?
5. Why would a Partnership dissolve?
6. What is the meaning of specialisation and how does it benefit a Partnership?
7. When a partner dies, explain the procedure that follows.

8. Outline *three* advantages of a Partnership.
9. Outline *three* disadvantages of a Partnership.

Companies

There are six main types of company:

1. State bodies: those totally funded by the government/state, e.g. the Army.
2. Semi-state bodies: those that are part funded by the government (public sector) and part funded by the private sector (firms and companies), e.g. the Electricity Supply Board (ESB).

State and semi-state bodies can be sub-categorised into trading and non-trading organisations as follows:

TRADING BODIES

Those which offer a service that you pay for.

Semi-state body examples are the Irish transport body CIE (Córas Iompar Éireann) (divided in three – Irish Rail (Iarnród Éireann), Bus Éireann (suburban) and Dublin Bus (city) transportation), ESB, Aer Lingus, Aer Rianta, and Bord na Móna (turf). An example of a state body is the Health Services Executive (HSE). Public hospitals are under the control of the HSE and public patients and out-patients have to pay for services.

Some essential services would be loss-making services and are semi-state for this reason. The government subsidises CIE for unprofitable routes in order to provide a full service to the public.

NON-TRADING BODIES

A semi-state body like the IDA (Industrial Development Authority), which looks after new and existing investment in Ireland, is a non-trading body providing important grants and incentives for any new iniatives. State bodies like the Army, Garda Síochána and the Blood Bank are non-trading bodies because they do not trade in goods or services for any fees, but they provide a free service to the public.

3. Unlimited companies: unlike partnerships, must register under the Companies Act 1983 but, similar to partnerships, do not enjoy the benefits of limited liability. Capital is provided by shareholders. Each individual amount is called a share.
4. Companies limited by guarantee: usually non-profit making like clubs registered under the Companies Act 1983 and liability is limited to the amount each individual member invests if the company gets into financial difficulty.

5. Private Limited Company: any business that applies to the CRO (Central Registrations Office) in order to gain limited liability and can place Ltd after the company name. Greater financial security is gained as the business is now a separate legal entity from the people that own it. Debts of the business are cleared by the business and money is not taken out of the owners' personal funds. The business, however, might be subject to Corporation Tax.

6. Public Limited Company: any well-established private limited company that has a good business track record and decides to float the shares of the business on the Stock Exchange, offering them to the public, and gaining a trading certificate allowing the business to place plc after their company name. The business is now a public company. More money or capital can be generated by going public through share capital. The company accounts have to be published and profit-sharing increases.

What is the CRO?

The Companies Registration Office is the statutory authority for registering new companies in the Republic of Ireland. It also deals with the registration of post-incorporation documents and ensures the enforcement of the Companies Acts (1963–2006) and companies' filing obligations.

The CRO (www.cro.ie) is where business people or the public in general can locate public statutory (or legal) information on Irish companies. Business people are also legally required to register with the CRO before commencing trading. The CRO operates under the rules of the Department of Enterprise, Trade and Employment.

Its website (search facility available) includes details of:
- The Register of Companies.
- Business names.
- Registered/disqualified persons.

The main functions of the CRO are:
- The incorporation of companies and the registration of business names.
- The receipt and registration of post-incorporation documents (after a business has been given company status).
- The enforcement of the Companies Acts in relation to the companies' filing obligations.
- Making information available to the public.

The CRO's website has been referred to as the main Irish companies' online registration environment.

There are three ways to register a business name, or a change made to a business name, with the CRO. You can register as:
- an individual (Form RBN1)
- a partnership (Form RBN1A)
- a body corporate (Form RBN1B).

(Forms can be downloaded from the CRO website, **www.cro.ie**.)

Formation of a Private Limited Company

(Converting from a Sole Trader, Partnership or Unlimited Company to a Private Limited Company)

You must decide on a company name. Look up the 'Frequently used numbers' section of the phone directory and find the Companies Registration Office – telephone (01) 804 5200. You must check with the office that the company name you have decided on is not already in use and you must get three forms:

1. An A1 form will be sent to you on request by the Companies Registration Office, more formally known as the Registrar of Joint Stock Companies.
2. A 'Memorandum of Association' form.
3. An 'Articles of Association' form.

   Both the memorandum and articles are in booklet form and must be purchased from a law stationery office. Look up 'Stationery Offices' in the phone book.

PROCEDURE

1. When the legal documents have been drawn up by yourself or by a solicitor (Solicitor's Act 1954) they must be lodged with the Registrar of Joint Stock Companies. They are:
   (a) Memorandum of Association: containing information on the name and objectives of the company, a statement verifying that the company has limited liability, two signatures which are witnessed verifying the formation of the company, and the location of the registered legal office where all the legal documents are sent.
   (b) Articles of Association: containing the list of internal rules and regulations connected with the company such as voting rights, powers and duties of directors, and procedures regarding meetings.
   (c) A formal declaration of compliance with the Companies Act 1983.
   (d) A statement denoting the amount of Authorised or Nominal Share Capital of the company.
2. The documents are inspected by the Registrar and must comply with the Companies Act 1983.
3. When the documents are verified, the Registrar issues a 'Certificate of Incorporation', the birth certificate of a limited company.
4. The company can now commence business with the protection of limited liability and can place Ltd after its company name.
   Note: Limited liability indicates that the company is a legal entity separate from the owners. Regarding debts of the company, the company is sued, not the owners. Refer to **www.cro.ie** for further information.

Formation of a Public Limited Company

(Converting from a Private Limited Company to a Public Limited Company)

The Companies Registration Office must be contacted (telephone (01) 804 5200) to clarify the requirements regarding capital turnover and size of business.

1. The company wishing to become public must satisfy the following conditions:
   (a) have a stated minimum authorised capital of which at least a quarter must be offered to the public.
   (b) have a minimum market value.
   (c) have a minimum number of shareholders.
   (d) have a healthy track record – positive working capital.
   (e) have a minimum profit level.
   (f) accept full disclosure on its operations – salaries, profits and strategies. This is the reason why some businesses are reluctant to go public.
2. The legal documents that must be lodged with the Registrar of Joint Stock Companies are:
   (a) Memorandum of Association – with at least seven signatures verifying the authenticity of the memo, as well as the other contents of the memo mentioned previously.
   (b) Articles of Association – contents mentioned previously.
   (c) A formal declaration of compliance with the Companies Act 1983.
   (d) A statement denoting the amount of authorised or nominal share capital of the company.
   (e) A list of agreed directors.
   (f) Directors' written consent to become directors.
3. Company makes application to Stock Exchange Council through a stockbroker where shares are quoted.
4. The company employs a merchant banker, and the stockbroker and the merchant banker together inspect the books of the company:
   (a) to verify that the books meet the Stock Exchange Council's requirements regarding the financial state of the company.
   (b) to verify the healthy future prospects of the company.
5. When the Stock Exchange Council accepts the company's application to trade on the Stock Exchange, the Registrar of Companies issues the company with a trading certificate.

TRADING CERTIFICATE

A public limited company must not commence business or exercise any borrowing powers until the trading certificate entitling it to commence business has been issued by the Companies Registration Office (CRO). Before such a certificate can be issued, the company must file *Form 70* in accordance with section 6 of the Companies (Amendment) Act 1983.

6. Before shares are quoted on the Stock Exchange, the company must produce a prospectus after receiving the trading certificate (the birth cert. of the public limited company).

PROSPECTUS

The word 'Prospectus' is defined in the Act as 'any prospectus, notice, circular, advertisement or other invitation, offering to the public for subscription or purchase any shares or debentures of a company'.

An offer to existing holders of shares or debentures is also regarded as coming within the scope of this definition.

7. Once the Trading Certificate has been received and the Prospectus has been organised, the company can now commence trading on the Stock Exchange, quoting the shares of the company, and can place plc after its trade name. Refer to **www. cro.ie** for further information.

Company Law

Irish company law is mainly laid down by the Companies Acts 1963–90. In addition, there is the Company Law Enforcement Act 2003, which aims to strengthen supervision and business compliance with some parts of company law. It was framed in response to a number of incidences of company fraud and malpractice that had been identified in the early years of the twenty-first century.

Areas that needed particular attention included:

- The appointment of a Director of Corporate Enforcement, to head a new multi-disciplinary agency to enforce company law, and to conduct investigations and prosecutions.
- More rigorous enforcement of the rules on filing annual returns and provision for 'on-the-spot' fines for late returns.
- Court powers, on the application of the Director, to order individual companies to comply with company law.
- Extended powers for the court to impose restrictions and disqualifications on individuals acting as directors.
- Costs of most investigations, prosecutions and court proceedings imposed on delinquent companies.
- New obligations on auditors to report suspected breaches of the Companies Acts by client companies.

In 2005 the then Minister for Trade and Commerce Michael Ahern gave the go-ahead for the new Investment Funds, Companies and Miscellaneous Provisions Act 2006. This Act allows a company to authorise a person to be its Electronic Filing Agent to simplify filing and doing business with the CRO.

Changes have also been introduced by the European Communities (Companies) (Amendment) Regulations 2007 Act with regard to new disclosure requirements of company information on websites and electronic communications. It is now mandatory to include the following information on all websites, electronic order forms and emails:

- Name of the company and its legal form.
- Place of registration of the company, the company number and its registered office.
- In the case of a company exempt from the obligation to use the word 'limited' or 'teoranta', the fact that it is a limited company.
- In the case of a company being wound up, the fact that this is so.
- If there is a reference to share capital of the company, the reference should be to paid-up share capital.

If a company has a website, it must display this information in a prominent and easily accessible place on the site.

(Source:**www.lowtax.net**.)

Changes to Private Limited Company formation

In 2007 the Company Law Review Group suggested that Irish company law be consolidated into one Act, the Companies Consolidation Act 2008. This law is intended to change the profile of a private limited company from its current form.

The main changes are:

- The current memorandum and articles of association will be replaced by a single document.
- Companies will be allowed to have just one director and a company secretary instead of the previous requirement to have a minimum of two directors. The director and secretary must be different individuals.
- Clauses will be introduced so that companies' obligations to other parties are more copper-fastened and companies cannot any longer evade these obligations by using loopholes in company law.

Other Categories of Company

Other categories of company that are covered by the Companies Act) include:

- Private Company Limited by Shares (private shares, 50 members only, no shares transfer).
- Non-resident Company. (The Finance Act 1999 rendered all incorporated companies resident in Ireland, with some offshore exceptions: now it is not as easy to benefit unfairly from favourable taxation conditions if you are a non-resident.)
- Public Company Limited by Shares (minimum seven members, maximum capital of €38,092).
- Company Limited by Guarantee (used for charitable and non-profit-making purposes such as a local community membership raising funds for buildings or facilities).
- Branch of Overseas Company (same CRO registration rules apply, with an authorised representative in Ireland).

- General Partnership (under Partnership Act 1890): partners are individually liable for debts of company.
- Limited Partnership (under Limited Partnership Act 1907): one or more general partners with unlimited liability and one or more limited partners where their liability or debt responsibility is limited to the amount they contributed to the business.
- Investment Limited Partnership (ILP) (under the Investment Limited Partnership Act 1994) allows collective investors to obtain double tax relief, which is unavailable to unit trust investors. The minimum share capital is €127,000 and at least two directors must be Irish. Partners must be approved by the Central Bank and monthly accounts must be submitted to the Central Bank.

What is a Public Private Partnership?

A Public Private Partnership (PPP) is a partnership between the public and private sector for the purpose of delivering a project or service traditionally to do with infrastructure, e.g. public road construction, school buildings, water treatment projects, etc. This type of partnership involves a public authority (such as a government department) delegating to a private organisation the responsibility for financing, executing and maintaining a project in return for the right to operate the facility for an extended period. This enables its investment to be amortised, that is, the private sector takes the financial risk.

Sample projects are listed on **www.ppp.gov.ie**.

Note: Irish Legal Acts referred to above and other Acts not referred to here are available as hard copy from the Department of Enterprise, Trade and Employment website (**www.entemp.ie**, under Company Law Financial Services Publications) or from the Government Publications Office, Molesworth Street, Dublin. Company Acts are also available to download from **www.cro.ie/en/downloads**.

What is the Financial Regulator?

The financial regulator (or the Irish Financial Services Regulatory Authority, IFSRA) is the single regulator of all financial institutions in the Republic of Ireland. Its powers are outlined in the Central Bank and Financial Services Authority of Ireland Act 2003, Section 26.

IFSRA was established in May 2003 and is a distinct element of the Central Bank and Financial Services Authority of Ireland. It has clearly defined regulatory responsibilities that cover all Irish financial institutions, including those that were previously regulated by the Central Bank of Ireland, the Department of Enterprise, Trade and Employment (DETE), Office of the Director of Consumer Affairs (ODCA) and the Registrar of Friendly Societies. The regulator has a major role in the protection of the consumer.

In 2005, IFSRA called itself the Financial Regulator, rather than its formal legal name, for simplicity. Businesses and financial institutions now include the information, 'This institution is regulated by the Irish Financial Services Regulatory Authority', in their media advertisements as a matter of course.

Friendly Societies

A friendly society was traditionally one that had an essentially community-based ethos and was a not-for-profit type of organisation. From the mid-1800s until 2003, the Registrar of Friendly Societies was the body that had statutory responsibility for the registration and general regulation of Friendly Societies, Trade Unions (social economy enterprises), Industrial and Provident Societies (mainly Co-operatives), Building Societies, and (from the 1960s) Credit Unions.

The government decision to set up the Financial Regulator (IFSRA) meant that responsibility for the regulation of these friendly societies passed to IFSRA.

The last (2004) report of the Registrar of Friendly Societies is available from the DETE website **www.entemp.ie**.

These societies are categorised in the Report of the Registrar of Friendly Societies 1994–1996 as follows:
1. Industrial and Provident Societies
2. Credit Unions
3. Friendly Societies registered under the Friendly Societies Acts.
4. Some trade unions.

1. Industrial and Provident Societies
These are divided in the following way:
Dairy societies, livestock breeding societies, meat-processing societies, livestock marketing societies, horticultural societies, egg and poultry societies, fishing societies, public utility societies. (Group water schemes and housing development are separate categories.)

Examples are Thurles Co-operative Creamery Ltd, Waterford Co-operative Society Ltd, Clover Meats Ltd, Donegal Potatoes Ltd, Goldenvale Co-operative Mart Ltd, Monaghan Poultry Growers Co-operative Society, Cappagh Group Water Scheme Society Ltd, Carlow Town Housing Co-operative Society Ltd, Clondalkin Community Enterprise Co-operative Society Ltd, and many others.

Most of the above-named industrial and provident societies are co-operative societies and have a co-operative organisational structure. The history of the co-op movement laid the foundation for the type of structures that exist today.

The co-operative movement had its origins in an English town in Lancashire called Rochdale. The father of the co-operative movement was a Welshman, Robert Owen (1771–1858). He gathered together a number of colleagues who called themselves the Rochdale Pioneers and they drew up a set of rules called the Rochdale Principles which still govern the thinking and conduct of co-operatives:

1. Open membership – anyone can join.
2. Democratic rule – one vote per person.
3. Limited return on capital.
4. Surplus profit to be distributed according to number of purchases.
5. No credit – cash sales only.
6. Some profit is set aside for educational purposes.
7. Neutral on political and religious issues.

Characteristics of the Co-operative

1. Must register under the Industrial and Provident Societies Act 1893–1978 with the Registrar of Friendly Societies and if they convert to companies they must conform to the Companies Act 1990.
2. Can be formed by eight or more people.
3. One person, one vote, irrespective of number of shares held.
4. A member may not own more than an agreed number of shares.
5. As more capital is acquired, no further authorised share capital can be issued.
6. Shares are non-transferable and a member must sell back shares to the co-op and they are withdrawn.
7. Surplus on profits is distributed to members in proportion to their holding. Some is used for educational purposes.

Retail co-operatives, producer co-operatives and worker co-operatives exist; however, the co-operative movement has undergone dramatic change in recent years and must now compete to survive. Many have become public companies, having successfully adjusted to the competitive position required in the business world today. Examples of plcs like this are Kerry Group plc and Avonmore Waterford plc (who merged in September 1997 to form Glanbia). Activities like milk processing, dairy produce trading, pig farming and meat processing are carried on by the Kerry Group. Talks of mergers or take-overs of any remaining suitable co-ops have been common in recent times due to the benefits attached to this type of venture:

1. Extra finance from share issues.
2. Top-class management improving efficiency and productivity.
3. Benefits attached to large-scale operations (economies of scale). Examples of economies or benefits are bulk buying with large discounts, lower advertising costs per unit output, and top-class specialised workers.

Retail Co-operatives

Some co-operatives, such as Thurles Co-operative Creamery Ltd, have a retail outlet (shop attached to the co-op). In this they sell fresh produce as well as a range of household items to the public. Retail co-operatives like this are listed in the Registry of Friendly Societies under 'Industrial and Provident Societies – Dairy Section'. Other co-operatives, such as knitwear co-ops, can also have shops attached to them. They are listed under the 'Other Productive Societies' section of the same publication.

What is a Credit Union?

A Credit Union is an organisation of people, for people. It exists only to serve its members, not to profit from their needs. History has shown that people can achieve far more through co-operation and working together than by individual effort. Credit Unions have ingrained this philosophy in their operations. They are are non-sectarian and non-political, and continue that Irish tradition of co-operative self-help.

Credit Union Operating Principles are founded based on the philosophy of co-operation, equality, equity (fairness), and mutual self-help. They are:

* Open and voluntary membership.
* Democratic control (one member one vote).
* Limited dividends on equity capital.
* Return of surplus to members.
* Non-discrimination in race, religion and politics.
* Services to members.
* Ongoing education (promoting the education of members, officers and employees).
* Co-operation among co-operatives (serving the best interests of members at local, national and international level).
* Social responsibility (extending services to those who need them; abiding by the interests of the broader community).

There are over three million members in Ireland and savings amount to approximately €12.6m. There are over 9200 active volunteers involved in the movement and over 3500 people are employed in Credit Unions in Ireland.

What is a 'Credit Union Chapter'?

Each Credit Union was traditionally a member of a particular Chapter (or geographical grouping), e.g. the Tipperary Chapter or the Limerick City Chapter. These chapters acted as a forum for the exchange of information, shared promotion and training programmes. There are 25 chapters with Chapter Liaison Officers in charge of each individual chapter.

Credit Unions in the Republic of Ireland are now regulated by the Financial Regulator (IFSRA) and Credit Unions in Northern Ireland are regulated by their Registry of Credit Unions and Industrial and Provident Societies.

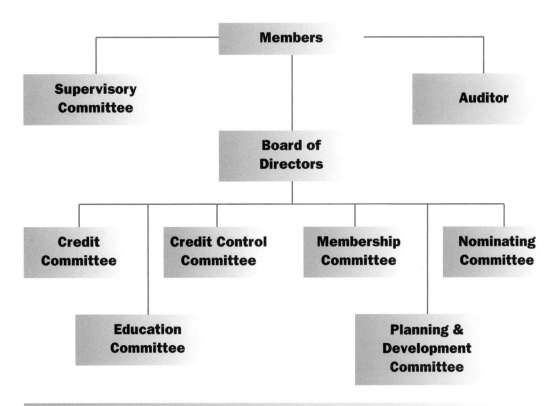

Figure 1.1 The Organisational Structure of the Credit Union

The members of a credit union elect a board of directors at its AGM (Annual General Meeting). The board is responsible for the control, direction and management of the affairs, funds and records of the credit union. Only credit union members are eligible for election to the credit union board and its committees. It is important, therefore, that members attend their AGM.

The Irish League of Credit Unions (ILCU) is the umbrella body for all credit unions in Ireland. It was set up in 1960 to represent and service affiliated credit unions on the island of Ireland. It now represents the interests of over 530 credit unions in Ireland.

Its main functions are to:
1. Promote the ideas and ethos (community-based) of credit unions.
2. Represent affiliated credit unions with government, the EU and other agencies.
3. Provide central services to credit unions.

The **Savings Protection Scheme Fund** protects the savings of individual members by making sure that the credit unions are financially and administratively sound and by providing remedial help to any credit union that shows signs of weakness in these areas. The savings of individual credit union members are protected up to a maximum of €12,700.

Credit Union services include:

- savings
- loans
- insurance
- ATM/EFT facilities
- money transfer
- foreign exchange.

Joining a Credit Union

Joining your local credit union is easy: all you do is apply for membership. To be a member there may be an entrance fee of not more than €1/£1stg and you will need to hold minimum savings of between one and ten shares. After this members can continue saving regularly – even small amounts – which encourages the saving habit.

Benefits of membership

Members of credit unions enjoy many benefits associated with membership, including:

- Control over members' own finances.
- Encouragement and advice on a regular savings programme.
- Loan availability at relatively low rates of interest that remain consistent even during times of economic turbulence.
- Security of savings through the credit unions fidelity bond and through the Irish League of Credit Unions Saving Protection Scheme.
- Loan Protection and Life Savings Insurance at no direct cost to the eligible member.
- The knowledge that their own savings are being used in their own community.
- All officials of credit unions, whether volunteers or staff, must be fidelity bonded.
- Under the rules of a member's credit union, confidentially is protected.
- The savings of eligible members are insured through Life Savings Insurance.
- Full financial statements are prepared and can be examined by members.
- Annual returns are independently audited and lodged with the relevant regulatory authority.

Savings are used to make loans to members. The interest received from loans and investments is used:

- to pay expenses
- to build up reserves.

The remaining income may be returned to members as a dividend. The rate of dividend can vary from credit union to credit union.

Will Credit Unions Survive?

Jim Aughney

The Irish credit union movement is facing into the most critical period in its 50-year history as a high proportion of its members shun its services in favour of credit card debt, motor loans and leases and electronic payments by debit card.

Credit unions' share of the post-Celtic Tiger credit boom has been falling for years. According to the Credit Union Development Association (CUDA) the market share has fallen from 8.9pc in 2000 to 5.5pc in 2004. We estimate it as being as low as 4.6pc in 2006.

Paradoxically savings built up over many years by the credit unions' 1.7million members means that most credit unions around the country now have loan books.

In all but a handful of cases, income from investments is now greater than fees and interest on loans.

For the vast bulk of credit unions, investment income — placing members' savings with third parties in search of a better rate — is used to meet the operating expense of the credit union.

Credit union savings are sizeable because credit unions operate a policy of increasing savings even while loans are being repaid. Regular saving is the way credit union members build up the collateral to borrow money and

they must continue saving while repaying their loans.

A major threat to credit unions' income is that stricter regulation of investments by the Financial Regulator, Brendan Logue, means that more risky investments have been ruled out and a lower safer return can be expected in future.

While credit unions were advancing loans at a healthy rate, in the 1960s to the 1990s, these savings were virtually gilt-edged as members were using them as collateral for loans. However as the flow of new lending has dried to a trickle, these savings become available for withdrawal by members.

Threat

Large financial institutions like Halifax, Allied Irish Bank and Bank of Ireland now pay around 7pc or more for monthly savings.

Anglo Irish, Irish Nationwide and Northern Rock pay top rate for lump sum deposits. Credit unions are under threat from members who want to beat the 3pc rate being set at the AGM each year.

Despite the fact that credit card debt is often much more expensive than its own rates, credit unions have not been able to sell the value-for-money message to any great extent. Convenience is a growing attraction for most

consumers today who can pick up a loan application at their local Tesco and go online to draw down funds.

Credit unions still require a loan application to a credit committee — a process which normally takes up to one week.

Credit unions' collective inability to sell their loans to consumers has been highlighted by their own Supervisory Committee. In the 2006 annual report the committee said 'the moneylender of old has been replaced by legalised credit sources which charge high interest rates in comparison to credit unions'.

Resources

This is an area where credit unions must focus their resources ensuring that 'good value credit' is available to all in their community. And they warn about the growing trend of advancing business loans: 'The strategy of using business loans to increase the loan book is, in our view, too speculative and credit unions should only engage in this area if the necessary expertise and underwriting skills are available to them' the supervisory committee warns.

The supervisors pointed to a number of factors inhibiting 'growth of lending'. These were the lack of a uniform national interest rate; the inability to provide full financial standards and operating procedures and the lack of a uniform public image.

Brendan Logue, the financial regulator with responsibility for the credit union movement, agrees with the committee's view on business lending.

'In some cases we have asked credit unions to look at their loans portfolios and asked for accounts and focused on loan arrears. In some cases loans have been made for property or business purposes. We would be sensitive to the idea that credit unions don't have the underwriting skills necessary to approve property or business loans,' Mr Logue says.

Some credit unions are seeing arrear mounting up on these property or business loans.

'Security is a key issue. Maybe credit union personnel are not as expert as the banks in this area in securing a first charge or letters of undertaking' Mr Logue says.

The financial regulator is compiling a guidance note for credit union lending which will provide a framework for loan approvals.

'It will cover the question of security and the issue of business lending. Where a loan goes into arrears we want to make sure re-scheduling is not ad hoc. We don't want to see an endless recycling of credit where it's inappropriate' Logue adds.

Bill Hobbs, former chief executive of CUDA, feels that credit unions must change rapidly if they are to compete in the savings and loans market.

'Credit unions have a fantastic brand image and they must be able to offer loans at competitive rates, they must also actively support a national marketing campaign and be willing to take in new people with modern financial and marketing skills,' he says.

The credit union movements in the US, Canada and Poland are competing strongly with banks. The question has been raised within the movement in Ireland whether credit unions should be renamed 'savings and investment unions' and drop the 'credit' tag.

However, this move would cause major disruption to the way credit unions operate. You do not require the same staff facilities or premises to run an investment club as you do to run a credit union.

As the level of lending falls credit unions are faced with trying to meet the expense of maintaining sizeable properties all over Ireland,' Hobbs says.

Unless directors of credit unions can correct the slide quickly, they may have to see the FOR SALE signs over their prized main street premises.

Source: *Irish Independent* 23 August 2007

Charities and Caring Groups

A charity is a not-for-profit organisation that must be constituted and operated exclusively for charitable purposes, e.g. St Vincent de Paul, Trócaire and Concern. It is a basic principle of charity law that an organisation's objects must be expressed in precise rather than broad or vague terms. This identifies it clearly as having a recognised charitable purpose.

There is no legal framework for the registration of charities in Ireland. However, the Office of the Revenue Commissioners, Charities Section maintains a database of organisations to which they have granted charitable tax exemption. A CHY reference number is then allocated to the charity.

Charitable organisations usually take one of three legal forms (as advised to them independently by a solicitor):

1. An unincorporated association with a Constitution or Rules.
2. A charitable trust established by Trust Deed.
3. A company governed by a Memorandum and Articles of Association.

Caring Groups are also not-for-profit organisations that fall under the 'charity' banner, but their services also consist of advice and counselling given by qualified trained volunteers e.g. CURA, the Samaritans and Alcoholics Anonymous. These organisations rely primarily on funding from donations and funds raised through charitable activities and events.

PRACTICE QUESTIONS

1. How do semi-state bodies and state-sponsored bodies differ?
2. Give *one* example *each* of:
    (i) a trading semi-state body
    (ii) a non-trading semi-state body
    (iii) a trading state body
    (iv) a non-trading state body.
3. Define the following:
    (i) Unlimited Company;
    (ii) Company Limited by Guarantee;
    (iii) a Private Limited Company; and
    (iv) a Public Limited Company.
4. What is the CRO?
5. Briefly explain Irish company law by referring to:
    (i) the Companies Act 1963–90
    (ii) the Company Law Enforcement Act 2003
    (iii) the Investment Funds, Companies and Miscellaneous Provisions Act 2006
    (iv) the European Communities (Companies) (Amendment) Regulations 2007 Act.
6. What are the procedures for unlimited companies to become private limited companies?
7. What are the procedures for a private limited company to become public?
8. What is a public private partnership?
9. What is the Financial Regulator?
10. Name *three* types of friendly societies. What characteristics are common to each?
11. What are the main functions of the ILCU?
12. How have co-ops changed in status in recent years?
13. What are the Rochdale Principles?
14. What is a chapter with regard to credit unions?
15. Give a brief account of how credit unions operate.
16. In your opinion, will credit unions survive into the future? Why/why not?
17. How are charities defined?
18. What is a Caring Group?

Features of Different Types of Organisational Structure

Factors Determining Organisational Design

1. **A Formal Organisation:** Functional divisions of labour that are based on the formal lines of authority affect the structure of an organisation.

    An organisation is structured to achieve specific goals with the formal functions of the organisation set out within a well-defined framework. Responsibilities are formally grouped to achieve specific tasks. Job specifications make the individual's position in the organisation clear. There are chains of delegated authority for different levels of decision-making and built-in channels of communication exist. Examples are banks, colleges, advertising agencies, software companies, etc.

2. **An Informal Organisation:** This operates alongside the formal framework, where individuals within the organisation form social groupings and relationships and often use informal methods to get things done. It is flexible and spontaneous and often speeds up the completion of tasks based on informal teamwork. Newcomers sometimes have to 'get accepted' into informal groupings.

THE ORGANISATIONAL HIERARCHY AND ORGANISATIONAL CHART SHAPES (FLAT, TALL)

The lines of authority should be clearly defined in every organisation (i.e. every employee should be able to see clearly to whom he/she is responsible). Since the employee is answerable to somebody he/she is said to be, in the formal sense, a subordinate. The organisational structure is best displayed by constructing an Organisational Chart of the organisation in question. This chart represents a framework within which staff are designated to perform required activities.

The main factors that dictate the shape of such a chart are referred to as the 'Principles of Organisation':

1. Unity of command and unity of purpose: is ensured when employees know who exactly they are answerable to (ideally one person) and no conflicts arise regarding authority.
2. Span of control: generally means one superior at the head of the organisation and a varying number of subordinates. The wider the span, the fewer the levels of authority, the flatter the shape of the organisational chart. A narrow span of control will tend to create a tall structure (see Figure 1.2).
3. Amount of delegation: Delegation means the dividing up of responsibilities and spreading them out among subordinates. A high level of delegation results in a greater number of levels of authority.
4. Size of organisation: A greater division of work, specialisation and delegation is required in a larger organisation. The larger the organisation, the taller the shape

of the chart; and the smaller the organisation, the flatter the shape of the chart.

5. Number and type of employees: The larger the organisation, the greater the labour force, and because of the need for greater departmentation and specialisation, there tends to be a greater number of levels of authority due to the workload and the need for delegation.

The horizontal and vertical dimensions of the pyramids are altered according to the factors listed above.

Question: Which in your opinion is more efficient?

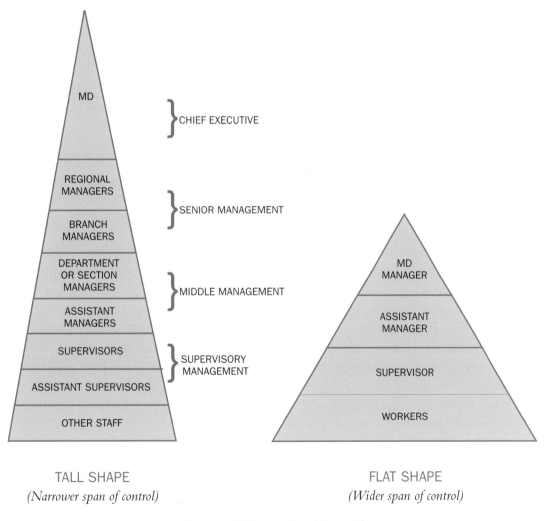

TALL SHAPE
(Narrower span of control)

FLAT SHAPE
(Wider span of control)

Figure 1.2 Organisational Pyramids

Tall Shape

CHARACTERISTICS: larger business with more departmental divisions, specialisation and delegation; greater number and variation of type of employee; work involves more analysis, research and development.

ADVANTAGES:
1. Greater economies of scale (i.e. benefits) due to larger size, e.g. opportunities to specialise and divide up labour, increasing opportunities for improved productivity.
2. Greater efficiency in organisational methods.
3. Greater turnover – can afford to incorporate the most modern technology.

DISADVANTAGES:
1. Greater difficulty with maintaining unity of purpose due to communication problems – too many levels of authority.
2   Less consumer friendly – more informal due to size.
3. Decision-making may be slower due to time it takes to get from top to bottom and vital decisions might be made too late.

Flat Shape

CHARACTERISTICS: smaller business with a small number of employees where work passes through fewer hands – few levels of authority.

ADVANTAGES:
1. Information and decisions pass from top to bottom quickly via fewer levels.
2. Top management are closer to the ground, ensuring efficiency – close and orderly planning and control of work.
3. Greater personal consumer attention and resulting consumer loyalty.

DISADVANTAGES:
1. Less specialisation or division of labour – usually lower wages for lower-level workers.
2. Smaller economies of scale.
3. Lower turnover – restricted ability to invest in expensive modern technology as it may not be cost effective.

PRACTICE QUESTIONS
1. How does a Formal Organisation differ from an Informal Organisation?
2. What is an Organisational Hierarchy and how is it illustrated?
3. What are the differences between a Tall and a Flat Organisational structure?
4. Which do you think is more efficient?
5. What is the meaning of the term 'Specialisation'?
6. How might it affect the shape of the Organisational Chart?

7. What is the meaning of the term 'delegation'?
8. What is the meaning of the term 'subordinate'?

Departments within an Organisation

(Role of Departments in achieving the Objectives of an Organisation)

Nearly every organisation has five main functional areas, to which departments can be linked, depending on the type of enterprise in question. These functional areas are:

1. Technical: including production, manufacture, and adaptation of materials (Production Department).
2. Commercial: including buying, selling and exchange (Purchases and Sales Departments).
3. Financial: activities designed to obtain capital and to make the best use of it (Financial Department).
4. Accounting: including payroll, tax returns, stock-taking and the preparation of balance sheets, cost statements and business statistics (Accounting Department).
5. Managerial activities: dealing with staff incentives and documentation, manpower planning and selection and general administration regarding staff (Personnel Department).

The divisions above would represent departmentation by function – a logical and traditional method which allows the division of work into specialist areas and is especially evident in large organisations. Within each department workers are specifically skilled and are allowed to concentrate on one task or a group of linked tasks. This process is referred to as specialisation or the division of labour. The aim is to increase efficiency and productivity in the organisation. Departmentation involves the clarification and grouping of tasks allotted to groups of people. It allows the organisation to complete targeted tasks that it has set itself.

The various means of departmentation are:

1. by function (functional)
2. by product (product – divisional)
3. by region (geographical or territorial)
4. by a mixture of the above (matrix).

DEPARTMENTATION BY FUNCTION
(with further sub-departmental divisions based on function)

DEPARTMENTATION BY PRODUCT

Managing Director (e.g. large supermarket)

sales	purchases	finance	production	personnel
home export	buying stores	costing records	assembly service	recruitment staff welfare

Figure 1.3 Functional Division of Organisation

Most companies have a mix of products at different stages of their life cycle. A single product might become outdated or unfashionable. Divisional managers might be given responsibility for a product or a brand line of products. This encourages expertise in sales and service areas.

Managing Director (e.g. a car, truck and aircraft components manufacturer such as Volvo)

Divisional Manager	Divisional Manager	Divisional Manager
Cars	Trucks	Aircraft Components

Figure 1.4 Product Division of Organisation

DEPARTMENTATION BY REGION OR TERRITORY (GEOGRAPHIC DIVISION)

Suitable for organisations where similar activities are carried out in widely different locations. On the spot decision-making is required based on local knowledge and the duplication of accounting tasks could be costly, e.g. insurance companies or travel agencies.

Managing Director (e.g. Dunnes Stores Branches Ireland)

Regional Manager North-east Branch	Regional Manager North-west Branch	Regional Manager Midlands Branch	Regional Manager South-west Branch	Regional Manager South-east Branch

Figure 1.5 Regional Division of Organisation

DEPARTMENTATION BY MIXTURE (MATRIX)

Within functional departments staff might be organised by region or by product. There may also be a subdivision of functions within product departments.

Functional departments organised by product:

Managing Director (e.g. Sales reps organised based on products) e.g. Roches Stores Ireland

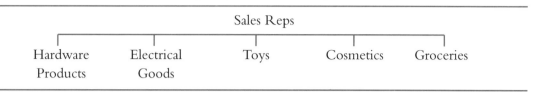

Figure 1.6 Matrix Division of Organisation – Function by Product

PRODUCT DEPARTMENTS SUBDIVIDED BY FUNCTION:

Managing Director (e.g. bank servies organised based on staff functions)
e.g. AIB, Bank of Ireland or Ulster Bank

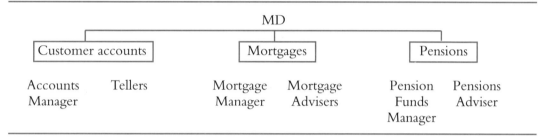

Figure 1.7 Matrix Division of Organisation – Product by Function

Departmental divisions are dictated by the size, type of business, nature of work involved, numbers, shifts, type of customer, and equipment specialisation.

Departmentation is the division of work into different areas. Dividing people into groups within each department or sub-department and allocating a head of department will ensure a greater level of efficiency and specialisation, where the lines of authority and decision-making responsibilities are clearly defined.

Larger organisations find it cost effective to engage in this type of division of labour to increase sales and profits by utilising the expertise in each department, thereby linking the whole organisation in this way. Some of these organisations have a department specifically for research and development of product in order to out-manoeuvre their nearest competitors.

PRACTICE QUESTIONS

1. Define the term Departmentation.
2. Name and explain the *five* main functional areas to which departments may be linked.
3. Pick an organisation and outline and discuss the duties attached to each functional area (i.e. Departments).
4. Pick any business and make illustrated divisions based on the process of:
   (a) departmentation by function (i.e. departments in a business such as sales, personnel)

(b) departmentation by product (i.e. products in a business)

(c) departmentation by region (i.e. branches in the country).

Environmental Features affecting an Organisation (A PEST plus C Analysis)

The factors that affect an organisation are:

1. *Political and Legal*

Conservation and environmental groups backed by political pressure can affect an organisation's activities by highlighting health and safety risks usually linked to noise, water or atmospheric pollution caused by the organisation. Regulations like registration, tax and VAT returns, as well as health and safety regulations, laws regarding employment practices and legislation, trade union laws, etc. all restrict an organisation's activities.

Fiscal (tax and government spending changes and decisions) and monetary decisions, including changes in interest rates, sometimes have a profound effect on organisations.

2. *Economic*

The level of economic activity in an economy will dictate consumer income and purchasing power. The higher the level of disposable (spendable) income, the greater the demand for goods. Price and changing interest rates will also affect consumers' decisions to purchase. Government fiscal policies (budget decisions on taxes and government spending) and monetary policies (interest rates and the availability of credit in banks) influence the cost of living and exchange rates, and therefore this also directly influences demand for goods and services from the organisation. The value of the domestic currency will influence investment in industry based on business confidence and the ability to borrow to invest, as well as confidence in future healthy economic activity. The number of competitors and their current success will also impact on an organisation from an economic point of view.

3. *Social and Cultural*

The ethical conduct of organisations is measured against legal and public standards. Organisations must carry out business in a responsible way that is both morally and legally acceptable. Certain attitudes, customs, beliefs and education, as well as behaviour and values, are generally adhered to by organisations. This will ensure that the business will remain a success or survive, whatever the case may be. Tribunals of inquiry are one example of social factors that will affect an organisation's reputation (e.g. the 1998 Blood Bank Tribunal) in a positive or negative way, depending on the outcome.

4. *Technological*

New high-tech equipment and computers have made work less time-consuming and more capital-intensive rather than labour-intensive. Work patterns have changed totally as a result. The need for retraining and constant modernisation of product due to processes and products becoming obsolete (out of date) has been highlighted in recent times. This can incur extra costs for organisations. The development of the Internet is good from an educational point of view as well as being a medium for payment (for example by credit card), intercommunications and advertising for a business all over the world.

5. *Competitive Factors*

If a similar business becomes established locally, it may affect the business – depending on the nature of the business. Retail organisations are more likely to be affected than services like hairdressers or beauty salons, which tend to retain custom based on customer loyalty because of the hands-on nature of these businesses.

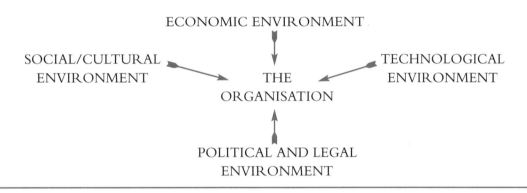

Figure 1.8 Environmental Factors impacting on an Organisation

Note: This analysis can be simply memorised by students, if they remember 'PEST plus C' (political, economic, social and technological factors that impact on an organisation, as well as competition factors).

Functions of Management

Henri Fayol (1841–1925) popularised the concept of the 'Universality of Management Principles', the idea that management should apply the same broad principles, no matter what sort of business is being managed. He is known as the 'father of modern operational management theory'. His work was published in 1949. He identified the following main functions of management:

1. Planning and Directing: to predetermine future action involving important areas like forecasting, objective-setting, decision-making and policy formation; also to direct events, as the organisation progresses towards achieving specific objectives. Planning is an essential element of good organisation and a manager must always be sure of goals.

2. Organising/Staffing: the activity of organising involves arranging and relating the work (a structure of tasks) to be performed, so that it can be accomplished most effectively by staff. It involves progressing plans from the decision stage to the activity stage by grouping tasks into specialised jobs for each individual, where each individual's responsibilities are clearly defined. Organising also involves delegating authority (dividing up tasks) and clearly defining the lines of authority so that each person knows who is superior and who is subordinate. It also involves the co-ordination and supervision of performance at all times. Staffing involves finding and training suitable successors, as well as the responsibilities for hiring and firing where appropriate.

3. Communication: the key to good organisation where information flow is accurate and all inclusive with regard to staff. The manager will organise successfully by being open to change, by seeking new ideas and implementing them, and by incorporating new technology into the organisation.

Importance of Effective Communication within an Organisation

Communication is one of the factors of management which, when used appropriately, is the key to good organisation and which influences the efficiency and effectiveness of an organisation. Efficiency means 'doing things right'. Effectiveness means 'doing the right things'.

Effectiveness comes first and is the key to managerial success – as dictated by the style of management and how the functions of management are undertaken. All the other functions rely on the existence of a good information system within the organisation. If planning is to be effective, i.e. if there is to be an effective planning environment, the goals, strategies and policies of the organisation have to be communicated appropriately to those who need to know them. The single greatest cause of unco-ordinated planning is a manager's lack of understanding of his goals, company strategies and policies when he is endeavouring to make decisions. Otherwise, a planning gap is caused by a lack of communication: senior management understand goals and plans; workers know what they have to do; but middle management do not understand how their departmental goals and policies tie in with those of the organisation as a whole. Effective planning is fostered when proper communication is established and all levels of management are given opportunities to contribute to plans which affect their areas of authority.

Efficiency can only be maintained when a high level of effectiveness is present and will be dictated by the individual skills, talents and styles of staff. Speed and efficiency with regard to work will gain the organisation a good reputation which will foster further future efficiency with results and productivity being based on good communication within the organisation.

4. Commanding: the activity of instructing subordinates, the demonstration of leadership skills. The roles regarding the 'Command' function can be subdivided into the following categories:

    (a) Interpersonal: the manager is the figurehead, leader and facilitator for liaison purposes.

    (b) Informational: the manager is a monitor, disseminator (sender of information in and out of the organisation), spokesperson (giving information to the organisation, having received it from either external or internal sources).

    (c) Decisional: the manager makes decisions about internal disturbances, and is the initiator of change and innovation.

    (d) Resource allocator: the manager takes charge of budgeting and the efficient management of time, money, materials, equipment and personnel.

    (e) Negotiator: the manager must deal directly with staff, customers and suppliers.

5. Co-ordinating and Motivating: the activity of co-ordinating involves harmonising activities of the different groups within the organisation; making sure each section and subsection operates efficiently and relates its efforts to the others. Motivating involves encouraging greater work effort aimed at achieving better results, the activity aimed at satisfying needs and drives within the work situation.

6. Controlling: activities and methods used by managers to ensure that previously agreed plans are in fact working (clarity of purpose, the awareness of objectives and targets). Henry Gantt, a specialist in scientific management, developed a type of bar chart which mapped actual and planned performances of the organisation based on agreed and established goals and standards. The chart provided a reviewing technique to compare target with actual performance over time. It allowed the effectiveness of the organisation to be judged in the light of specific targets. Based on mapping performance in this way, the organisation could take corrective action if a decline was detected.

GANTT CHART

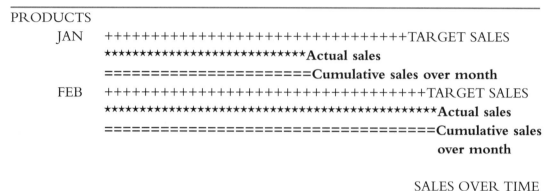

PRODUCTS		
JAN	+++++++++++++++++++++++++++++++++++++TARGET SALES	
	★★★★★★★★★★★★★★★★★★★★★★★★★★★★★Actual sales	
	=====================Cumulative sales over month	
FEB	+++TARGET SALES	
	★★★Actual sales	
	==================================Cumulative sales over month	

SALES OVER TIME

Figure 1.9 Gantt Chart

Explanation of Gantt chart:
- In January sales fell short of the target, so corrective action is required – either improvement of product or marketing improvements.
- In February sales exceeded the target. More money through higher profits might allow for spending on product diversification or spending on research and development of product.

PRACTICE QUESTIONS
1. List the environmental features that make an impact on an organisation and explain them briefly.
2. Carry out a PEST plus C analysis of an organisation of your choice.
3. What are the *six* functions of management?
4. Briefly explain each.
5. Why is the function 'communication' linked with organisation?
6. How does Effectiveness differ from Efficiency?
7. Explain the roles of the manager with regard to the command function.
8. Why is motivation so significant?
9. What is a Gantt chart and which function is it connected with?

Knowledge Management

Knowledge management is the method used by employers and managers to leverage knowledge to improve overall performance. (The analysis of performance in an organisation is known as performance appraisal).

Knowledge Management Systems Involve:

1. Examining how an organisation's knowledge is maintained, accessed and exchanged. This knowledge comes from staff. Managers aim to encourage the sharing of knowledge and sometimes this requires a cultural change within the organisation.
2. Sharing information among different departments.

Modern management thinking aims to reinforce in employees' minds that if business performance improves due to intelligent sharing and use of knowledge, then everyone gains.

Advantages of Knowledge Management Systems Are:

1. The more people involved the easier it is to spread and collect information.
2. Employees are more involved in company decision-making and the development of the business, which in turn stimulates greater work effort and productivity and leads to much lower staff turnover.
3. They keep the organisation ahead of the curve and cut costs.

Knowledge management is an umbrella term for making more efficient use of the human knowledge that exists within an organisation. Sharing knowledge in any company is vital but in order for a knowledge management activity to succeed, it must be tied into a business strategy.

The major focus of knowledge management is to identify and gather content from documents, reports and other sources and to be able to search that content for meaningful relationships.

Knowledge management can also be defined as the twenty-first century equivalent of information management. It is essentially an industry trying to distinguish itself with specialised groupware and business intelligence (BI) products that offer a wide range of solutions.

Knowledge management: from lifelong employment to lifelong learning

by Gerry McGovern

Knowledge management is often thought of as a process by which an organisation gets its staff to share their knowledge for the benefit of the organisation. Of equal importance to the success of knowledge management is how an organisation shares knowledge for the benefit of staff.

The traditional organisation made a promise to its staff: Work hard, show talent, and you will have a long and progressive career with us. Downsizing, outsourcing, and a general environment of rapid change, has meant that this promise is less common.

The response of many staff is to no longer expect lifelong employment. In fact, to stay a long time with a particular organisation is now seen in a negative light by many people. They want to stay fresh and move on before they are moved out.

The increase in interest in the discipline of knowledge management finds some of its roots in the decline of the lifelong employment promise. The organisation sees itself in danger of becoming a knowledge sieve, with knowledgeable staff continuously leaving, bringing their knowledge with them. A key question of knowledge management is: How do we tap this knowledge before it flows away?

Naturally, many staff have taken a cynical view. It looks to them that knowledge management initiatives are a way of draining knowledge from them. Some believe that once their best knowledge has been sucked out, they become even more dispensable.

The way to create a positive and realistic environment is to answer the question: What's in it for me? If you take away the promise of lifelong employment, what do you replace it with? Lifelong learning.

Lifelong learning is a direct response to the decline in lifelong employment. The age of lifelong employment was reflected by gradual change and a formal education for a fixed period that, by and large, lasted you through your career.

The age of lifelong learning is reflected by rapid change and the need to constantly update your skills. Rapid change has brought with it a tremendous rise in complexity. The emergence of the Internet combines access to vast quantities of information with powerful communication and collaboration tools.

Knowledge workers — those who get paid to think — live in a giant network that is constantly in flux. The opposite of a network is an individual. Hoarding of information is a natural defensive reaction, but it doesn't work if you want to succeed in a network.

In an Internet-driven economy, it simply pays to share. Getting connected and sharing is one of the surest ways to become a lifelong learner.

The organisation can offer a new set of promises to the knowledge worker:

- Our intranet will be full of useful things that will help you learn smarter and faster.
- We reward those who share and collaborate. The more quality knowledge you share the more your career will progress.
- Because everyone in this organisation shares, our collective knowledge is a powerful resource.
- We offer you opportunities to publish and promote your best ideas. This will enhance your reputation.
- In essence, we offer you a lifelong learning university. We provide you will the tools, content and environment that makes learning a form of sharing and sharing a form of learning.

www.gerrymcgovern.com

What is Information Management or Knowledge Transfer?

Most customer service organisations today will admit that effective knowledge transfer is the most crucial element in resolving customer problems. When done correctly, knowledge transfer accelerates problem resolution processes, fuels customer satisfaction and leads to greater organisational efficiency.

Information management can be defined as the discipline that analyses information as an organisational resource. It covers the definitions, uses, value and distribution of all data and information within an organisation, whether processed by computer or not. It evaluates the kinds of data/information an organisation requires in order to function and progress effectively.

What is Data Administration/Management?

Information can now be stored on networked computer systems (via LAN; a local area network) and instead of the outdated practice of keeping information in hard-backed form in filing cabinets and the constant photocopying of sheets, businesses can use intranet and extranet systems to store information and allow staff and/or customers/clients limited or unlimited access. This also helps retain information for the business more efficiently.

In Summary:

- Knowledge Management is the collection of information from staff.
- Information Management is the analysis of information and business intelligence (often part of a business's R&D (research and development) function).
- Data Administration and Management refers to the modern, high-tech methods employed by businesses to store and transfer large volumes of information and enable access to this information by managers, staff and customers. (Examples are intranets and extranets.)

What is Facility Management?

A facility can be defined as a physical place where business activities are done – the building itself.

Facility Management has been defined by Tuveson as 'the co-ordination of the physical workplace with the people and work of an organisation' (*Facility Management in the 21st Century* (1998)).

The Facility Manager has a very responsible job, making facility plans in accordance with the needs and demands of business activities. It involves leadership skills and attempts to integrate the principles of business administration, architecture and the behavioural and engineering sciences.

In summary it focuses on how to keep an organisation operating, specifically in relation to its buildings.

Examples of facilities include grocery stores, sports complexes, jails, office buildings, hospitals, hotels, retail outlets and government institutions.

The responsibilities involved in this type of management include a wide range of function and support services, including caretaking services and security, health and safety considerations, property and buildings management, space planning and accounting, telecommunications and mail and messenger services, management of records and other support duties.

It is the job of the facility manager to create an efficient environment that encourages productivity, safety (reducing the risk of liability, or of being sued), one that is pleasing to clients, customers and staff and meets legal and/or government requirements.

Different businesses generally have different facility needs in terms of buildings, space, an office or a suite of offices (urban/rural) and other physical aspects. A good facility manager will address these needs in the best and most cost-effective ways possible.

Typical responsibilities include:

- Monitoring operating efficiency within the organisation (identifying physical problems like machine breakdown, problems with products, deliveries, etc.) and finding solutions.
- Keeping a check on facility-related expenditure based on available monies.
- Real estate procurement (buying buildings for the business), leasing or sale of buildings, renovation or relocation of buildings.
- Monitoring of upkeep of buildings (high-capacity operation is essential).
- Ordering office supplies.
- Tracking and responding to environmental, health, safety and security issues. (Ergonomics – the design of tasks and work areas to maximise the efficiency and quality of employees' work.)
- Making sure business complies with codes and regulations.
- Planning future facility needs – e.g. new spaces, new wiring, lighting, technology/automation, wheelchair access, etc.
- Identifying needs for educating workforce in line with new plans and putting in place suitable training regarding standards and procedures (policy formulation).

Until recently, senior managers in Irish organisations have as a matter of course taken on the responsibilities of a facility manager. Now, however, in line with the knowledge economy, and due to senior managers' excessive workload and greater expectations of facilities by both staff and customers, many organisations employ facility managers for their expertise, in order to ensure that they have state-of-the-art, constantly updated and monitored facilities (buildings, etc.), in this increasingly competitive modern work environment.

The Need for Quality within an Organisation

Quality control is part of an organisation's overall control mechanism used to maintain standards and to identify deviations that are unacceptable compared against an agreed standard of quality. It involves taking corrective action, if deviations are significant, to restore the agreed acceptable level of quality. The role of quality control is to ensure that appropriate standards of quality are set and that variances beyond the tolerances are rejected. It is, however, possible to mass produce items that are almost identical but are not defective and conform to quality standards.

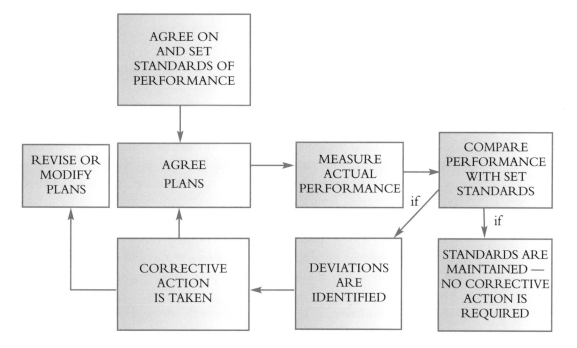

Figure 1.10   How Control is maintained

Quality control is needed in an organisation because it is linked directly with such factors as:

1. Price: Businesses ascertain the quality of their products and charge selling prices which should correlate with these standards. Products such as highly priced porcelain will be subject to far higher quality controls than run of the mill household earthenware.
2. Consistency: Must be maintained to justify prices and for businesses to maintain competitiveness.

3. Safety: Products like pharmaceuticals and food require the highest standards of quality to ensure the good health and safety of the community. Vehicles in general, e.g. public transport vehicles, cars, etc., are also subject to intensive testing to ensure public safety.

4. Legal requirements: Pharmaceutical products are subject to health controls which are backed by legislation. The general public expect the highest quality with regard to products that they purchase. Legal action taken against businesses will affect their reputation and appropriate corrective action will be necessary to restore public confidence.

Quality Controls and Measures

THE MOST WIDELY USED TECHNIQUES ARE

1. 100 per cent inspection: this is used when perfect quality is required, e.g. in the construction of a nuclear reactor plant or pharmaceutical product.

2. Random Sampling: where batch production takes place, 100 per cent inspection is not always necessary, nor is it always effective, where inspectors' ability to concentrate might be affected by noisy or busy surroundings. (Up to 15 per cent of defective items pass unnoticed, recent studies have shown.) Better results can sometimes be achieved by random sampling. Random sampling means that a batch is accepted or rejected on the basis of the number of rejects found after taking a random sample from the batch.

3. Continuous Sampling: this is used in mass-production systems, and entails an initial 100 per cent inspection until a predetermined number of correct items have passed in succession; then random sampling begins and continues until a further reject appears; then 100 per cent inspection is recommended, and the cycle is repeated if necessary.

4. Quality Circles: a quality circle is a group of people within an organisation who meet together on a regular basis to identify, analyse and solve problems in relation to quality, productivity or other aspects of day-to-day working arrangements using problem-solving techniques. The idea of quality circles is based on the Japanese ethos of quality.

ESSENTIAL FEATURES OF QUALITY CIRCLES

1. Membership is voluntary.
2. Group usually between five and ten members.
3. Group selects the problems to be tackled and methods of operation.
4. Leader is usually the immediate supervisor.

EFFECTIVENESS DEPENDS ON

1. Commitment and support of top management.
2. Full consultation with staff.
3. A participative approach by management.
4. Delegation of decision-making.
5. Trust and goodwill on all sides.
6. An effective support structure of consultation and negotiation.
5. Group members will receive training in communication and problem-solving skills, quality control techniques and group processes.
6. The group recommends solutions to management and, where possible, has authority to implement agreed solutions.
7. Support of trade unions and/or staff representatives.
8. An effective training programme including development of quantitative skills.
9. Continuous monitoring and review of result

BENEFITS OF QUALITY CONTROL

1. Reduction in costs of scrap or re-working.
2. Reduction in complaints from customers.
3. Enhanced reputation of company's products.
4. Feedback to designers and staff about performance of products and the machines required to produce them.

QUALITY CONTROL IN SERVICE-TYPE ORGANISATIONS

This concerns staff and their approach to clients as well as their skills and professional performance in these organisations (efficient human resource management). Quality with regard to service will be maintained by:

1. Attention to monitoring staff performance and refresher retraining to update staff.
2. Management should be open to new innovative ideas and be willing to implement them.
3. Lines of communication should be kept open to avoid staff-management relationship problems.
4. Corrective action should be taken to restore damaged reputation due to bad client-handling techniques.
5. Prompt and efficient response to client enquiries or problems should take priority.
6. Efficient manpower planning and back-up mechanisms for handling absenteeism. Manpower planning is the activity of matching the labour need with suitably skilled labour and making appropriate projections with regard to future expected shortfalls of labour in order to ensure efficiency and quality of service.
7. Maintain a professional image at all times.

Quality Awards

THE MAIN QUALITY AWARDS PRESENTED TO ORGANISATIONS ARE:

1. Quality Mark: information available from the Excellence Ireland Quality Association.
2. Hygiene Mark: information available from the Excellence Ireland Quality Association.
3. ISO 9000: information available from the National Standards Association of Ireland (NSAI).

Smaller organisations whose market share is mainly in the domestic market would tend to apply for the Quality Mark and/or the Hygiene Mark.

THE Q-MARK

The Q-Mark from EIQA has become one of the most sought-after trademarks in the Irish business world. To be awarded a Q-Mark an organisation is independently audited on key operational criteria and business results.

Benefits of the Q-Mark:
- widely known by consumers
- recognised as a reliable and trustworthy indicator of quality
- means significant operational efficiencies
- improves morale and teamwork
- will increase your bottom line.

The steps to achieving Q-Mark certification are simple. If you have not sought Q-Mark certification before, all you have to do is:
- fill in the application form
- submit it to EIQA
- wait for an audit to be scheduled
- have the audit completed and the result submitted to a board of independent assessors.

If your organisation passes the minimum threshold then it will be awarded the Q-Mark for a period of twelve months.

Many organisations, particularly first-time applicants, may need some practical assistance such as training, a mock audit or some direct in-company help. EIQA will be happy to provide any or all such assistance.

Hygiene Mark (Assessment areas)

Structural hygiene	Operational hygiene	Food storage & protection	Staff facilities & personal hygiene	Hygiene management system
Size/Layout/ Design/Finish	General operational hygiene	Deliveries from suppliers	Sanitary (toilet) conveniences	Records
Water supply	Equipment & utensils	Cold food storage	Handwash facilities	Hazard analysis
Lighting	Cleaning & disinfecting	Temperature control	Locker areas	Hygiene training
Ventilation	Equipment requirements	Food storage	Eating facilities (canteen)	Other
Proofing	Storage of cleaning equipment	Defrosting of food	Protective clothing	
Grounds	Handling of money	Cooking	Jewellery	
	Sawdust	– hot food handling	Cosmetics	
	Internal waste control	– cooling of hot food	First aid	
	Food hygiene practices	Food display	Unhygienic habits	
	Cleanliness of grounds & premises	Returns area		
		Stock rotation		
		Pest control		

Source: Information leaflet from 'Excellence Ireland'

Recognition (The Hygiene Mark)

Successful applicants (typically grade C or above) are presented with **The Hygiene Mark**.

Companies who secure a consistently high score over a three year period are awarded **The Triple Hygiene Mark.**

Awards (The National Hygiene Awards)

The annual audits are used to select award winners in various industrial categories.

The overall best performance is recognised by **The Supreme Hygiene Award.**

THE HYGIENE MARK

The National Hygiene Mark Programme is open to any company in the food or non-food sector. Companies are assessed under the following headings (with some variations depending on the company):

- Structural Hygiene
- Operational Hygiene
- Food Storage and Protection
- Staff Facilities and Personal Hygiene
- Hygiene Management System.

A written report is issued and graded on a scale of A to F. A corrective action and surveillance system is in place.

ISO 9000

Companies with international links will tend to have a preference for ISO 9000. ISO 9000 registration is a logical move for a company demonstrably committed to quality, i.e. a company that already holds both or either of the other two awards. Some companies may consider ISO 9000 not relevant to their particular needs or too expensive, since generally speaking a small to medium-sized company can expect to pay €4,000–€5,000 plus expenses on consultation fees. Added to this is the staff time devoted to preparing the quality system and the cost of the audit of this system, as well as the production of a quality manual. The National Standards Association of Ireland (NSAI) is the certification body for ISO 9000.

THE MICHELIN GUIDE – STAR RATINGS

The Michelin Guide awards restaurants between one and three stars based on the quality of the cuisine served: *three stars* indicate that food, wine, décor and service are exceptional; *two stars* indicate perfection; and *one star* means that food is very good and there is a pleasant environment.

The Guide warns readers not to compare the very fancy 'de luxe' restaurant that has *one star* to a simpler restaurant 'where you can appreciate fine food at a reasonable price'. (Refer to **www.cuisinenet.com**)

FÁILTE IRELAND QUALITY ASSURANCE

Tourism Accommodation Approval (B and B approval)

This organisation allocates Fáilte Ireland approval to bed and breakfast accommodation. It is located in Donegal (tel: 072 52760).

EXCELLENCE IN TOURISM (HOTEL, GUESTHOUSE, CARAVAN AND CAMPING PARK ACCOMMODATION APPROVAL)

This organisation awards different Fáilte Ireland grades of excellence to accommodation within the tourist industry as indicated above. It is located in Dublin (tel: 01 676 8018).

QUALITY TRAINING

Any entrepreneur wishing to enter the food and drinks industry (i.e. restaurants or hotels) should at the very minimum consider the FÁS Certificate Course in Foundation Hygiene for Food Handlers as it ties in very nicely with the requirements of the three quality marks.

The Excellence Ireland Quality Association provides training and information on quality systems and FÁS may grant aid attendance on these training programmes by qualified applicants under the FÁS Training Support Scheme. The applicants would need to apply for grant aid to FÁS before attendance on the course.

WEBSITE QUALITY CERTIFICATION

What is the W-mark?

Launch of Global Website Quality Mark
www.rte.ie/business, Thursday 1 July 2004

The Minister for Transport, Seamus Brennan, today launched the first ever global website quality certification process, which will be known simply as the W-mark.

It will allow organisations to have their websites independently audited under a number of criteria to ensure excellence and best practice. Ireland will be the global headquarters for the certification process. The Excellence Ireland Quality Association product brings together quality associations from the UK, USA, Asia and Europe.

Websites will be rigorously audited under a number of headings including consistency, appearance, accessibility, privacy, navigation and service commitment. A certification report will be issued to the organisation following the initial audit. There will be two audits per annum conducted to ensure consistency in awarding the globally recognised website certification symbol.

Phase one has been launched in Ireland, UK, and USA today and will be rolled out globally over the coming months. Hewlett-Packard Galway Limited will be one of the first organisations to be audited. Friends First, the financial services group and REHAB will also be audited for website certification.

'340,000 people use the internet in Ireland each day, accessing websites from around the world. This is a major new innovation with a global reach and I am delighted that an Irish company is at the forefront in leading the way to ensure rigorous standards of excellence are adhered to for websites globally,' said Minister Brennan, speaking at the launch.

PRACTICE QUESTIONS

1. What is Knowledge Management?
2. List two advantages of knowledge management systems in an organisation.
3. Distinguish between knowledge management, information management and data administration management.

4. What is facility management?
5. How does the basic control mechanism in an organisation operate?
6. Briefly explain the factors that dictate the need for quality in an organisation.
7. Explain the *four* main techniques used to maintain quality in organisations.
8. What are Quality Circles and have they a good chance of being effective, in your opinion?
9. What are the benefits of quality control in an organisation?
10. Why does quality control in service type organisations differ from quality control in manufacturing organisations?
11. Name the *three* main quality awards.
12. Why does ISO 9000 differ from the other two awards?
13. What are the Michelin Guide Awards?
14. How does Fáilte Ireland guarantee quality with regard to accommodation in Ireland?
15. What is the W-mark?

How Students can Research Organisations

Methods to Collect Data

A survey is a framework used to collect primary data (raw data). Surveys are usually carried out using the following methods:

1. Observation or Direct Measurement.
2. Enumeration.
3. Personal Interview (face-to-face).
4. Telephone Interview.
5. Postal Interview.
6. Internet Interview.

OBSERVATION AND DIRECT MEASUREMENT

This describes the counting or measuring of items of data. The Roads Authority often employs this type of survey technique when it is carrying out a traffic survey. The survey can involve counting the number of cars that pass a particular location in a given time period.

ENUMERATION

This involves the distributing of questionnaires and the follow up collection of them. An example is the Census of Population. Due to the length and detail required on the Census Questionnaires, households need time to complete them. The collectors are called enumerators.

THE PERSONAL INTERVIEW

This is a face-to-face interview in which 'the interviewer' asks 'the respondent' (person being interviewed) a series of questions that are contained on the interviewer's questionnaire. The interviewer records the responses. Example: Detergent and washing powder manufacturers often use this survey technique. They carry out door-to-door household surveys, the results of which can be used as part of their advertising campaigns.

THE TELEPHONE INTERVIEW

This is an interview by telephone where the interviewer asks the respondent a series of questions that are contained in the interviewer's questionnaire. The interviewer records the responses.

THE POSTAL INTERVIEW

This questionnaire is posted to the respondent when a survey is being conducted.

THE INTERNET INTERVIEW

Many marketing research agencies have websites on the Internet and offer services including constructing questionnaires, fieldwork, collecting data, processing data and analysing the results of research. Companies and businesses find that this is a useful way of analysing business performance and making comparisons with competitors. Email (electronic mail) allows questionnaires to be sent to respondents via computer and increasingly the Internet is being used to collect data and show results and the analysis of these results.

QUESTIONNAIRES & QUESTIONNAIRE DESIGN

A questionnaire is a group of questions compiled to do a survey. Types of questionnaires include:
1. The questionnaire for a Census
2. The questionnaire for the personal interview
3. The questionnaire for the telephone interview
4. The postal questionnaire
5. The Internet questionnaire.

QUESTIONNAIRE DESIGN

In order to put a useful questionnaire together – where information can be easily collated and coded – the investigator must be aware of different types of questions that can be asked.

OPEN-ENDED QUESTIONS: These are questions that lead to opinionated answers and are difficult to code but inject a useful level of variety and variability into a survey when they are constructed correctly. For example:

- Q What do you think of the performance of the current government?
- Q How in your opinion can we improve this product?

MULTIPLE-CHOICE QUESTIONS: These questions allow the respondent to choose from a range of options:
- Q What kind of telephone manner does Mary have?
  - (a) Fair
  - (b) Good
  - (c) Very Good
  - (d) Excellent

- Q What daily newspaper do you buy most often?
  Choose *one* only.
  Independent
  Times
  Evening Herald
  Examiner
  Belfast News
  Belfast Telegraph
  Irish Sun
  Irish Mirror

DICHOTOMOUS QUESTIONS: These questions allow the respondent to answer either yes or no.
- Q Will you support Labour in the coming General Election?
  Yes   No

- Q Did you shop on Grafton Street today?
  Yes   No

TYPES OF PROBLEM QUESTIONS: These are the type of questions that lead to unreliable answers and are best avoided.
- Leading Questions: Is it not true that Mary speaks well on the telephone? (The question is suggesting the answer is 'yes'.)
- Ambiguous Questions: Do you think that Mitsubishi Lancers are better than Volkswagon Jettas?
  (What does 'better' mean? – maybe cheaper or better quality? It is open to interpretation.)
- Irrelevant and Unnecessary Questions: Keep to the point and make sure that the survey only asks the questions that it needs to fulfil its purpose.
- Complicated Questions that involve other instructions: If the answer to this

question is 'yes', enter a tick at the top of the form and move to question 53. If 'no' answer question 52.

- Unreasonable Calculations: How much do you clock up on your phone bill in a week?
- Multiple Questions: Do you travel to work by car or by bus or do you walk? Some people might use all three modes on different occasions.
- Questions containing difficult, not easily definable words: Do you think that President Clinton should be impeached?
- Offensive or Tactless Questions: Do you go to Mass every Sunday?
- Emotive Questions: Based on Catholic beliefs, do you think that contraception is acceptable?
- Questions based on Memory: How many times do you go to the supermarket in a year?

SWOT and PEST Analyses

The SWOT and PEST analyses should be carried out when the student has done all the fieldwork and all possible avenues of questioning have been exhausted. The student should then compile comprehensive analyses in these two areas based on both facts (data collected) and the student's own opinions of the organisation being examined.

SWOT ANALYSIS
SWOT stands for the Strengths and Weaknesses of the business as well as the Opportunities afforded to the organisation and the Threats that endanger its performance or continued existence.

Examples of questions useful for analysis:

Strengths:
1. Are management structures well organised? Are there good communication structures between management and staff?
2. Is technology future-focused and of help to staff?
3. Is the organisation well located?
4. Does infrastructure (road, rail transportation) benefit the organisation?
5. Are social conveniences for customers like car parking, crèche facilities etc. available to customers?
6. What type of pricing policy exists?

PEST ANALYSIS
PEST means the Political, Economic, Social and Technological factors that affect the business in its own right, as well as in the context of the industry of which it is a part.

Examples of questions useful for analysis:

Political:
1. Have new political decisions had beneficial or non-beneficial effects on the business?
2. Has the business applied for and/or received any government grants?
3. Has the business had to register with particular bodies connected with the industry itself and/or connected with health, hygiene and safety? For example, leisure centres may look for grants from the Irish Sports Council.
4. Have the owners had to look for planning permission?

SWOT ANALYSIS continued

Weaknesses:

1. Is there bad management? How can it be improved?
2. Is there a problem with personal hygiene?
3. Is customer service poor?

Opportunities:

1. What future plans does the business have? — New ideas/possibilities/product or service diversification/more cost-efficient and higher quality operations?

Threats:

1. Has the conversion to the euro currency affected the business?
2. Have new European regulations affected the business?
3. Are new or existing competitors a problem?
4. Are the cost of new technology and the pace of business innovation causing products or services to be obsolete (out of date)?

PEST ANALYSIS continued

5. Has the government had to intervene to settle disputes and what effects has this had on the business?
6. Does the business play a part or benefit from the industry being placed high on the political agenda?

Economic:

1. Has the boom/recession in the economy affected the business/sales? Has new business developed? Has there been a positive or negative impact on the business?
2. Has expansion of product/service and/or premises taken place?
3. Have product and/or service diversification and/or change taken place?
4. Has new technology been employed due to the economic boom?
5. Have closures/job losses taken place due to the recession or are there more employed due to the boom? Is there a shortage of appropriately skilled labour?
   (A Business Employment Profile in the form of a chart would be useful and impressive — line graph, bar chart, pie chart — refer to 'Simple ways to illustrate the results of research.')

Social:

1. Has there been a change of ownership resulting in a new work ethos (competitive urge) which is more customer-orientated (more consumer-friendly atmosphere)?
2. Have new infrastructural developments (improved roads and rail accessibility) and better customer facilities like car parks and crèches made a direct impact on the business — by making it easier for people to avail of the service or to visit and purchase?
3. Have pollution and/or noise controls made it more difficult for the business to operate?
4. Have changes in fashion and popularity of certain products forced the business to change or lose money?

Technology:

1. Has the purchase of more modern equipment given the business the 'competitive edge' or have competitors won out in this way?
2. Has new technology meant redundancy or job losses (labour saving for management)?

Sample Assignment Brief

You are required to investigate and analyse topics appropriate to the structure and functions of any organisation of your choice. Please explore:
1. Internal organisational structures and functions.
2. External organisational structures.
3. The impact of these structures/functions on the performance of the organisation.
Choose either the company where you have completed your work experience or any other organisation of your choice.

Sample Questions for Student Research on 'The Organisation'

These questions or a sample thereof may prove useful to students when carrying out a personal interview (face to face) for any assignment on *The Organisation*.

HISTORY & SIZE OF ORGANISATION
1. When was the business established?
2. Did it relocate and or change its name? (Is the business name registered in Dublin Castle?)
3. How many staff are employed? How many males/females?
4. What goods/services does the business offer?
5. How large (square footage/no. of floors etc.) is this branch of the organisation? Could I sketch a plan of the building? Or take a photo of it?
6. Are there branches nationally/internationally? Please specify.

ORGANISATIONAL STRUCTURE
7. Could you provide me with an organisational chart of the staff and departments displaying regional, functional and product and/or service divisions?
8. Are there many lines of authority (middle managers)? (Is there a flat or tall hierarchy?)
9. What are the functions of the staff mentioned on the organisational chart and/or other staff?

OWNERSHIP, INSURANCE AND BUSINESS CONTROLS
10. Who owns the business? Tick which category the business falls into:
    * Sole Trader
    * Partnership
    * Private Company

- Public Company
- Friendly Society
- State Body
- Semi-State Body
- Other – please specify.

11. Is there a Board of Directors?
12. How is shareholding split?
13. Has the business got a:
    - Certificate of Incorporation.
    - Trading Certificate.
    - Other?

    Can I include a copy in my project?
14. What general category of finance was used to set up the business? E.g. bank loan, overdraft, venture capital.
15. How is the business insured?
16. How are the following controls handled in the organisation?
    - Financial Control (Cash flow etc.)
    - Credit Control (Debt Collection and Payment/Credit terms).
    - Stock Control (EPOS, Stock-takes etc.)
    - Quality Control (quality testing, quality circles, etc.)
17. Does the business possess a quality mark? E.g. Q-Mark, Hygiene Mark, ISO 9000, Star Ratings etc. If yes, is this beneficial?

INTERNAL ORGANISATIONAL STRUCTIRES (COMMUNICATION AND STAFFING):

18. Is the business represented by any lobby group, e.g. ISME, SFA, IBEC?
19. How is the formal organisational structure arranged? E.g. timetable, roster, rota, shifts.
20. How do staff complete tasks informally? E.g. swooping shifts.
21. How are staff interest and motivation maintained? E.g. Staff days, bonuses, commission.
22. Tick which communication systems are used to make the business operate well and rate their effectiveness:

	Not Effective	Fairly effective	Very Effective
Intercom	❑	❑	❑
Meetings	❑	❑	❑
Notice boards	❑	❑	❑
Networked computer systems (e.g. staff email/ ICT access and usage)	❑	❑	❑
Internal phones	❑	❑	❑
Staff knowledge management	❑	❑	❑
Other	❑	❑	❑

23. Have recent global events affected the organisation? In what ways?
24. Has the change to the currency and European Union affected the business? In what ways?
25. Have recent political decisions affected the business?
26. What types of advertising, marketing and PR methods are used by the business to gain exposure?

FUTURE FOCUS

27. Does the organisation have a five-year plan? What main plans are envisaged?

Student Analysis
(Impact of internal and external organisational structures/functions on the performance of the organisation)

Note: The student should carry out SWOT and PEST analyses (check previous information on this) and conclude by summarising what impact they think the functions and structures of the organisation have on its performance.

The student could take the following structure for this section:

My opinions on how effective and efficient the organisation is. (Being effective means making the right choices. Being efficient means having a tight and well-run organisation.)

The following are examples of how students could analyse the impact different structures or functions have on the performance of the organisation:

Efficiencies	How these efficiencies affect the organisation	Inefficiencies	How these inefficiencies affect the organisation
Good staff management interaction	Leads to good productivity and a happy working environment	Problem with customer service	Bad for company image
Up-to-date ICT and well-constructed website	Higher sales than nearest competitor	Frequent office equipment breakdown (photocopier)	Slows down completion of work and causes staff irritation

Simple Ways to Illustrate the Results of Research

Please refer to information on graphs and charts and the display of business information in Chapter 3. The following is a simple explanation and example of how to show the results of research in graphical form. The Chart Wizard in Microsoft Excel could be used to create these graphs.

Q1. How many staff are employed? Male/female?

Answer: 250 in total – 100 female and remainder male. There are 20 females in sales, 10 females in production and remaining females in administration. There are 50 males in sales and the remainder in production.

Summary Figures:

	Sales	Production	Administration	Total
Males	50	100	0	150
Females	20	10	70	100
				250

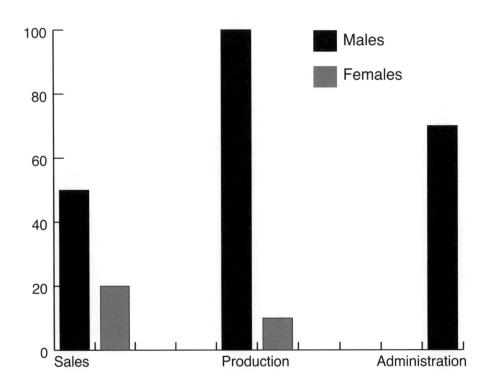

Staff Numbers

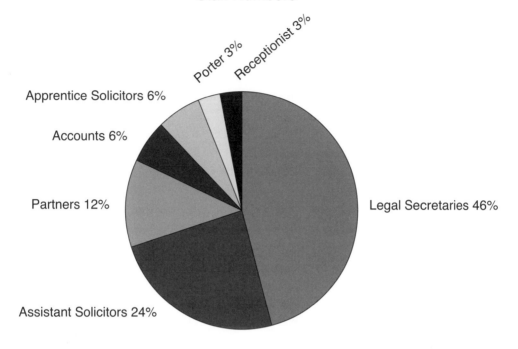

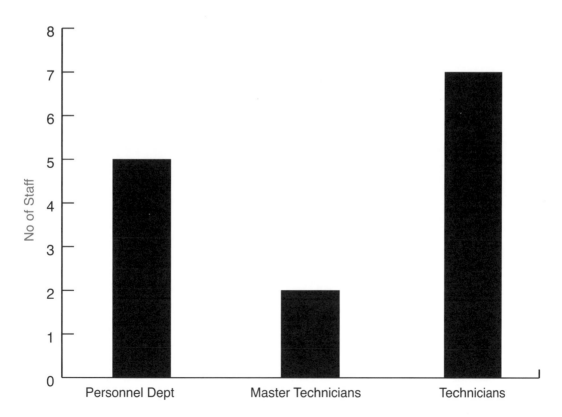

Sample Assignment Brief – 'The Organisation'

1. Candidates are required to investigate and analyse topics appropriate to the structure and functions of an organisation of the candidates' vocational area, e.g.
   a) internal organisational structures (staff structures, communications, quality, human resources, etc.)
   b) external organisation (PEST plus C factors affecting the business, suppliers, customers or clients, etc.)
2. Evidence will include reference to the impact of such structures and/or functions on the performance of the organisation, i.e. the candidate's opinion on efficiencies and inefficiencies of the organisation and how they affect its performance.

Sample Assignment

The Organisational Structure of St Munchin's — The Family Resource Centre, Limerick

Table of Contents
Introduction
Aim, Objectives and Methodology
History, Size, Type, Ownership and Services provided by St Munchin's
Internal Structures/Organisational Chart
External Structures (PEST plus C Analysis)
SWOT Analysis
Impact of the Structures on the Performance of the Organisation
Efficiencies and Inefficiencies
Conclusion
Bibliography
Appendix

Introduction

This project was compiled based on two weeks' work experience at St Munchin's Family Resource Centre, Ballynanty, Limerick.

Aim

My aim is to explore and analyse the internal workings of the centre and to look at external factors affecting it, and in so doing to make the reader more aware of how much the centre is needed by the community.

Objectives and Methodology

The primary data was collected by using a questionnaire and by observation. The questionnaire can be found in the Appendix. Secondary sources of information, including the centre's leaflets and the Community Link website, were also used.

Mission Statement

St Munchin's Family Resource Centre provides a safe, welcoming and supportive environment which encourages and enables our community to reach its full potential based on the principles of equality, empowerment and justice.

History, Size, Type, Ownership and Services Provided

St Munchin's is a non-profit-making organisation that exists to serve the community. Established by Sr Ursula in 1987, it was first set up in a normal three-bedroomed house. Significant expansion has taken place since then and the old centre was demolished in March 2007, having served the community for the previous twenty years. Funding has been secured for the new building. The centre is not owned by the people who run the centre but by Limerick Corporation.

Over the years the work and profile of the centre changed in many ways. In 1994, the International Year of the Family, St Munchin's Family Resource Centre was one of a small number of such centres (the other sister community centres include Our Lady of Lourdes Centre, Southill Community Services Centre, Moyross Community Enterprise Centre, and St Mary's) that were funded for the first time under the Department of Social Welfare.

The main rationale behind the funding was the perception of a possible gap in the statutory support for community development activities focused on support for family and tackling child poverty.

The centre's aims are listed on its website, indicating that it responds to the needs of the local community by providing:

- Structures that facilitate local people to support each other and search for ways to improve the quality of life in the area.
- Services in answer to the needs of families and family members.
- Support for those most disadvantaged and socially excluded.

It acts as a drop-in centre in the community and people are always welcome to come in for a cup of tea and a chat.

The following are the main services it provides:

SENIOR CITIZENS' OUTREACH AND SUPPORT

This provision includes meals on wheels, a counselling service, bereavement support, money advice and budgeting, chiropody, general information and a secretarial service.

Outreach visits the elderly, dinners are provided three times a week, minor repairs, cleaning and painting are looked after, alarms and lights installed for the elderly and a crafts group and clubs and social events are organised.

WOMEN'S GROUPS

The centre runs a local book project, a Young at Heart project, a mothers' group and a Follow your Dreams mothers group.

CHILDCARE AND CRÈCHE FACILITY

This facility (which includes an outdoor area) caters for up to 24 children per session ranging in age from three months to three years.

YOUTH SERVICES

These initiatives provide a combination of youth counselling, a Go 4 It programme (supported by Limerick Institute) and a first years' personal development club. There is also an after school club (for children aged eight to thirteen years), a homework club for six young people, computer clubs for twelve primary pupils and a summer project catering for sixty young people.

IT TRAINING AND COMPUTER CENTRE

ECDL classes are on offer, together with driver theory tests, beginners', intermediate and advanced computer training and anti-racism training.

FAIR TRADE PRODUCTS

Fair trade products are highlighted, promoted and used at the centre.

LITERACY PROJECT WITH A STEERING GROUP

Literacy research is carried out and funded by the Salesian Trust Fund and RAPID (a city rejuvenation group), the aim being to find out how many people in the community and parish area have literacy needs.

COMMUNITY EDUCATION

Lifelong learning and equality are promoted and literacy classes and art classes are also offered, either certified or non-certified, depending on the needs of the participants.

Organisation Chart of St Munchin's Family Resource Centre

BOARD OF DIRECTORS

CHAIRPERSON   SECRETARY   TREASURER

SUBGROUPS AND COMMITTEES

CENTRE CO-ORDINATOR

ADMINISTRATOR

Education Committee	Literacy Steering Group	PR Committee	Senior Citizens' Committee	Senior Citizens' Advisory Group	Bereavement Group Committee	After School Club Committee	Follow Your Dream Steering Group	Childcare Management Committee	Finance Sub-committee	Personnel Group
Administrator	Principal, St Lelia's	Community Person	Outreach Worker for the elderly	Outreach Worker	Manager	Centre Co-ordinator	Centre Co-ordinator	Centre Co-ordinator	Centre Co-ordinator	Centre Co-ordinator
Class Participant	HSCL Teacher	Development Workers (4)	Community Persons (3)	CDP	Outreach Worker for the elderly	Youth Services Co-ordinator	Youth Diversion Project, Moyross (2)	Barnardos Member	Admin Person	Management Committee Member
Development Worker	Learner Development Worker	Management Worker (1)	Senior Citizens' Club Leader	RAPID	Community Worker	Home/School Liaison Teacher	Youth Development Co-ordinator	PAUL Partnership Member	Management Committee	MidWest Support Agency
AISS	ALSS	Centre Co-ordinator	Development Worker	PAUL Partnership	Bereavement Facilitator	Staff ASC	Youth Project Worker	Childcare Manager	Treasurer	Crèche Management Committee Member
VEC	ALSS			Senior Citizens' Club Leader	Development Worker	Community Garda Co-ordinator, School Completion Programme	Remedial Teacher	Parent Chairperson		HR Consultant
Tutor	Literacy Worker			Development Worker		Parent Resource Teacher		Community Representative		
Chairperson	Local Community (2)					Management Community Representative		Pre-school Parent Representative		
Centre Co-ordinator	Centre Co-ordinator					ALSS: Adult Literacy Support Service		Crèche Parent Representative		
								Social Service Centre Member		

Functions of Staff

- **Centre Co-ordinator**. Responsible to the Board of Management for all aspects of centre operations and sits on all the committees listed in the chart. It is her function to hire staff and to get approval for appointments from the Board of Directors.
- **Administrator**. Responsible for administrative duties connected with the centre, including wages and enrolment, and assisting the Centre Co-ordinator.
- **Development Workers**. Organise individual projects at the centre, e.g. women's groups, community education, PR, etc.
- **Child Services Co-ordinators** have a range of child-centred functions.
- **Youth Development Co-ordinator** is responsible for looking after all aspects of youth development and support.
- **Youth Project Workers** work with the Co-ordinator to help the youth project members.
- **Crèche Manager** manages the Crèche.
- **Crèche Workers** look after the day-to-day running of the crèche.

The internal functions of the centre depend on the funding received. The centre is a company limited by guarantee and also a charity and they have a Chargeable Status Certificate, which means they are essentially non-profit-making and in existence for the good of the community. They are funded by the Department of Social Welfare.

Communications

Regular weekly meetings are held by each committee to discuss problems and/or future plans. Phone systems are efficient and there is also an email facility in the centre.

Advertising

The centre advertises using the Community Links website in co-operation with its sister centres. In the drop-in centre there are information leaflets available to any members of the community interested in visiting the centre or taking part in activities there.

Resources at St Munchin's

The communication systems in the centre are very high-tech in most areas. A computer room connects you to the Internet. The new Dell Dimension Computer is one of the newest additions to this room. There is a notice board in the main entrance to the building. Of the four telephones, three are for internal use only, in the reception, the crèche and kitchen. The telephone with the external line is located in the head office on the second floor of the building. Leaflets, the newspaper and sometimes the radio are also used to communicate with the public.

The centre is not recognised by any Quality Mark, but as there is a kitchen and crèche in the building there are occasional visits from health inspectors. They are always satisfied with the standards upheld by St Munchin's Family Resource Centre. The family resource centre has a Safety Statement that I was not allowed to include in this project.

External Structures

The external structures of St Munchin's Family Resource Centre are what happen outside the building. The tutors who take the education classes are all from outside the centre. Some are from primary schools or colleges and teach at the centre in the evening also.

As the centre cannot make a profit, they have to depend on grants and donations from people outside. Those who make such donations include the VEC, PAUL Partnership and also the Mid-Western Health Board. Without these donations the centre would not survive.

There are many visits from outside inspectors to ensure the centre maintains high standards for the public. All those unemployed who attend classes or visit the centre are from the community.

A PEST Analysis

Factors affecting the organisation

Political Factors	Department of Social Welfare makes decisions regarding funding and allocation of numbers of staff
Economic Factors	The economic boom and the desire to have a good job helped people realise that going back to education is a good idea
Social Factors	Amenable surroundings and community spirit: good facilities to help the community participants
Technonogical Factors	New computers and generally efficient equipment
Competition Factors	Little competition evident: not a problem since this is a community initiative

A SWOT Analysis

Strengths	Good for community motivation and collective support for the area
Weaknesses	Could have better technology and buildings
Opportunities	Drive for more funding from the Department and new initiatives into the future
Threats	n/a

The Impact of the Structures on the Performance of the Organisation

This section is divided into the following headings:

- Efficiencies
- Inefficiencies.

The following information will show in my opinion the efficiencies and the inefficiencies of St Munchin's Family Resource Centre.

EFFICIENCIES

1. *Security*

The security system in the centre was very good. A camera in the main reception area is connected to a TV system showing everything that was happening in the reception area.

2. *The centre's good image*

When on my work experience I found that the centre had a good image which attracted people there.

3. *Interaction of staff*

All staff members interacted well with each other and with all members of the public.

INEFFICIENCIES

1. *Building facilities*

The centre is held in three houses. It would be better if more space was available.

2. *The use of only one external telephone*

The use of a telephone with an external line in the reception area would make the work in head office a lot easier.

3. *Depending on funds*

The dependence on funding means there is no job security in the centre. If funding stopped, staff would lose their jobs.

Conclusion

While completing my work experience and this project, my knowledge of St Munchin's Family Resource Centre has grown dramatically. I hope that some day the centre will not have to depend so much on grants as it does now.

Bibliography

Douglas, Arlene, *Business Administration*, Chapter 1. Dublin: Gill & Macmillan.
Website: www.communitylink.ie
Leaflets from St Munchin's Centre

Appendix

QUESTIONNAIRE

1. When was the business established?
2. Did it relocate or change its name at any time?
3. How many staff are employed?
4. What goods/services does the business offer?
5. Have you an organisational chart of staff and departments?
6. Is there a Board of Directors?
7. What are the functions of staff?
8. Has the business got a:
   − Certificate of Incorporation
   − Trading Certificate
   − Other?
9. Who owns the business?
10. Does any lobby group represent the business?
11. How is the formal organisational structure arranged?
12. How do staff complete tasks informally?
13. In your opinion how is the business
    − efficient
    − inefficient?
14. How are staff motivated?
15. What communication systems are used to make the business operate well?
16. Has the organisation got a five-year plan?
17. Is the business insured?
18. What general category of finance was used to set up the business?
19. What are the main factors that affect the business (negative/positive)?

20. How is finance controlled?
21. What types of advertising, marketing and PR techniques does the business have?
22. Has the business gained a Quality Mark?
23. Does the business have a Safety Statement?

2. Finance, Business Controls and Ratios

Why is Control so Important in Business?

It is a managerial task aimed at:

1. Setting standards.
2. Measuring performance against standards.
3. Feedback of results.
4. Correcting deviations that stray from set standards.

(Refer to Figure 1.9 (Gantt chart) and Figure 1.10 (How control is maintained) in Chapter 1.)

Control is one of the functions of management. The different types of control necessary in business are:

1. *PLANNING CONTROLS:* This involves the determination of instructions to be used as directives for activities within the company and to determine standards that are to be used for comparison. There must be clear, unambiguous plans to enable managers to carry them out efficiently and effectively. (Refer to the Functions of Management in Chapter 1.)

2. *FINANCIAL CONTROL:* This involves budgeting – the formulation of plans for a given future period, expressed in quantitative terms; money management using cost and revenue controls.

    The following are the different types of financial controls that are used, depending on the nature of the business in question:

    1. Non-budgetary Controls
    Marginal Costing and Breakeven Charts:
    Marginal costing involves monitoring any extra costs incurred in a business and can help with price-fixing. Breakeven analysis is an extension of marginal costing. The breakeven chart maps total costs and total sales revenue and where the two lines intersect is the company's breakeven point. Below this line the company will see what output is making a loss, and above it what profit is being made on the other output. Total Costs are made up of Fixed Costs and Variable Costs.

        Fixed costs are for example rent, rates, permanent wages, insurance of premises – the type of costs that do not change as output or production increases.

Variable costs are for example part-time wages, raw material costs and overhead expenses like heat and light, telephone and general day-to-day bills that increase as output or production increases.

It is also important to note that there is a difference between direct and indirect costs.

Direct costs, like direct labour, are those costs that contribute directly to production. Production cannot take place without them.

Indirect costs, like indirect wages, selling expenses, administration and insurance, do not contribute directly to the physical production process. They are costs that are difficult to attribute to specific products or cost units. A good understanding of the terms mentioned will help students to answer the questions on breakeven charts, which will appear later in the section.

2. Budgetary Controls:

This involves Standard Costing, which is costing out a job in terms of labour, materials and overheads. This is done together with monitoring total costs. Higher profits are gained by minimising costs.

Departmental Budgets are an integral part of the functional budget which forms part of the Master Budget of a business – the departmental expenditures being generally sales, production, stocks, administration, capital expenditure, R & D (research and development), cash and credit control (debtors and creditors), purchasing, and profit & loss and balance sheet forecasting.

A clearly defined financial policy allows management to authorise specific expenditures. The tight monitoring of costs using comparisons between actual and budgeted costs can allow the mismanagement of costs to be traced to a particular department. The correction of such deviations can then take place in order to minimise costs and maximise profit levels.

3. Financial Ratios

Liquidity, primary, current, sales, expense and operating ratios are used to measure efficiency and to summarise and assess overtrading, solvency and profitability in a business. Financial control can be maintained by observing the resulting ratios and making improvements where necessary.

4. PPBS – Planning, Programming and Budgeting Systems

This is a method used by government to control expenditure and to make decisions based on choices regarding money allocation for planned public expenditure. Calculations and benefit analyses are carried out by the programme.

3. CREDIT CONTROL: This involves the monitoring of debtors' and creditors' records – a system to ensure payment (into and out of the business): the means employed by a business to control the amount of credit it allows to its customers/debtors (the people that owe the business money) and to negotiate the amount of credit it is allowed to take from its creditors (the people to whom the business owes money).

The term 'credit terms' is the amount of time allowed to pay a bill. Suppliers can give 30 days (one month's credit) 60 days (two months' credit) or 90 days (three months' credit). Trade discount and settlement discount agreements are usually built into the terms of credit (discussed further in Chapter 6, 'Processing Business Documents').

4. *QUALITY CONTROL:* This involves the establishment of appropriate standards of quality. Variances beyond certain tolerances are rejected. The main methods used to control quality are 100 per cent inspection, random sampling inspection, continuous sampling, quality circles, and applying for quality awards (refer to the latter half of Chapter 1 for an explanation of these methods). Control charts are also often used and represent a graphical method to identify tolerance limits within which an item produced is acceptable and is not a reject. These charts have 95 per cent and 99 per cent tolerance limits.

5. *STOCK CONTROL:* Businesses must strive to maintain the optimum level of stock. This, however, depends on the following factors and the relationship between them:

1. The cost of holding stock – dictated by the type of goods in question – perishable/non-perishable, deterioration period, how long before the good becomes obsolete (out of date), and the cost of warehouse space.
2. Discounts available through bulk buying (warehouse space needed).
3. The variability of consumer demand.
4. On time, scheduled production supply to meet the demand: the shortage of materials or late delivery of materials can lead to major decreases in profits.

Keeping these factors in mind, a happy medium (optimum level) regarding stock levels must be reached, where a maximum and a minimum level of stock is set per item.

Minimum Stock: There exists the problem of holding the minimum amount of stock necessary to satisfy production (supply) and consumer demand, but at the same time not understocking. *Understocking* can lead to shortages of materials, with consumers switching to the nearest competitor (a loss of business and damaged reputation) – supply not keeping up with demand.

Maximum Stock: *Overstocking* can lead to excess supply (goods that do not sell) and the price must be reduced to dispose of the excess, like a sale (a loss-making venture).

Purchasing managers often make use of the Economic Order Quantity formula (EOQ) to estimate acceptable levels of stock per annum:

$$EOQ = \sqrt{\frac{2DS}{IC}}$$

D = Annual demand
S = Ordering costs (storage & delivery)
IC = Annual cost of holding stock (like the cost of the administration of stock (documentation etc.) and the cost of the security of stock)

QUESTION

The annual demand (D) for a product is 3,000 units and the cost of placing an order is €8 (S).

The annual cost of carrying a unit of stock is 10% (IC).

Using the EOQ formula, work out:

(a) How many units should be ordered each time.

(b) How many times during the year the order should be placed.

ANSWER

$$EOQ = \sqrt{\frac{2DS}{IC}}$$

$$\sqrt{\frac{2 \times 3,000 \times 8}{10\%}}$$

$$\sqrt{\frac{2 \times 3,000 \times 8}{\frac{1}{10}}}$$

- Turn the divisor upside down and multiply – divisor is the fraction under the line in the case above.

$$48,000 \times \frac{10}{1}$$

Answer to Part (a)   692.82 = 693 units
Annual Demand = 3,000
Each Order = 693

Answer to Part (b)   4.3 = 4 times

- 693 units should be ordered each time – 4 times a year.

Average Cost is estimated as follows $\dfrac{\text{Total Cost}}{\text{Output (number of items produced)}}$

Weighted average cost is total cost weighted against proportion of income spent on goods.

REPLACEMENT COST OF STOCK: any stock that does not sell or is damaged in transit or in the process of selling is calculated as wastage (e.g. perishable items or stock that goes off easily like vegetables, fruit and bread). In these cases consumers like these goods to be very fresh. The stock must be replaced. Sales agents who deliver bread, in particular, must bear the loss of bread that does not sell and the amount taken out is the replacement cost. Systems have been developed in recent times to minimise waste, helping to achieve low stock levels without causing shortages.

PRACTICE QUESTIONS

1. Why is control so important?
2. Revise how control is maintained (Fig. 1.10) and link it with the Gantt Chart (Fig. 1.9).
3. Name the *five* main controls that managers have to maintain in day-to-day business.
4. Distinguish between Fixed Costs and Variable Costs.
5. Distinguish between Direct Costs and Indirect Costs.
6. Explain how financial controls apply to business.
7. What is Credit Control?
8. Distinguish between a Debtor and a Creditor.
9. What is Quality Control? Link Fig. 1.9 with Quality Control.
10. With reference to Stock Control, what factors will affect a business that is looking to maintain an Optimum level of Stock? Explain these implications in your own words.
11. Differentiate between Minimum Stock and Maximum Stock and the problems with both.
12. What is the purpose of the Economic Order Quantity formula?
13. When trying to estimate the cost of stock, distinguish between Average Cost, Weighted Average Cost and Replacement Cost.

Ordering Stock – Re-order Levels and Quantities

Re-order level: indicates when to purchase more stock.
Re-order quantity: indicates how much to purchase.

When shelf space is freed up, it indicates the speed at which stock is being bought up by consumers. This will dictate the need to re-order stock. Trained personnel in retail outlets carry out stock-takes on a regular basis, to make sure that the appropriate levels of stock are being maintained. In large retail outlets like supermarkets, it is usually the responsibility of individual sales distributors and agents to keep their shelf space well stocked and to contact their suppliers and make further deliveries based on the retail outlet's requirements. From time to time, based on changing consumer choice, seasonal factors and other factors, shortages occur and either the retail outlet manager, department manager or the stores supervisor will inform the sales distributor/agent of the extra requirements. Some unsold stocks, like bread and perishables, are taken back by the suppliers. However, this is not always the case.

How the Retail Outlet Monitors Incoming and Outgoing Stock

In some supermarkets, deliveries are checked in through the stores area at the back of the supermarket. This is usually the responsibility of the stores supervisor.

1. *COMPUTERISED STOCK CONTROL AND THE ROLE OF ELECTRONIC POINT OF SALE IN STOCK CONTROL (EPOS):* In some supermarkets, a stock scanner is used to check in each individual delivery and to check out any returns (unsold/out of date stock) – last in, first out. A separate printout of the check-in and check-out is given to the agent/distributor. The number of goods sold is estimated by taking the number of goods delivered *minus* the returns.

    Some supermarkets do not have stock scanners and in this case each agent has a separate stock card. The number of goods sold per day is noted on the stock card. The agent can estimate how many goods he/she should put on the shelves by looking at last week's sales column. An example of a stock card is shown on page 73.

    Stock control computer programs incorporate stock ratios to indicate the efficiency of stock control in a business. Examples of these ratios are:

    (a) Raw material/Total sales turnover
    (b) Work in progress/Total turnover
    Both of these ratios show stock-holding in relation to amount sold – detects level of overstocking or understocking.
    (c) Raw materials/Purchases, i.e. total purchases/average stock – shows how many times stock is turned over or replaced – indicating the frequency of restocking.

New computerised stock control systems can monitor and track orders and balances and can indicate to the stock controller that stock renewal is required and 'best before' dates can also be estimated.

Other advanced stock control systems have good forecasting techniques incorporated into them in order to evaluate certain degrees of error, i.e. degrees of overstocking or understocking. The mistakes are noted and adjusted using statistical methods like 'exponential smoothing'. Using this method, stock levels are adjusted by a proportion of the most recent errors in stock numbers and a new forecast of stock requirements results. The Box-Jenkins statistical method is based on the adjustments of errors themselves, based on past errors. Both methods are accurate and satisfy the requirements of larger organisations and those that deal in stock that could be a risk to the health and safety of the community. Examples are pharmaceutical products and nuclear products.

EPOS Systems:
New Solutions for the Retailer
and the Consumer

From the smallest huckster shop to video stores to supermarkets, electronic point-of-sale (EPOS) and scanning systems are in operation. What used to be seen as a high tech novelty are now part of the norm, but instead of functioning purely as a counting system (goods sold, stock received, stock remaining etc.), today's EPOS systems are focusing more and more on the consumer, for the mutual benefit of retailer and customer alike. Modern retailers are becoming ever more aware that information is everything, and the more they know about the erratic spending habits of modern society, the better they will be able to cater for its needs. Today's retailing wars are being fought with technology in the quest for understanding the customer, tracking their purchasing habits, adding systems that help them decide on a purchase, speeding up service and literally trying to take the hassle out of shopping.

What is becoming increasingly clear is that information technology systems are essential in helping solve the riddles of what people want to buy, why they buy it and what makes a happy shopping experience. Software is being created and updated for PC-based EPOS tills, which include a vast range of functions including bar code scanning, card readers, receipt printing, dockets, loyalty schemes and communications. The advantage this technology gives to the retailer is instant information on what products they're selling, which are the more popular and, most importantly, who they're selling it to. Proper use of this information has led

to the success of loyalty schemes introduced by retail chains over the last few years. Basic loyalty schemes offer the customer price reductions tantamount to the frequency of their visits to the outlet. Alongside, products can be given a boost in exposure to the consumer by the addition of extra points; for example, "Buy a bottle of Yankee Cheez-in-a-Can today and receive 300 points!" This allows the popularity of the product to be gauged by the EPOS system; it will suggest whether Cheez-in-a-Can should be replenished and advise what time of year it sells best. Affinity schemes involve a wider network of companies based on the same premise (such as the "SuperClub" card) and similarly give retailers a mutual boost, while attracting the same demographic of customers.

EPOS systems have also developed to account for theft or "shrinkage", with compatible software being introduced to combat it. Most retailers have an idea as to when suspicious dealings are most likely to occur at the service till, such as the refund or exchange of goods, excessive voiding of transactions, and multiple manual entries of credit card details after the initial swipe. Although instinct is an advantage to any retailer, what EPOS systems offer is an effective means of detection. All of these events are identifiable while they take place, and the data can be processed quickly and efficiently. With EPOS systems in place with the relevant software, retailers have solutions that enable them to detect "shrinkage" patterns and prevent theft before it occurs.

For the consumer, information technology in stores and shops adds a vibrant new element to the way they spend money. The introduction of easy to use touch-screen kiosks give customers access to services, from locating the deli counter to what wine might suit the lasagne they just bought. In Britain, some car showrooms allow the prospective buyer to create the car of their choice on-screen, while music stores give the customer a chance to browse through CDs, check the prices, listen to selected tracks and print a list of what they've chosen. With interactive kiosks in place, the next step is integrating them with the advantages of loyalty cards, allowing retailers access to a very comprehensive profile of what their customers want.

The attention being focused on the individual has led to concern from some consumers. There are those who think that personal information stored by retailers can be construed as intrusive. What people gain from the developments in EPOS technology is accurate pricing, a much higher level of service, and discount advantages through loyalty schemes. The customer's involvement in loyalty schemes is voluntary, and any information held by the retail company is available to the customer. On the subject of credit card confidentiality, the retailer cannot hold on to any credit information after the transaction has been completed. So with the initial fears of EPOS systems having been allayed, one can truly say that both retailer and consumer are helping each other into the next millennium.

EPOS means Electronic Point of Sale. The point of sale occurs at the check-out when the product has just been sold to the customer. Goods are checked through an electronic check-out scanner system where bar codes automatically program prices into the cash register. The till receipt is the proof of purchase and proof of the point of sale of goods to the customer. Using till details on how much stock is left, the outlet is a means of controlling stocks.

2. *CONTINUOUS WRITTEN RECORD:* This is based on the same idea as EPOS. However, the account of goods coming in and taken out is handwritten on stock cards. The supervisor takes account only of the difference between the goods that come in and returns taken out.

3. *PERIODIC WRITTEN RECORD AND OBSERVATION:* Trained personnel who work in the supermarkets/stores might do a check on the stock position at the end of every month. This would act as a double check on agents. Discrepancies possibly due to theft or numerical mistakes would be noted when sales volume is compared to till takings.

4. *BIN CARDS:* An account is also kept of changes in stock, in item order. For example, a bin card might exist detailing the change in the stock of jars of jam. The balance of the remaining stock of jam is recorded on the card (example of a bin card below).

BIN CARD No.			
ITEM Flour		UNIT 1.5 KG	
DATE	RECEIVED	ISSUED	BALANCE
1 Mar	12	3	9
5 Mar	–	4	5
8 Mar	12	4	13

It would probably not be cost effective for other smaller retail outlets like boutiques, jewellers and small shops to have a computerised stock control system. However, it is becoming the norm in most businesses now.

Note: Not all suppliers allow returns to be taken back. In most cases sales agents for bread and other perishable goods have to bear the cost of overstocking. To avoid this, they streamline stocks to a minimum level. Most shops such as clothes shops only return items when they are damaged or when more were delivered than were ordered.

STOCK AND ORDER CARD

Department 16 Bread & Cakes   Sales from :
Order from:

Store
Supplier
Phone

Product Description

MONDAY		TUESDAY		WEDNESDAY			THURSDAY			FRIDAY			SATURDAY			SUNDAY	
Stock Sales	Floor Order	Stock Sales	Floor Order	Stock Sales	Floor Order	Stock Order	Floor Sales	Stock Order	Floor Order	Stock Sales	Floor Order	Stock Order	Floor Sales	Order	Order	Sales	Order
3		2		3	3		1	3		3	4		4			0	
1		1		2	2		4	3		3	5		3			0	
2		1		2	3		5	3		6	4		6			0	
3		5		7	8		11	6		20	16		18			0	
3		4		7	16		7	-		15	9		10			0	
5		7		13	-		7	8		18	15		12			2	
0		0		0	-		0	-		0	-		0			0	
1		7		7	2		8	10		14	5		8			0	
4		7		5	9		7	-		13	9		9			0	
2		0		2	6		2	-		2	6		3			4	
3		1		2	5		6	7		3	5		8			0	
0		1		5	-		5	10		8	10		11			0	
0		2		3	-		9	10		2	5		4			0	

Total:

Signed for . . . .   by: . . . .

Supplier: . . . .

Stock Card example (agents and sales distributors fill these cards in on a daily basis in some retail outlets).

- Stock Sales column – indicates the quantity sold the previous week.
- Floor Order column – the aim is to match or improve on the quantity sold the same day the previous week. This will, however, depend on the amount still on the shelves from the previous day.

For example on Friday, where 20/16 appears, this indicates that 20 items were sold that day last week. Only 16 items are replaced because 4 must have been left unsold on the shelf from the previous day. The previous week's sales (Stock Sales column) provide a guideline as to how many items should be put on the shelf to avoid shortages occurring.

Stock Turnover is measured using the following formula:

$$\frac{\text{Cost of Sales}}{\text{Average Stock}}$$

Average Stock is Opening Stock *plus* Closing Stock divided by 2.

Stock turnover describes the number of times stock is replaced. Jewellers generally have low levels of stock turnover because the goods for sale are expensive. Shops, supermarkets and pubs would have high levels of stock turnover, with perishable goods (milk, fresh cream) and fresh goods (bread, some vegetables such as carrots and broccoli) having a very short shelf life. The deterioration period, together with the fluctuation of consumer demand, will dictate the profitability of the retail outlet. The level of stock turnover will be indicated by the stock re-order levels.

Factors that Influence the Levels of Profits and Stock Turnover of a Retail Outlet

The following factors have beneficial influences on the levels of stock turnover and profitability:

1. More competitive prices.
2. Supplier advertising via television, radio, newspapers, direct mail, leaflet drops, personal selling (e.g. cooking food in a supermarket), public relations exercises (creating an image that the public relates to the product) and special offers will usually increase consumer demand. Publicity in the form of the short sharp shock method is a marketing technique that can also increase sales.
3. Sunday and late opening hours will increase stock turnover.
4. Customer service: consumer friendly shop layout, self-service with helpful and friendly back-up customer service and free home delivery.

5. Material service: safety and hygiene, as well as the assurance that the outlet is always well stocked, with a wide and varied choice of stock which is always fresh. If the lines of authority are clearly defined when problems arise, prompt and efficient service should be provided in response to customer complaints, returns and replacement of damaged goods.

The following factors have undesirable effects on the levels of stock turnover and profitability:

1. High prices in relation to competitors can discourage demand.
2. The deterioration period together with the fluctuation of consumer demand, which can sometimes be unpredictable and perhaps seasonal, will dictate levels of wastage and unanticipated losses.
3. When supply falls short of demand due to badly managed re-ordering, failure to deliver or late delivery, the nearest competitor could win out (the substitution effect). This depends greatly on individual suppliers' relationships with their sales distributors and sales agents.
4. If stock returns are not taken back by suppliers, sales agents will streamline stock which is likely to cause understocking and shortages from time to time.
5. The cost of holding stock and warehouse space will dictate stock re-order levels and quantities.

Breakeven Charts

PRACTICE QUESTION

Morton and Murphy Ltd project sales for the next twelve months at 100,000 units sold at €10 per unit.
The firm expects the following expenses:

Direct material cost	€3 per unit
Direct wages cost	€2 per unit
Administration expenses	€150,000
Rent of the premises for the year	€100,000
Advertising fixed budget (yearly)	€10,000

Based on the twelve-monthly financial information given:

A. Make the appropriate pre-calculations to prepare to draw a Breakeven chart.
B. Draw a Breakeven chart and include the following detail on it:
    (a) The Breakeven point.
    (b) The 100% Present Capacity position.

(c) The Profit or Loss when 20,000 units are produced.

(d) The Profit or Loss when 60,000 units are produced.

(e) Comment on your findings.

SOLUTION

In order to draw the chart, Variable Costs must be grouped together and then Fixed Costs must also be totalled. Sales *less* Variable Costs = Contribution (an amount that is contributed to the business – a type of profit figure). When Fixed Costs are then deducted, depending on how high these fixed costs are, an overall loss could result. If Fixed Costs are lower than Contribution, then a profit will result.

QUESTION (A) PRE-CALCULATIONS:

	€	€
Sales (100,000 x €10 per unit)		1,000,000
Less VARIABLE COSTS		
Direct Material costs	300,000	
Direct Wage costs	200,000	
Administration expenses	150,000	
TOTAL VARIABLE COSTS		650,000
CONTRIBUTION		350,000
Less FIXED COSTS		
Rent of premises for year	100,000	
Budgeted advertising	10,000	
TOTAL FIXED COSTS		110,000
Net profit		240,000

TOTAL COSTS (650,000 + 110,000) = 760,000

PROCEDURE TO DRAW THE CHART

1. Graph paper must *always* be used to ensure accuracy.
2. 'Output or number of units produced' is plotted on the X axis and Sales revenue is plotted on the Y axis.
3. The 100 per cent Capacity line should be drawn in first – vertical line
4. Then the Total Costs line should be drawn in – horizontal line.
5. The Sales line should extend from the Origin to the Present Capacity Sales revenue level.
6. The Variable Costs line should extend from the Total Costs line. It should intersect the sales line at the Breakeven point which can now be read from the graph, above which there is a profit and below which there is a loss made.
7. To read the profit figure or the loss figure from the graph, draw a straight dotted line from the given output level intersecting both the Sales line and the Variable Costs line.

8. If a Loss is detected, the output level will be below the breakeven output level and the straight dotted line will hit the Sales line first. The Loss is the DIFFERENCE between the two intersections and is read from the Y axis.

9. If a Profit is shown, the output level will be above the breakeven output level and the straight dotted line will hit the Variable Costs line first. The Profit is the DIFFERENCE between the two intersections and is read from the Y axis.

QUESTION (B) (a) TO (d) Breakeven Chart Morton & Murphy Ltd

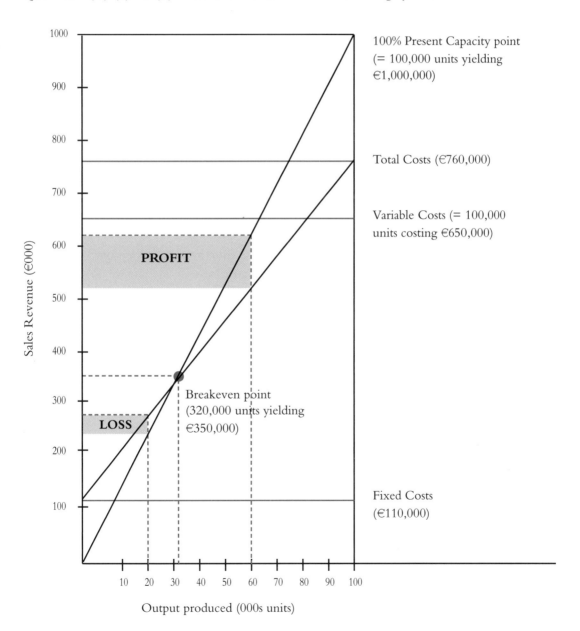

QUESTION 1B (e) COMMENT

The Breakeven point indicated on the chart is where 23,000 units of production yield €230,000 in Sales revenue. Any output/production level below this will show a Loss, and above it will generate a Profit.

The 100% present or current capacity line indicates the maximum point of production to which the business can go, given present resources available. This business is capable therefore of generating a maximum of €1,000,000 (€1m) in Sales revenue by producing 100,000 units. This would always be difficult to achieve due to problems that occur, like employee absenteeism, shortages or damaged materials, machinery breakdown and other unpredictable occurrences.

The first small shaded area represents the Loss that would be incurred if the business only produced 20,000 units. This amount (€270,000 *minus* €230,000 = €40,000 loss made) means 20,000 units is too low a level of production and indicates an under-utilisation and wastage of resources. This means that resources like labour and materials would not be used to the fullest capacity at this level of output.

The large shaded area represents the Profit that would be generated if the business produced 60,000 units. This profit (€600,000 *minus* €515,000 = €85,000 profit made) indicates good productivity (output per person) and the level of production is above breakeven point. Resources are being well employed to generate a good profit. The business is, however, a good distance away from optimum capacity.

The Fixed Costs line indicates costs that remain the same irrespective of any other activities in the business. In this case a set figure for rent and also for advertising has been agreed and will not change over the year.

PRACTICE QUESTIONS

1. What are Re-order Levels and Quantities?
2. How are stock levels monitored in retail outlets?
3. What are Stock Ratios?
4. What is EPOS?
5. How is a Stock Card written up?
6. How is Stock Turnover calculated? What does it indicate?
7. Explain *five* factors that have a good effect on Stock Turnover and Profitability.
8. Explain *five* factors that have a bad effect on Stock Turnover and Profitability.
9. The financial breakdown of the business owned by James and Sons Ltd is as follows:

	€	€
Sales (3,000 units at €120 each)		360,000
Direct labour	100,000	
Direct materials	50,000	
Factory overheads – variable	12,000	
– fixed	18,000	180,000
		180,000
Selling expenses – variable	30,000	
– fixed	16,000	
Other fixed overheads	12,000	58,000
Net profit		122,000

From the information provided:

(A) Make appropriate pre-calculations to draw a Breakeven chart.

(B) Draw a Breakeven chart and include the following details on it.

    (a) The Breakeven Point.

    (b) The 100% Present Capacity position.

    (c) The Profit or Loss when 250 units are produced.

    (d) The Profit or Loss when 1,250 units are produced.

(C) Comment on your findings.

Sources of Finance for Business

The acquisition of money, often called capital, is the first step necessary to set up or develop businesses. Different interpretations of capital exist but it usually means money either in a liquid (cash) or non-liquid form (in the form of an asset). Together with the other three factors of production – Land (premises), Labour (workers), Enterprise (the entrepreneur co-ordinates activities) – Capital is the basis of successful business start-up or expansion. The four factors are known as the Factors of Production.

    Business people usually avail of the following possible Sources of Finance to commence or develop businesses:

1. Bank or financial institution loans.

2. Personal savings.

3. Loans from family or friends.

4. Grants and incentives from public bodies (like the IDA, Forbairt).

5. Investment by promoters, partners or shareholders.

Capital can be defined as follows:

FIXED CAPITAL: the non-liquid form of capital – money in the form of land, buildings, machinery, equipment – usually not for resale and used as part of the running of the business.

WORKING CAPITAL: the difference between Current Assets and Current Liabilities of a business. Current liabilities generally consist of creditors (the people to whom the business owes money) and short-term loans. The lesser the current liabilities of a business the better because it allows for more working capital or current accessible money for immediate use in the business. Current assets are generally stock, debtors (the people who owe the business money) – there is money out there to be collected. The more debtors there are, the better. A healthy working capital figure ensures that the business has sufficient funds in the form of current assets to cover its current liabilities.

VENTURE CAPITAL: This is investment received from an investor who wishes to take a high risk, keeping in mind the possibility of making a higher than average positive return, as well as the possibility of making a negative return. An example of a venture capitalist is Richard Branson. Some promoters would also fall into this category.

SOCIAL CAPITAL: This refers to the infrastructure of the state i.e. roads, state schools, hospitals, public libraries. The basis for this public capital is through government spending of public monies

Short-Term, Medium-Term and Long-Term Finance

The sources of finance mentioned previously can be broken down into the following categories.

SHORT-TERM FINANCE (DURATION = UP TO ONE YEAR)

1. Bank overdraft: involves permission to overdraw an account in a bank to a specific amount, as sanctioned by the bank manager. It is a cheap source of finance, only available to customers who have a satisfactory record. Interest charged is allowable against profits or taxes. The facility can, however, be withdrawn at any time.
2. Bill of Exchange: could be described as similar to a post-dated cheque of sorts which is given in exchange for goods delivered. A bill may be discounted by the holder, should they require finance immediately, and the level of discount is normally agreed at the outset. The basic criterion applied to a bill transaction is that it should be self-financing by the date of maturity – this is usually thirty, sixty or ninety days, but can be arranged for longer periods. It is an unconditional order requiring the person to whom it is addressed to pay on demand a certain sum of money at an agreed fixed future date (an IOU).

3. Amounts due to be paid by Debtors still outstanding, but yet to be collected: these amounts can be used by a business as finance. Debtors are current assets to a business in this way.

4. Credit terms agreed by Creditors (people to whom the business owes money): When a business purchases goods on credit, rather than demanding payment up front, creditors allow either thirty or sixty days before the payment is due. This time lapse allows the business to use the money it has to finance the business until creditors' payments fall due. Businesses like Dunnes Stores can sell goods for cash (cash up front) and purchase their materials on credit, sometimes availing of ninety days' credit. During this time they can bank their takings and earn interest, thus benefiting. This method of financing, involving rapid turnover generating small profits, is often called 'Leaning on the Trade' or Trade Credit Taken.

5. Letters of Credit: requests from the issuing bank to its foreign agent to honour all cheques presented by the holder only up to the limit specified in the letter of credit. It is an undertaking of a bank to honour demands for payment and is usually the means by which trade is carried out between companies in different countries.

6. Factoring: the sale of debts for less than their actual value to a finance company – this company being called 'the factor'. The debtors are no longer the debtors of the supplier but the debtors of the factor. It means immediate cash to finance the business. A loss is made, however, where the value of the debtors might have been €100,000 and sold to the factor for €94,000.

7. Taxation and Expenses Due: There is a period of time, i.e. six to twelve months, before interest is levied on unpaid business taxes. A business can allow the money that is to be used for payment to accumulate interest. It is sometimes used for something else and in this way acts as a short-term loan to the business. Unpaid VAT and taxation on profits are often used as finance for businesses in this way. The same criterion can be applied to overheads and short-term expenses like ESB bills, rent and rates and advertising bills. If payment can be delayed, the money acts as short-term finance.

MEDIUM-TERM FINANCE (DURATION 1 TO 5 YEARS)

1. Term Loan: These are usually designed to finance the purchase of fixed assets. Repayments are made by agreed stated amounts as negotiated. Repayments are usually paid monthly or quarterly and the borrower knows exactly what his commitment is. Term loans are usually more expensive than overdrafts.

2. Hire Purchase: Also called Instalment Credit, it is a method of paying for equipment in instalments, while gaining possession of the equipment immediately. An example is payment for televisions, fridges etc. as part of the household ESB bill. An initial contract is signed on receipt of the article purchased and the repayment might be six payments over a year, every two

months, included on the ESB bill. The purchaser does not own the article, however, until the final instalment is paid. A computer might be purchased over five years in the same way.

3. Leasing: This gives a business the opportunity to use an asset, without ever owning it, for a specified number of years for set payments. The ownership of the article will never pass from the leasing company. This is availing of non-liquid capital to advance a business.

LONG-TERM FINANCE (DURATION 5 YEARS AND OVER)

1. Investment/Owner Capital: Promoters, partners, shareholders, venture capitalists can all be owners of a business and are responsible for investing and contributing long-term capital to the business. The more the investment, the greater the ability for a business to grow and expand and to become more competitive by being able to purchase the most modern equipment and to employ highly skilled staff and pay them accordingly.

   Ordinary shareholders, preference shareholders and debenture holders contribute the capital to the business. These shares are said to be the Equity Share Capital of the business – this means the holders are entitled to the equity or balance of profits.

   Ordinary shareholders are the risk-takers because there is no guaranteed dividend (money paid out of profits, not out of the original capital). They are the last people to get money. (Generally they have voting rights.)

   Preference shareholders carry a fixed dividend and must be paid before ordinary shareholders. (Generally they have less or no voting rights compared to ordinary shareholders.)

   Debenture holders contribute the capital in the form of a long-term loan, carrying a fixed rate of interest and a specified repayment date (maturity date). Debenture holders are paid before the other shareholders, even if profits are inadequate to cover the repayment. There is a risk of court action if a business defaults on the interest payments, and this could force receivership. (Generally they have no vote.)

2. Sale and Lease Back: Large companies often run short of ready finance and may decide to sell their premises to an investment institution. These companies then lease the same buildings or offices (a long-term lease – usually twenty years) from the investment institution. Business continues as before, but on a rental basis. The rent is reviewed every few years. Ready finance is received up front on the sale of the premises, allowing the business to become liquid again, despite having to pay rent in exchange.

3. Government and semi-state grants: New domestic small businesses as well as export-orientated businesses tend to gain finance in the form of grants because these producers help to improve the balance of trade through import substitution and capital inflow.

nding?

ɔ the practice of making loans (extending credit) to
fy for market interest rates because of problems with
of borrowers who would otherwise not have access to
ɪe loan is offered at a higher rate than regular loans due
ɔrime borrowers typically have histories of payment

a number of credit instruments including sub-prime
ans, and sub-prime credit cards. Sometimes these types
ɪve regular higher fees and up-front charges attached as
reement. Many house repossessions have resulted from
ɔrrowers to keep up with the payments.
ɪe sub-prime lending industry have criticised loan
ɪey engage in predatory practices – targeting borrowers
ɪcial resources to meet the terms of the loans they are
ɔɪɪɛɪɛᴅ ᴏᴠɛʀ ᴛɪɛ ___ ɡ   n.

Northern Rock background

www.rte.ie/business, Friday 14 September 2007

Northern Rock has a long history providing home loans as a mutual building society.

However, like most building societies in the UK and Ireland, it demutualised and became a bank with a stock market listing.

It entered the Irish market in 1999 and up to yesterday was best known as an aggressive player in the savings market where it offers both telephone and post banking.

It has around 24,000 to 25,000 Irish customers, and at its half-year results it said 13,400 of these were online customers and that its customer base in Ireland had around €2.4 billion on deposit.

That means the average deposit could be in the vicinity of €100,000, which indicates the bank attracted people with plenty of cash.

Northern Rock is also the fifth largest mortgage lender in the UK, though it does not do home loans in the Republic of Ireland.

There is a good reason for that, as the bank offers a very attractive 4.75% interest rate. That is just about the most attractive in the market, according to the Financial Regulator.

Borrowing practices

Northern Rock ought to be a healthy business. But it is part of a trend in banking that those who do not work in the sector are coming to grips with. And that is 'how do banks get money to lend to borrowers?' Usually we associate this with taking in deposits, which are then loaned on.

However this is not how Northern Rock operate. It borrows most of the money it lends from other banks at the interbank lending rate.

Currently, there is huge nervousness in this market, with central banks having to provide money to keep money circulating in the system. This nervousness is associated with sub-prime mortgages.

Thousands of sub-prime mortgages were issued in the US – many at a time when interest rates were low. US interest rates have risen, leading to economic problems. Consequently, sub-prime borrowers have been failing to meet their loan repayments. The level of foreclosure is at such a level that it has caused a crisis.

This crisis has spread around the world because sub-prime lenders have sold on their mortgage debt in the market. This is called securitisation.

Investment funds have bought into these debts over which there are now sizeable question marks. This makes assets almost impossible to value. If one bank doesn't know the value of another, then it is reluctant to loan money.

The two consequences have been falling share values and banks finding themselves unable to raise money. Even if they can raise the cash, they are have to pay very high interbank lending rates.

These rates are currently at ten-year highs. Yesterday, Northern Bank was simply unable to get money at all.

Mortgage fall-out will take time – Bush

www.rte.ie/business, Friday 14 September 2007

US President George W Bush has announced a package of measures to help US home-owners struggling to pay their mortgages amid the sub-prime loan crisis.

He said the turmoil on financial markets stemming from the problem would take time to play out. But he said the mortgage market worries represented only a small part of the economy and would not undermine what he said were 'sound fundamentals'.

Financial markets around the workd have been affected in recent weeks as defaults have risen on so-called sub-prime mortgages.

President Bush urged US lenders to work with home-owners to renegotiate their mortgages to prevent default. He called on Congress to approve legislation he proposed last year to modernise the Federal Housing Administration, which provides mortgage insurance to borrowers through a network of private sector lenders.

The FHA will soon launch a new programme to allow home-owners with good credit history, but who cannot afford their current payments, to refinance into FHA-insured mortgages, Bush said.

He also pledged to work with the Democratic-controlled Congress to temporarily reform a key housing provision of the federal tax code to make it easier for home-owners to refinance their mortgages.

Financial analysts said Bush's proposals were unlikely to have an immediate impact on home-owners who may be in danger of defaulting on their mortgages.

PRACTICE QUESTIONS

1. List two short-term, two medium-term and two long-term sources of labour.
2. What are the *four* Factors of Production?
3. What are the differences between Fixed Capital and Social Capital?
4. What are the differences between Working Capital and Venture Capital?
5. What are the differences between a Bank Overdraft and a Term Loan?
6. What is a Bill of Exchange?
7. How do Letters of Credit and Credit Terms differ?
8. Why are Debtors regarded as sources of short-term finance and how is Factoring connected with debtors?
9. Why is Taxation regarded as a source of short-term finance?
10. Are Leasing and Sale and Lease Back one and the same?
11. Define Hire Purchase, giving a current example.
12. How do Ordinary, Preference Shareholders and Debentures differ with regard to ownership of a business?
13. What is Equity Share Capital?
14. Explain the following: Dividend, Sale and Lease Back, and Government/semi-state grants.
15. Why are domestic entrepreneurs given grants?
16. What is sub-prime lending? What do sub-prime lenders do?
17. Explain the sub-prime lending crisis.

Commencement Finance or Seed Money (Seed Capital)

Seed Capital (start-up finance) is the initial money or capital used to start a new venture or business.

The amount of this equity capital is initially quite small because the venture is at the idea stage and there is a high risk that it will fail. This type of finance is usually quite expensive than later-stage financing because of the high risk involved.

Possible Sources

- Friends and family (family members providing security/guarantor facility to other family members).
- Traditional financing sources such as banks and venture capital firms.
- Enterprise Boards (non-profit organisations dedicated to providing seed capital to new businesses).

Seed Capital Scheme

The SCS (1993) formed part of the BES (Business Expansion Scheme), which was introduced in 1984.

It included the facility to provide a refund of tax already paid by an individual who set up or took up employment in a new qualifying business. This investment of money had to be in certain listed qualifying Irish companies, thus raising seed capital for these new businesses. It was also allowable for an employee who left employment and invested by means of shares in one of these companies to claim a refund of income tax they had already paid in previous years.

The BES scheme ended officially in 2006. However, both schemes have now been modified and extended, with increases in the annual investment requirement limit from €31,750 to €150,000 for the BES and to €100,000 for the SCS.

Welcome for EU approval of BES extension

Jim Aughney

Business leaders have welcomed EU approval of Brian Cowen's planned extension of the Business Expansion Scheme (BES) and Seed Capital Scheme (SCS).

The European Commission announced that it will not raise any objections to the changes in the schemes announced in Budget 2007.

This follows a review of the operation of BES in Ireland carried out by the Department of Finance in conjunction with the Department of Enterprise, Trade & Employment and the Revenue Commissioners.

The review found that 58pc of BES companies classed themselves as manufacturing, while 22pc classed themselves as international services.

Over 70pc of companies were new, being set up in the past ten years and one third of all firms were start-ups or in the development phase. The survey also found that the bulk of firms, over 60pc, employed less than 15 staff and in two-thirds of cases their annual sales were less than €1m.

The chief executive of the Irish Taxation Institute, Mark Redmond, has welcomed the approval by the EU Commission to changes in the schemes.

'As the recent Government report on BES and Seed Capital illustrated, these initiatives are key contributors to economic activity. Policies like BES are central to getting new businesses up and running,' Mr Redmond said.

Source: *Irish Independent,* 30 August 2007

Development Finance

This is expansion capital and is regarded as being less risky than seed capital because the business has a guaranteed track record.

Ways of Raising Development Money

- Traditional financing sources, e.g. banks and venture capital firms.
- Equity Investment (in shares in the business) – issuing shares (share capital). Different company share details are on public record and available from **www.cro.ie**.
- Investment Fund Managers will fund small speculative infrastructure projects – the investor will expect returns in excess of their standard yield.
- Project Finance – some investment banks will advance funds for projects.
- Creating Debenture or Loan Notes (Loan Capital) – interest has to be paid to debenture holders.
- Factoring – selling some debts to a finance company at a discount.
- Sale and Lease Back of high-depreciation equipment that costs the business money – a bank may agree to raise finance based on the value of these assets.
- Lease and Lease Back – assets are leased to the bank, not sold to them, for an upfront lease payment

What is an IPO?

The term IPO means Initial Public Offering and was central to the dot-com era in the late 1990s during the technology bull market (rising shares). The term siliconaire described the dot-com entrepreneurs in their early twenties and thirties who suddenly found themselves gaining from the proceeds of their Internet companies' IPOs due to positive share deals.

The IPOs were the first sale of stock by these private, small, young internet-based companies *seeking capital to expand* and this was also done by larger privately owned companies wishing to gain public company status. These were very risky investments and it was difficult to predict what stock values would result: however, the positive entrepreneurial economic environment of the era benefited many young business people.

Matching the Sources of Finance with Particular Needs of the Organisation or the Individual

Long-term finance is usually sought by businesses who run short of finance or wish to commence or expand businesses, where the amount of capital required is large. The decisions and commitments are long term and costly and require serious consideration before they are undertaken.

Medium-term finance need not necessarily apply to a business. Someone might want to buy a home computer for their children or change a car by availing of a term loan. They might wish to lease a photocopier or buy the computer in instalments by availing of hire purchase.

Short-term finance is usually required by businesses. A bank overdraft, however, can be sought by ordinary individuals who have a good track record with their bank. It will be reviewed after a year, whereas a term loan (medium-term finance) might have a repayment deadline of up to five years. Other sources like credit terms and taxation and expenses due represent short-term ways of maintaining the use of money, that would otherwise be used to pay creditors, to finance the business. (This concept is explained under 'Short-term Finance' in the previous section.) Also, quick money can be acquired by factoring, but a loss is made in the short term.

Cash Flow Forecasts

These are charts which analyse a business's inflows of money compared with outflows of money in order to predict whether a business will have enough money coming in to adequately cover outgoing expense payments due. Every business should compile a cash flow prediction chart or forecast each year or half yearly depending on the business. Typical inflows are sales, loans, investment capital raised, grants and refunds.

Typical outflows are interest on loans, purchases, wages, commission, advertising, rent and rates, light and heat, telephone, administration expenses, general expenses, personal drawings, and any capital expenditure like spending on fixed assets (office equipment/furniture, premises, plant, motor vehicles for the business).

THINGS TO BE KEPT IN MIND WHEN COMPILING A CASH FLOW CHART

1. Debtors' and Creditors' Credit Terms: For example, if we allow our debtors (people that owe us money) one month's credit, this means that if we bill them in January, the inflow will not occur until February (February entry into chart).

    If our creditors (people we owe money to) allow us two months' credit, this means that if they bill us in January, we will not have to pay until March – outflow will not occur until March (March entry into chart).

    Important: It is only at the moment that the inflows and outflows occur that the figures are lodged into the Cashflow chart and **not when the bills are dated**. This appears to be the most common mistake made by students.

2. Terms like 'month in arrears' and 'in the month incurred': Wages paid out by us a month in arrears (often referred to as a lag in the payment of wages by a month) means, for example, work done by employees in July will not be paid for by us until August (August entry into chart).

    Expenses paid out by us per month or in the month incurred means, for example, in June itself (June entry into the chart).

3. If a wage increase of 15% is due from June onwards, the increased figure will appear in the months from June onwards (including June). Note: the wages figure *never* reverts back to the original amount.

4. Terms like 'quarterly in arrears': Bills due for payment quarterly in arrears means at the end of every three months. Sometimes the first payment date due will be given, for example, a light and heat bill of €2,000 payable quarterly in arrears beginning on 1 February. Entries into the chart would be €500 in February, €500 in May, €500 in August and €500 in November. If no first payment date is given, and the chart is a twelve-monthly forecast starting in January, the entries into the chart would be €500 in March, €500 in June, €500 in September and €500 in December.

5. A cash purchase of goods: This is recorded in the chart as stock – an amount bought and paid for on the same day. March cash purchases of goods for stock, paid for immediately, is entered into the chart as an outflow in March only.

6. Calculation of Commission: (This exercise is probably the one that students find the most difficult.) If staff are to receive a 5 per cent commission of total sales, it means that the calculations should be worked on the question given and not the chart the student is compiling. Cash and Credit Sales will be listed in the question and these are added per month to get each month's Total Sales.

   For example: if the sales information in the question is

SALES	Cash	Credit
January	2,000	3,000
February	5,000	2,500

   and the commission is to be calculated at 5 per cent of Total Sales, payable to staff each month one month in arrears, then 5 per cent of €5,000 = €250 is entered into the chart in February. (This represents January wages not paid out until February.) Five per cent of €7,500 = €375 is entered into the chart in March. (This represents February wages not paid out until March.)

7. If new equipment or machinery is purchased, it is entered once in the month that it is purchased. The equipment is assumed to be purchased and paid for immediately, unless other information is provided where a lease exists. If this is the case, it becomes an ongoing bill that is either paid monthly or perhaps quarterly.

Note: Depreciation has *nothing to do with cash flow*, so it is ignored in this regard.

PRACTICE QUESTION

Frank Smith is expected to have the following inflows and outflows of money from 1 January to 30 June 2008. The cash balance at 1 January was €1,000.

1. Expected Sales

Month	Cash €	Credit €
January	2,300	1,000
February	2,000	1,500
March	3,000	1,800
April	2,800	1,400
May	3,300	1,500
June	3,500	1,900

2. Expected Expenses

	Jan	Feb	Mar	Apr	May	June
Purchases (credit)	700	1,500	1,300	1,000	1,000	1,000
Cash purchases	300	2,000	800	1,000	1,100	1,400
Wages	1,000	1,000	1,000	1,000	1,500	1,500
Purchase of office equipment		7,000				
Rent and rates	300	300	350	350	350	350
Administration	70	60	60	60	60	65

3. Purchases are on credit, where one month's credit is taken from suppliers.
4. Debtors are allowed two months' credit.
5. Commission is 2% of total sales and is paid to employees one month in arrears.
6. A yearly light and heat bill of €2,000 is payable quarterly in arrears, with the first payment starting in February.
7. The lag in the payment of wages is one month.
8. Administration expenses are payable a month in arrears.
9. Any other expenses are paid out in the month incurred.

Based on the information given, you are required to:
(a) Compile a Cash Flow Forecast for Frank Smith for the period 1 January to 30 June 2008.
(b) Identify the sources of shortfall of cash.
(c) Recommend any provisions that should be put in place to avoid shortfalls of cash.

SOLUTION TO PRACTICE QUESTION

(a) Cash Flow Forecast for Frank Smith for the six months ending 30 June 2008

CASH INFLOWS	Jan	Feb	Mar	Apr	May	Jun
	€	€	€	€	€	€
Cash sales	2,300	2,000	3,000	2,800	3,300	3,500
Credit sales	-	-	1,000	1,500	1,800	1,400
TOTAL INFLOWS	2,300	2,000	4,000	4,300	5,100	4,900
CASH OUTFLOWS						
Cash purchases	300	2,000	800	1,000	1,100	1,400
Credit Purchases	-	700	1,500	1,300	1,000	1,000
Wages	-	1,000	1,000	1,000	1,000	1,500
Commission		66	70	96	84	96
Office equipment		7,000	-	-	-	-
Rent and rates	300	300	350	350	350	350
Admin. expenses	-	70	60	60	60	60
Light and heat	-	500	-	-	500	-
TOTAL OUTFLOWS	600	11,636	3,780	3,806	4,094	4,406
NET *(inflows – outflows)*	1,700	–9,636	220	494	1,006	494
BALANCE 1/1/xx	1,000	2,700	–6,936	–6,716	–6,222	–5,216
BALANCE 30/6/xx	2,700	–6,936	–6,716	–6,222	–5,216	–4,722

(b) Mr Smith will experience a shortfall of cash in February. This is due to the proposed purchase of office equipment. Cash inflows for credit sales are not due in until March and this is also a major cause of the shortfall.

(c) The following provisions should be put in place to avoid the cash shortfall:

1. Either postpone the purchase of the office equipment or acquire a loan to cover it in January.
2. The length of payment time allowed to debtors needs to be reviewed and reduced to one month's credit. Money from credit sales would come in in February if this could be agreed.

PRACTICE QUESTIONS

1. Distinguish between Commencement and Development Finance. What bodies provide these monies?
2. List two ways of raising development finance.
3. What were the purposes of the (a) the BES and (b) the SCS?

4. What were IPOs and how were they linked to development finance?
5. Why are Cash Flow Forecasts so vital to organisations?
6. Is Depreciation part of a cash flow chart?

Note: In order to understand fully the detail in the following section, the student should be able to prepare a cash flow forecast as has been explained.

Credit Control and Cash Flow/Liquidity

The frequency of cash inflows and outflows will be regulated by the credit terms agreed between purchaser and seller. Control on credit allowed means, in simple terms, chasing up money that is due to you. It is in the interest of all retail outlets to have a tight credit control policy.

Liquidity Ratio

Accountants measure liquidity using the Liquidity Ratio which ideally should be 1:1.

$$\text{Formula: } \frac{\text{Current Assets } less \text{ Closing Stock}}{\text{Current Liabilities}}$$

Answer will be CA *less* CS: CL

Current assets consist of valuable items in a business that can be easily converted into cash. Debtors (people who owe you money) are an example – money due to come in. Current liabilities consist of debts that we owe to creditors (people to whom we owe money). Closing stock is excluded because it is regarded as the current asset that is the most difficult to convert into cash. A business's current assets must be able to cover its current liabilities. In other words, the money it has must be able to cover the money it owes.

If a business shows a Liquidity Ratio of 2.5:1 this indicates a bad credit control policy and an under-utilisation of resources (meaning credit control personnel are not doing their job properly and debts are not being collected on time). There is a danger in this case that outstanding debts could turn into bad debts and would have to be written off – causing unnecessary losses that could be avoided.

If a business shows a liquidity ratio of 5:1 this indicates that its current assets are unable to cover its current liabilities, so even if the debtor payments due are collected on time, there would not be enough money generated to allow current liabilities to be paid off. The business in this case has a very serious liquidity problem and must substantially increase sales and profitability in order to break even.

Cash flow charts were discussed in the previous section. Since they are a means of measuring future requirements with regard to money needs, they therefore help a business to avoid shortfalls of cash and allow for appropriate future cash planning.

Irish business need to cheque out e-payments

John Kennedy

Credit control and late payments are often a matter of life and death for small Irish business and the sector is believed to be behind the European norm in adopting e-payment methods.

According to the European Central Bank, 24pc of non-cash transactions in Ireland are made by cheque. This amounts to 79pc of all euro changing hands via non-cash methods.

Electronic credit transfers account for only 15pc of the volume of payments in the Irish economy each year.

The need to address this in order to boost productivity is paramount.

The introduction of the Single European Payments Area (SEPA) could trigger more Irish businesses to pursue electronic payments and shake free of the administrative burden of a cheque-based economy.

'The Irish market is still lodging 180 million cheques every year,' says Colm Lyon of Dublin-based Realex Payments.

Realex processes up to €4bn per annum worth of online payments for Irish-based businesses like Aer Lingus as well as overseas merchants like CD Wow.

Accounting software player Sage is also about to launch e-payment services for Irish small and medium-sized businesses.

'Cash flow is the biggest concern to small businesses and being paid on time is vital,' says Jessica McIntire, head of products at Sage Ireland.

She adds that productivity is becoming an urgent issue for Irish firms and that electronic payments will boost SME performance; 'Increasing productivity is pivotal for Irish businesses to compete.'

Lyon said SEPA will work as a single domestic payments market in which citizens and businesses will be able to make payments as easily and inexpensively as they can locally.

SEPA is a project of the European banks and the intention is to harmonise bank systems throughout the eurozone so as to make cross-border payments easier and eventually to facilitate eurozone banking from a single account in any one country.

'This is great news for Irish businesses. At the moment they are writing cheques to one another. But in the future, to remit money, they will use a sort code and international bank account number (IBAN) and simply send the money.

'We see this being expanded to handle direct debits, as distinct from credit card payments. At present a book shop in Paris won't accept a Laser card, but in the future we expect this will be harmonised.

'If you want to remit money to someone in France today you would need to set up a French bank account, but from next year the French bank must accept your e-payment from the Bank of Ireland, for example,' Lyon says.

McIntire says that compared to the time involved with cheques — from chasing payments, waiting for the cheque to arrive (if indeed it does), reconciling the payment to accounts and then lodging the physical cheque into the bank — paying electronically in only a few seconds makes sense.

'We have feedback from our customers that managing cash flow is one of the most difficult elements of their business and it's the cause of too many businesses going bust. We're offering an opportunity for businesses to improve their cash flow by taking payment immediately over the phone and directly into the bank.

'The average salary per individual in the workplace is not increasing, while at the same time we need to increase the productivity per individual.

'It's a growth market. We are predicting a 30pc increase in the market place in the next two years,' she concludes.

Source: *Irish Independent,* August 2007

Impact of Credit Control Policy on the Liquidity and Profitability of a Business

A tight and regulated credit control policy is essential to ensure *on time* cash inflow and outflow.

DEBT COLLECTION: making sure that debts are collected and money is received when it is supposed to be received will:

1. Reduce the liquidity ratio and bring it nearer to the ideal 1:1 ratio.
2. Allow accurate cash flow forecasting, with planned spending being postponed if a shortfall occurs. If spending is essential, loan arrangements can be put in place.
3. Skilled credit control personnel will be able to estimate monies that are likely to be paid late, as well as possible bad debts. Money can then be put aside to cover these eventualities.
4. Future investments can be confidently planned, e.g. the purchase of new premises or equipment.
5. Costs can be minimised once sufficient monies are collected to pay off debts. This, combined with appropriate price competitiveness, advertising mechanisms, materials and customer service, will ensure a higher level of sales and will increase profit margins.

DEBT PAYMENT: making sure that money owed by the business is paid out to creditors on time will:

1. Avoid unnecessary interest accruing on loans, overdraft facilities and credit cards.
2. Ensure a good reputation with regard to debt payment and will help to gain new customers/sales through goodwill (reputation).
3. Allow an accurate picture to be drawn with regard to how much money is available to either put aside or invest.
4. Uphold good reputation with regard to business management and profitability and attract new investors. Greater capital investment means business expansion and further profitability.

Once a business remains within the credit term agreed (payment within a month or two months) and once this degree of flexibility is respected, creditors will usually be thankful for the business and may put more business in the direction of the company.

When a business has:

1. a satisfactory level of stock turnover, as indicated by how many times stock is replaced (empty shelves that are efficiently restocked) – discussed previously under the heading 'Stock Control';
2. an effective and efficient Credit Control Policy, indicating a well managed cash flow record; and
3. a 1:1 Liquidity Ratio (or as near to this as possible), indicating that the business has enough money in current assets to cover its current liabilities;

this will imply that the retail outlet is operating at a high level of efficiency and profitability and it has a healthy turnover per annum.

PRACTICE QUESTIONS
1. What is Credit Control?
2. How might a business know that there is a problem with its credit control policy?
3. What does a Liquidity Ratio of 3:1 indicate?
4. What does a Liquidity Ratio of 8:1 indicate?
5. How are Cash Flow Forecasts linked to Credit Control policy?
6. Why would e-payments help a business's cash flow and credit control?
7. Explain *five* benefits of prompt debt collection.
8. Explain *four* benefits of prompt debt payment.
9. Why might efficient cash flow and credit control policies indicate profitability?

Unit Cost and Selling Price Calculations

The easiest way to understand Cost Analysis, and how Selling Prices are arrived at, is to take a question as follows:

PRACTICE QUESTION
You are the administrator of a restaurant and in the business of monitoring costs. The following information is made available to you:

Ingredients to produce ten portions of Irish stew.

1 kg lamb	@ €1.35 per kg
1 kg potatoes	@ 4c per kg
1 kg onion	@ 13c per kg
2 leeks	@ 5c each
1 head celery	@ 10c
1 kg button onions	@ 18c per kg
1 bunch parsley	@ 5c

You are required to:

(a) Calculate the Total Cost of the ingredients used.

(b) Find the Average Cost per portion.

(c) Work out the Selling Price so that the business can achieve a 40% profit on materials.

(d) Calculate the Profit in money terms.

SOLUTION

(a) Cost of ingredients Total = €1.95

(b) Average Cost per portion = $\dfrac{€1.95}{10}$ = 20 cent

(c) Selling Price = Cost *plus* Profit (the Selling Price formula is a formula that must be learned)

Selling Price is always 100%

Therefore 100% = Cost *plus* Profit

Related to question:

$$100\% = \text{Cost} + 40\%$$

therefore　　Cost = 60%

from (a)　　Cost = €1.95

$$60\% = €1.95$$

What are we looking for? Answer 100% Selling Price

So　　　$1\% = \dfrac{€1.95}{60}$

$$100\% = \dfrac{€1.95 \times 100}{60}$$

Answer = €3.25

The Selling Price that would be charged for the dish is €3.25

(i.e. $\dfrac{€3.25}{10}$ = 33 pence per portion based on 10 portions, which was not asked).

(d) The Profit in money terms is found in the following way:

Apply the Selling Price formula again but this time in money terms rather than in percentage terms.

Selling Price = Cost + Profit

€3.25　　　　= €1.95 + Profit

Answer: therefore Profit = €1.30

It is important to note that different businesses have different profit margins and therefore the percentage profit levels will vary. Larger businesses can afford to charge lower selling prices because they can avail of large trade discounts through bulk buying or buying raw materials cheaper abroad. They create unmatchable price levels (too price competitive) that have contributed to smaller traders having to close their businesses.

Specialised businesses often have to charge higher prices because it is more expensive for them in terms of their costs and they combat their cost problems by passing on the cost to the consumer in the form of higher prices.

Warning! The last practice question only deals with Material costs in the catering industry.

There are three main costs in every business.
1. Materials (e.g. shampoos and conditioners for hairdressers and food and drink for chefs).
2. Labour (payment for labour is wages – a rising cost in business).
3. Overheads (like electricity bills, telephone bills, insurance, advertising, stationery).

All three costs have to be taken into account when a business is setting selling prices.

Competitors' prices also have to be considered. It must be remembered that unless a business can secure a solid market share, it cannot charge extraordinarily high prices, because consumers generally look for a mixture of 'value for money' and 'quality'. Some consumers will continue to buy a good or avail of a service based on consumer loyalty.

Securing a good reputation (through advertising and a good marketing strategy) and resulting consumer loyalty will allow greater flexibility regarding selling prices.

PRACTICE QUESTIONS
1. What *three* types of costs are connected with every business?
2. How is Selling Price defined?
3. Why can larger businesses afford to charge lower prices?
4. List *four* factors that will have an influence on Selling Prices set by business people.
5. You are a chef and owner of a business and the cost of the ingredients of an Irish stew (which is divided into four portions) is as follows:

425 g stewing lamb	@ €2.20 per kg
400 g potatoes	@ 70c per kg
100 g celery	@ 50c per kg
100 g button onions	@ 50c per kg
10 onions	@ 10c each
100 g leeks	@ 55c per kg

(a) Calculate the Total Cost of the ingredients.

(b) Find the Average Cost per portion.

(c) Work out the Selling Price so that the business can achieve a 40% profit on materials.

(d) Calculate the profit (on materials only) of the dish as a whole, in money terms.

Note: Be careful to calculate the cost based on 1,000 g = 1 kg.
In the case of drink 1,000 ml = 1 litre.

Sample Assignment Briefs

1. You have decided to start your own business. You are required to prepare a cash flow chart for the first six months of trading and a breakeven chart to present to your bank as you require an overdraft facility.

2. Candidates should investigate finance and business controls within an organisation of their choice under the following headings:
   - Brief History, Size, Ownership and Staff Structure.
   - Management Controls which include Planning Controls, Stock Controls, Quality Control, Financial Control, Credit Control.
   - Overall Performance Appraisal.

CHOOSE QUESTION **A** OR **B** BUT *NOT* BOTH

A. Downey and Sons Incorporated produce goods and have recently received worrying cost information.

One product exists within the range of goods that is making a loss. Financial Cost and Sales information on this product is as follows:

Sales (2,500 units at €120 each)		€300,000
Direct Labour	€200,000	
Direct Materials	€40,000	
Factory Overheads – variable	€10,000	
–fixed	€30,000	€280,000
		€20,000
Selling Expenses – variable	€15,000	
– fixed	€8,000	
Other Fixed Overheads	€6,000	€29,000
Net Loss		€9,000

(i) Make the appropriate pre-calculations to prepare to draw the Breakeven chart.
(ii) Draw the Breakeven chart and include the following details on it:
    (a) The Breakeven point.
    (b) The 100% Present Capacity position.
    (c) The Profit or Loss when 500 units are produced.
    (d) The Profit or Loss when 2,000 units are produced.

    Comment on your findings.

(iii) What recommendations would you suggest that would improve the Breakeven level and convert the Net Loss to a Net Profit?

B. Based on your knowledge of stock control, analyse the stock control procedures that are operated by a supermarket or superstore in your home locality or wherever is most convenient. (The student should prepare well by summarising the appropriate parts of the text material in Chapter 2.)

3. Freebird Ltd manufactures rail engines and carriages. The business expects cash shortages to occur. The following details apply to the business:

1. Sales are expected to be €2 million in January 2008 and are expected to grow at 3% per month until December 2008. Debtors are allowed one month's credit.
2. The business has €300,000 in the bank in January 2008.
3. The issuing of company shares is expected to raise €600,000 in July.
4. Redundancy payments of €400,000 have to be paid out in May.
5. Purchases are calculated at 20% of sales. The company avails of one month's credit.
6. Wages are calculated at 30% of sales, and paid to employees one month in arrears.
7. Administration costs are expected to amount to €550 per month.
8. The outright purchase of premises is expected in February at a cost of €7.2 million.
9. Government grants of €40,000 will be received every quarter, beginning in March.
10. A tax refund of €3,000 will be received in April.

    (a) Prepare a Cash flow forecast for Freebird Ltd, for the twelve-month period 1 January to 31 December 2008.
    (b) Identify the location of and reasons for any shortfall of cash.
    (c) Make appropriate suggestions to management of Freebird Ltd as to how to avoid shortages of cash, based on this twelve-monthly projection.

Sample Questions for Student Research on 'Finance and Business Controls'

1. Can you provide me with a little information about the history, size, ownership and staff structure of the organisation?
2. What types of planning controls are used by the business?
3. Are 'Knowledge Management Systems' used?
4. Is performance appraisal part of the business?
5. What financial controls are used in the business? E.g. breakeven analysis, budgeting, cash flow forecasting, cost analysis (income and expenditure analysis).
6. Are any specific types of computer software used for financial control within the business?
7. What are the main sources of finance in the business? Loans, overdrafts, investor capital, grants, savings? Please specify.
8. How is debt collection managed?
9. How is debt payment managed? Does the business still pay creditors by cheque, or is an online e-payments method used?
10. What terms of trade (credit terms, discounts) are:
    - Offered to debtors.
    - Taken from creditors.
11. How does the business control quality and maintain standards of excellence? E.g. 100% inspection, random sampling, quality circles, observation.
12. Who mainly supplies the business with:
    - Goods?
    - Services?
    (Include office stock)
13. How are stock levels monitored? E.g. EPOS system, stock cards, indexing, MBWA – management by walk around, ordering/reordering.
14. Have understocking or overstocking ever posed a problem for the business? If so, why?

3. Banking, Currencies, Visual Data and Insurance

The Euro and the European Central Bank

There were initially 15 EU countries in the EEA (European Economic Area) – Germany, Belgium, Spain, France, Ireland, Italy, Luxembourg, the Netherlands, Austria, Portugal, Finland and Greece, Denmark, Sweden and the United Kingdom. Later Norway, Iceland and Liechtenstein came into the EEA. More recently, Bulgaria, Cyprus, the Czech Republic, Estonia, Finland, Greece, Hungary, Latvia, Lithuania, Malta, Poland, Romania, Slovakia and Slovenia joined.

1 January 2002 marked the launch of euro bank notes and coins. The introduction of the euro as the single currency for around 300 million European citizens was a truly historic event.

The European Central Bank (ECB) has been at the centre of this development. The ECB was first established on 1 June 1998. The German Bundesbank in Frankfurt is the nerve centre of the ECB. It is the governing bank that covers the 12 different countries in the Eurozone (approximately 304 million men, women and children).

The ESCB or European System of Central Banks consists of the ECB and the National Central Banks (NCBs) of each individual member state. Three member states, Denmark, Sweden and the United Kingdom, are part of the ESCB but have opted not to adopt the euro currency.

the euro

On 1 January 2002 the euro banknotes and coins were put into circulation.

...banknotes, coins and more...

the **EURO.**
OUR *money*

The decision-making bodies of the Eurosystem are part of the ECB, namely:

1. The Governing Council – the central decision-making body in charge of monetary policy for the euro area. The Governors of each NCB are members of the Council.
2. The Executive Board.
3. The General Council — for those member states that have not adopted the euro.

The European Union (EU) was originally established as the European Economic Community (EEC) in 1957 by the Treaty of Rome. Transition to European integration began with the Maastricht Treaty in 1992. In 1997, countries wishing to adopt the single European currency had to strive to meet the following economic criteria known as the Maastricht criteria:

• Low inflation.
• Sound public finances.
• Low interest rates.
• Stable exchange rates.
• Political independence of its NCB.

These criteria laid a solid foundation for the new currency and a single monetary policy.

In January 1999, the locking of EMU (European Monetary Union) currencies against the euro marked the official beginning of EMU.

IRREVOCABLY FIXED EXCHANGE RATES

1 euro =	40.3399	Belgian Francs
	1.95583	Deutsche Mark
	340.750	Greek Drachmas
	166.386	Spanish Pesetas
	6.55957	French Francs
	0.787564	Irish Pounds
	1,936.27	Italian Lira
	40.3399	Luxembourg Francs
	2.20371	Deutch Guilders
	13,7603	Austrian Schillings
	200,482	Portuguese Escudos
	5,94573	Finish Markkas

Eleven print works were set up all over the euro area and the first euro coins were produced in August 1999. Approximately 14.5 billion euro bank notes were produced. The Irish mint (Currency Centre) producing euro notes and coins is located in Sandyford, Dublin.

The euro currency was introduced on 1 January 2002. In Ireland both the Irish currency and the euro were legal tender (acceptable in exchange for goods and services) until 9 February 2002. Since then, the euro has replaced the Irish currency.

The Euro and the ECB 2007/2008

As at 1 January 2007 there were 27 member countries of the European Union: Austria, Belgium, Bulgaria, Cyprus, Czech Republic, Denmark, Estonia, Finland, France, Germany, Greece, Hungary, Ireland, Italy, Latvia, Lithuania, Luxembourg, Malta, Netherlands, Poland, Portugal, Romania, Slovakia, Slovenia, Spain, Sweden and the United Kingdom.

The ECB is the central bank for Europe's single currency, the euro. The ECB's main task is to maintain the euro's purchasing power and thus price stability in the euro area.

European Integration

Economic and Monetary Union (EMU) in 2007

Of the 27 member countries **the euro area** comprises the 13 European Union countries that have introduced the euro since 1999, which means that they participate fully in Stage Three of EMU. They are: Belgium, Germany, Ireland, Greece, Spain, France, Italy, Luxembourg, the Netherlands, Austria, Portugal, Slovenia and Finland.

The Eurosystem comprises the ECB and the NCBs of those countries that have adopted the euro. The Eurosystem and the ECB will co-exist as long as there are EU member states outside the euro area.

The headquarters of the ECB is in Frankfurt, Germany – the nerve centre of the European Union. It is expected to move into a new building in 2011.

The ECB was established on 1 January 1998, and its first president was former Netherlands finance minister Wim Duisenberg. In November 2003 France's Jean-Claude Trichet became President and Lucas Papademos, formerly Governor of the Bank of Greece, became the ECB Vice President.

The Governing Council

The Governing Council is the main decision-making body of the ECB. It comprises:

- the six members of the Executive Board; and
- the governors of the national central banks (NCBs) from the 13 euro area countries.

Its responsibilities are:

- to adopt the guidelines and take the decisions necessary to ensure the performance of the tasks entrusted to the Eurosystem;
- to formulate monetary policy for the euro area. This includes decisions relating to monetary objectives, key interest rates, the supply of reserves in the Eurosystem, and the establishment of guidelines for the implementation of those decisions.

The Governing Council usually meets twice a month at the Eurotower in Frankfurt am Main, Germany.

At its first meeting each month, the Governing Council assesses monetary and economic developments and takes its monthly monetary policy decision. At its second meeting, the Council discusses issues mainly related to other tasks and responsibilities of the ECB and the Eurosystem.

The minutes of the meetings are not published, but the monetary policy decision is announced at a press conference held shortly after the first meeting each month. The President, assisted by the Vice-President, chairs the press conference.

FUNCTIONS OF THE ECB
(IN CO-OPERATION WITH THE NCBS JOINTLY KNOWN AS THE ESCB – EUROPEAN SYSTEM OF CENTRAL BANKS)

1. To support and contribute to the general economic policies in the Community with the main objective of price stability.

2. Open Market Operations in general – to steer interest rates, manage the liquidity (cash) situation in the market and signal the monetary policy stance within the euro area – the decision on which OMO instrument is to be used lies with the ECB. The executing of the instrument is carried out by individual NCBs. (OMO instruments are listed later.)

3. Standing Facilities – The ECB determines the effect of overnight liquidity on market interest rates and signals the general monetary policy stance following these events. The administering of standing facilities are dealt with by NCBs. (Types of standing facilities are listed later.)

4. Minimum Reserves – the application of minimum reserves by the ECB is intended to stabilise money market interest rates and to control monetary expansion that can cause inflation.

5. Counterparties – a broad range of counterparties participate in the euro system ensuring healthy foreign exchange swaps.

6. Eligible Assets – counterparties may borrow from their own NCB by using eligible assets located in another member state as collateral. This eligibility is controlled by the ECB.

ECB triggers rate hike fears

Tom McEnaney

The European Central Bank (ECB) reminded markets of its monetary policy stance yesterday in a move analysts interpreted as signalling a rate rise next month.

Meanwhile, European markets rose for the fourth day in a row on positive corporate news and growing hope the US Federal Reserve will cut its benchmark interest rate to further calm nerves in the credit markets.

The ECB said: 'The position of the Governing Council of the ECB on its monetary policy stance was expressed by its President on 2 August 2007.'

Auction

The statement came as part of a surprise announcement that the ECB would auction €40bn in three-month financing to money markets on Thursday, on top of regular funds.

The decision to add extra funds was agreed in writing by the ECB's entire Governing Council.

Unlike its weekly refinancing tenders, the ECB's monthly auctions of three-month liquidity are geared to ensuring banks have enough funding rather than implementing its monetary policy decisions.

Nonetheless, some analysts interpreted the reference to the ECB's August 2 policy stance as meaning that the ECB's Governing Council had not changed its view on rates despite heavy share price falls and tightening credit conditions since then.

'The deliberate choice of including that sentence suggests to us that the Council continues to view the chances of a rate increase in September as high,' said Jacques Cailloux, European economist with RBS.

There is evidence that investors, who have been seeking out safe harbours from recent turbulence, may be less risk-averse.

'All markets are in a risk taking mode again,' said Emiel van den Heiligenberg, head of the asset allocation at Fortis Investment. 'If you don't believe this (sell-off) is something structural, equities have been completely oversold, and tactical buyers were ready to jump in.'

In Dublin, the ISEQ gained 1.3pc. Around Europe both UK's FTSE 100 index and France's CAC 40 rose 1.8pc, while Germany's DAX index gained 1pc.

Alain Bokobza, head of strategy at Société Generale in Paris, said he saw scope for a rebound in equities. 'My case is for them to regain ground by year-end, but in a more volatile environment than we've had for a few years,' he said.

Today, investors will be looking at American jobless claims data for the week for clues in the health of the economy and to see how much room for manoeuvre the Fed has to cut.

Irish Independent, Thursday 23 August 2007

EU Energy Policy, Climate Change and Global Warming

What is the Kyoto Agreement?

The Kyoto Protocol is an agreement made under the United Nations Framework Convention on Climate Change (UNFCCC) aimed at the 'stabilisation of greenhouse gas concentrations in the atmosphere at a level that would prevent dangerous anthropogenic interference with the climate system'.

Countries that signed up as part of this agreement committed to reduce their emission of carbon dioxide and five other greenhouse gases. This rule now covers over 160 countries globally. As of June 2007, a total of 172 countries and other governmental entities have ratified the agreement. Notable exceptions include the US and Australia. Other countries, like India and China, which have ratified the protocol, are not required to reduce carbon emissions under the present agreement. This treaty expires in 2012, and international talks began in May 2007 on a future treaty to succeed the current one. Countries have to reduce their greenhouse gas emissions or they will be penalised by the UN.

The European Union has agreed policies to tackle climate change that European Commission President Jose Manuel Barroso describes as 'the most ambitious ever made'.

What are the EU's Aims on Climate Change?

Dependence on oil and gas has been a concern. The EU aims to boost wind power and other renewable sources of energy as well as increasing the use of bio-fuels to create a large percentage of the energy used for transportation. The EU wants to get countries to use renewable energy in power generation and heating. EU funding is being made available to countries for research with the aim of bringing down the price of renewable energy and low-carbon technology and finding new ways of increasing energy efficiency. As part of the energy strategy there are plans to encourage the construction of twelve plants that will demonstrate sustainable fossil fuel technologies, such as carbon capture, in action.

Research programmes on nuclear waste management are also a consideration but are controversial. Nuclear power is the cheapest low-carbon source of energy in Europe today. However, there are deep differences between pro- and anti-nuclear member states.

What are the EU's Targets?

The following have all been set as goals to achieve by 2020:

- A 20 per cent reduction in EU greenhouse gas emissions, as compared with 1990 levels, or 30 per cent if other developed nations agree to take similar action.
- An increase in the use of renewable energy, to 20 per cent of all energy consumed. This is a binding target. However, the plan allows flexibility in how each country contributes to the overall EU target.
- A 20 per cent increase in energy efficiency.

Functions and Services of the Central Bank of Ireland

The Central Bank of Ireland was first established in 1943 following the passing of the Central Bank Act 1942. It replaced the Currency Commission, which had functioned as the national currency-issuing authority until then.

In 1999 the bank became part of EMU (European Monetary Union) and together with the other NCBs (National Central Banks) and the ECB (European Central Bank) became part of the Eurosystem (Central Bank Act 1998).

On 1 May 2003 it was renamed and restructured and is now entitled the Central Bank and Financial Services Authority of Ireland (CBFSAI).

There are two sections of the CBFSAI:
1. The Central Bank is responsible for monetary policy functions, financial stability, economic analysis, currency and payment systems, investment and domestic assets and the provision of central services.
2. The Irish Financial Services Regulatory Authority (IFSRA – the Financial Regulator) is responsible for the financial sector regulation and consumer protection. (Discussed in Chapter 1.)

The main functions of the Central Bank are:
1. To maintain euro area price stability (low inflation) and a stable financial system by co-operating with the ECB and other NCBs by determining monetary policy and implementing Eurosystem monetary and exchange rate policy.
2. To co-operate with the Financial Regulator to ensure financial stability and help ensure economic growth.
3. To ensure safe and reliable inter-bank and customer payments implemented through the inter-central bank system known as TARGET (all EU credit institutions are linked to this system – it meets the needs of the single European currency).
4. To produce and distribute euro bank notes and coins and to ensure the integrity and security of the euro currency (the ECB has the sole right to issue the currency in euro area countries (euro notes and coins) and approves their volume, authenticity and quality).
5. To manage foreign exchange assets or reserves (that the Central Bank transferred to the ECB at the start of EMU in 1999) on behalf of the ECB in accordance with the investment policy of the ECB.

Mortgage lending growth slows again

www.rte.ie/business, Friday 31 August 2007

Figures from the Central Bank show that growth in residential mortgage lending was the slowest for five and a half years in July. The annual rate of growth was 17.9%, down from 19% in June.

The €1.6 billion increase in mortgage lending in July was down more than 30% on the same month last year.

Overall lending growth in the economy stabilised in July, with the annual rate at 20.3%, compared with 20.2% in June.

Non-mortgage lending continued to grow more quickly, though it also fell from 26.3% in June to 25.9%. The Central Bank says this is mainly due to a slowdown in lending to the property and construction sectors.

Central banks inject more money

www.rte.ie/business, Thursday 12 August 2007

The European Central Bank and the US Federal Reserve have taken fresh action to ease tightening credit linked to the home loans crisis in the US.

The ECB added €40 billion in three-month funds to the money market to cut borrowing costs in one of the areas hardest hit by the US sub-prime crisis.

The measure, designed to encourage lending by banks, was the first time the ECB had made a three-month injection outside its normal monthly schedule.

The ECB made the offer of the funds on Wednesday, saying it was 'a technical measure aimed at supporting the normalisation of the functioning of the euro money market'.

In its latest move, the US Federal Reserve injected $17.25 billion into the financial system. That brought the total added to money markets by the Fed to $120.5 billion over the past two weeks.

Central banks around the world began a series of major cash infusions on August 9 in response to the home loans crisis in the US. The ECB has pumped more than €200 billion into markets in recent weeks.

In a bid to ease lending between banks, the US central bank on Friday made a surprise cut in its discount rate to commercial banks to 5.75% from 6.25%.

Analysts says banks are now reluctant to lend to each other because of the uncertainty sparked by the US sub-prime mortgage crisis. The Fed move sent US markets lower as it seemed to indicate that fears of a credit squeeze had not abated.

Functions of the Central Bank (financial market operations) (continued) are:

6. To implement monetary policy acting as part of the ESCB (in co-operation with the ECB and other NCBs) to execute the main **instruments of the euro system as follows**:

(I) OPEN MARKET OPERATIONS

    (a) The main Refinancing Operations – concerning refinancing to the financial sector (short-term).

(b) The longer-term Refinancing Operations.

(c) Fine-tuning Operations – this involves managing liquidity in the market and steering interest rates to smooth them following unexpected liquidity changes. Occasionally the ECB will decide whether fine-tuning bilateral operations (two or more countries) are necessary and it will execute the instrument itself.

(d) Structural operations – when the ECB wishes to adjust the structural position of the euro system via the financial sector. The issuance of debt instruments is carried out by the NCBs.

(II) STANDING FACILITIES

To provide overnight liquidity to counterparties backed by eligible assets. These can be broken down into:

(a) The marginal lending facility – counterparties can get overnight liquidity from NCBs against eligible assets.

(b) The deposit facility – counterparties can make overnight deposits with the NCBs.

(III) MINIMUM RESERVES

NCBs must hold only minimum reserves of cash to avoid too much money being given out – contributing to inflation.

(IV) ELIGIBLE ASSETS

The types of suitable assets to act as collateral for counterparties loans and the eligibility criteria are established by NCBs, subject to the ECB's approval.

7. Acting as agent for and banker to the government.

8. It is legally responsible for the supervision of most financial institutions in Ireland including banks, building societies and a broad range of non-bank firms, exchanges and collective investment schemes.

9. Its Currency Centre prints euro bank notes and mints euro coins which are issued into circulation through the banking system. The Central Bank will accept all Irish bank notes and coins for years to come. (Note: other euro area foreign bank notes and coins cannot be accepted and must be exchanged for euros in their own NCB.)

10. The bank reports to the Minister for Finance annually (audited accounts) – its statement on annual accounts is published and is a primary source of financial statistics on the Irish economy. The Governor of the CB appears before the Oireachtas when asked to do so.

11. The vast majority of the Central Bank's net profit is paid to the Irish exchequer (Government).

Other responsibilities include:
- Contributing to the maintenance of a stable financial system in Ireland.
- Overseeing the domestic payment and settlement systems.
- Ensuring the provision and integrity of banknotes and coins.
- Managing the investment assets on behalf of the state.
- Acting as agent for and banker to the government.
- Providing advice and guidance on Irish economic policies.
- Serving the public interest – public accountability and external reporting.
- Helping government to draft and redraft legislation at home and EU level.

Functions and Services of Irish Commercial Banks

The most prominent commercial banks in Ireland are Allied Irish Bank, Bank of Ireland, Ulster Bank, Permanent TSB, National Irish Bank, Agricultural Credit Corporation (ACC), and Industrial Credit Corporation (ICC), Bank of Scotland/Halifax.

Other foreign banks that have branches in Ireland are Barclay's Bank, Banque Nationale de Paris, Chase Manhattan, Bank of America and Citibank.

Some of the functions of commercial banks are
1. Savings and Payment Facilities – deposit and current accounts (chequebook and cheque card), Special Saving Accounts (SSAs).
2. Giving out loans – bank overdrafts, term loans, credit cards.
3. Changing currencies, travel documents and mediums of payment abroad – foreign exchange, traveller's cheques, euro cheques.
4. Providing internal and external mechanisms to transfer money from account to account.
    (a) Internal – direct debits, standing orders, Bank Giro (credit transfer)
    (b) Bank drafts, money orders.
    (c) External–international payments: EFT (electronic funds transfer) and e-payments (IBAN bank numbers used).
5. Certain insurances – life assurance and pensions.
6. Payment of bills through commercial banks – electricity bills, telephone and mobile phone bills and student college fees – CAO etc.
7. Issuing credit cards and laser cards.

Refer to Chapter 6, 'Payment Methods', for full explanations of the payment methods mentioned and also refer to 'Sources of Finance' in Chapter 2.

OTHER BANKS

1. Industrial and Corporate Banks – AIB Finance and Leasing, Smurfit Finance and Leasing, Ulster Bank Commercial Services.
2. Merchant Banks – AIB Capital Markets, Ansbacher Bankers, Bank of Ireland Asset Management, Guinness & Mahon (Ire) Ltd, Smurfit Paribas Bank (Ltd).

Industrial, corporate and merchant banks provide financial and banking services for the business sector and are regarded as Wholesale banks.

How Merchant Banks differ from Commercial Banks

1. They do not deal with the public in general and are therefore wholesale banks.
2. Their services are for investors, large-scale business activities (private sector) and government (public sector).
3. No short-term loans are offered. These banks are only located in prominent city areas – unlike commercial banks they do not have a network of branches.
4. Some of the notable services, other than the regular range of financial and banking services, that are offered to large investors, private sector and public sector customers are:
   (a) The guarantee of the purchase of any issued shares not taken up by shareholders which contributes to the capital of the business – this service is referred to as Underwriting. (The fee is called a Spread.)
   (b) Factoring – the purchasing of debtors to give businesses ready cash for an agreed lower figure than the debtors are worth.
   (c) Leasing – car leases etc.
   (d) They give expert advice and consultation to the private sector, e. g. firms who want to go public, and they liaise with the Stock Exchange on their behalf.
   (e) They take active parts in mergers, take-overs and company rationalisation and liquidation.
   (f) They liaise with government agencies like Forfas, Industrial Development Authority (IDA) and Shannon Development regarding foreign investors.

PRACTICE QUESTIONS

1. When and under what conditions was the euro introduced?
2. How many countries are members of the EU?
3. What is the ECB and what are its functions?
4. Explain the terms:
   (a) ESCB.
   (b) OMO Instrument.
   (c) NCB.

(d) EMU.

(e) European integration.

5. What was the Kyoto Agreement?

6. List three EU targets aimed at controlling climate change.

7. Explain *five* functions of the Central Bank.

8. List *six* functions of Commercial Banks.

9. Explain *four* ways in which Merchant Banks differ from Commercial Banks.

What is an SSIA?

An SSIA is a Special Savings Incentive Account. This type of account was introduced in 2001 to encourage everyone in the state aged over 18 to start saving. The agreement was that the government would pay out a 25 per cent bonus on the investment if a set amount per month was saved (minimum €12.50, maximum €254 per month). The financial institution would also pay interest to the saver. The scheme was only available to savers from 1 May 2001 to 30 April 2002, allowing people twelve months to open an SSIA account. Savings were to be left in place for five years until their maturity date.

The main conditions (eligibility rules) of opening an SSIA and benefiting from the investment were:

- Account holders had to be resident in the Republic of Ireland.
- The amount saved had to be between €12.50 (IR£10) and €254 (IR£200) per month.
- If a withdrawal was made prior to the maturity date, an SSIA tax (23%) would be deducted from the amount withdrawn.
- A government declaration had to be signed for tax purposes.
- Only one SSIA was permitted per person.
- There had to be one lodgement per month into an SSIA for the first twelve months of the scheme.
- Joint SSIAs were not allowed.
- PPS numbers had to be supplied.
- Only persons over 18 years of age could open accounts.
- Savings could not be funded from a loan or the deferral of repayments of sums borrowed.
- Savers could not assign or otherwise pledge SSIA assets as security for a loan.

Over one million people had opened SSIAs by the time the scheme closed, many waiting until the last possible day, 30 April 2002. This meant that between 31 May 2006 and 30 April 2007 hundreds of thousands of Irish people experienced a positive and much welcomed maturing of their savings.

Effects of SSIAs on Business

- Companies offering SSIAs have benefited, as many savers will have opted to continue saving with that company (e.g. Quinn Life, Canada Life and other financial institutions).
- The economy benefited because a culture of savings has now been established and realisation of the need to save for a rainy day is now stronger in people's minds.
- More money is being spent in the economy (greater circulation of income) – some SSIA savings were used and reinvested in property or other assets.

What is Funds Administration?

Greater wealth in Ireland and globally has led to a growing trend of people investing their funds. This has created the need for special managers and administrators of funds that are invested – people need to know the best place to invest and the best time to invest.

The Hedge Fund industry has grown at a ferocious pace in the last decade, from as few as 300 funds in 1990 to more than 9,000 today. The funds have become highly visible in markets and the press, and are today estimated to manage up to 1.3 trillion in capital. Hedge funds, like other alternative investments such as real estate and private equity, are thought to provide returns that are uncorrelated with traditional investments. This has attracted an increasing number of individual and institutional investors who have realised that investing in hedge funds can further diversify their portfolios and produce higher returns at lower risk.

Funds administrators charge for their services and advise on the range of investment options open to the investor. Funds administrators offer a management service to manage these funds.

Financial Mismanagement and Tax Evasion

In recent years there has been a need to create a formal, transparent method of regulating monies in Ireland, probably due to the fallout originating in the misuse of taxpayers' money.

The realisation that money had been mismanaged dawned when it was discovered that public money had been used to fund former Taoiseach Charles Haughey's lavish lifestyle. Funds had been invested in an illegal Ansbacher account in the Cayman Islands. These facts emerged in the High Court inspectors' Ansbacher Report, published in 2002.

Other government ministers' financial affairs were also investigated by tribunals of inquiry.

Negotiations with the Revenue Commissioners led to estimates that Haughey may have spent up to £10 million (€12.7 million) during his time in politics (1977 to 1992). Many prominent businessmen were also party to the Ansbacher deposits and other exchanges of monies. Des Traynor, Haughey's accountant, was the mastermind and architect of the elaborate scheme that supported the former Taoiseach's personal finances at the expense of the taxpayer.

Nowadays the Revenue Commissioners and the Financial Regulator both control how monies are managed in the economy.

Taxpayers must file their tax returns on time and pay the monies due. If they do not, they are subject to somewhat draconian sanctions. Non-compliance means that the Revenue charges penalties, and penal interest will be charged on late tax payments. The Revenue Commissioners have also backtracked thirty years and have uncovered monies that were owed on illegal bogus non-residents' accounts and offshore accounts that were held by many taxpayers. This has yielded large tax payments over the last five years or more.

In this climate of zero-tolerance taxpayers are unwilling to take a chance that will cost them money and as a result most people file and pay their taxes on time.

Problems have also been uncovered in banking and financial institutions, including the systematic overcharging of customers. The Financial Regulator (part of the restructured Central Bank of Ireland) now monitors all financial institutions' activities and has the power to prosecute any financial institution on the grounds of mismanagement and illegal financial activities that are against the interests of the consumer. (Refer to Chapter 1, 'The Organisation'.)

The Internet

The Internet was the result of some visionary thinking by people in the early 1960s who saw great potential value in allowing computers to share information on research and development in scientific and military fields. J. C. R. Licklider of Massachusetts Institute of Technology (MIT) first proposed a global network of computers in 1962, and moved over to the Defense Advanced Research Projects Agency (DARPA) in late 1962 to head the work to develop it. Leonard Kleinrock of MIT and later UCLA developed the theory of packet switching, which was to form the basis of Internet connections. Lawrence Roberts of MIT connected a Massachusetts computer with a California computer in 1965 over dial-up telephone lines. This showed that wide area networking was feasible, but also showed that the telephone line's circuit switching was inadequate. Kleinrock's packet switching theory was confirmed. Roberts moved over to DARPA in 1966 and developed his plan for ARPANET. These visionaries – and many more – are the real founders of the Internet.

When Senator Ted Kennedy heard in 1968 that the pioneering Massachusetts company BBN had won the ARPA contract for an 'interface message processor (IMP)', he sent a congratulatory telegram to BBN for their ecumenical spirit in winning the 'interfaith message processor' contract.

The Internet, then known as ARPANET, was brought online in 1969 under a contract let by the renamed Advanced Research Projects Agency (ARPA), which initially connected four major computers at universities in the southwestern US (University of California Los Angeles (UCLA), University of California Santa Barbara (UCSB), Stanford Research Institute and the University of Utah). The contract was carried out by BBN of Cambridge, Massachusetts under Bob Kahn, and went online in December 1969. By June 1970, MIT, Harvard, BBN and Systems Development Corp (SDC) in Santa Monica, California were added to the network and within the next six months Stanford, MIT's Lincoln Labs, Carnegie-Mellon, and Case-Western Reserve University came on board.

Who First Used the Internet?

Charley Kline at UCLA sent the first packets on ARPANet as he tried to connect to Stanford Research Institute on 29 October 1969. The system crashed as he reached the G in LOGIN!

The Internet was designed in part to provide a communications network that would work even if some of the sites were destroyed by nuclear attack. If the most direct route was not available, routers would direct traffic around the network via alternate routes.

The early Internet was used by computer experts, engineers, scientists and librarians. There was nothing friendly about it. There were no home or office personal computers in those days, and anyone who used it, whether a computer professional or an engineer or scientist or librarian, had to learn to use a very complex system.

Did Al Gore Invent the Internet?

According to a CNN transcript of an interview with Wolf Blitzer, American Senator Al Gore said, 'During my service in the United States Congress, I took the initiative in creating the Internet.' Al Gore was not yet in Congress in 1969 when ARPANET started or in 1974 when the term Internet first came into use. Gore was elected to Congress in 1976. In fairness, Bob Kahn and Vint Cerf acknowledge, in a paper entitled 'Al Gore and the Internet', that Gore has probably done more than any other elected official to support the growth and development of the Internet from the 1970s to the present.

Source: www.walthowe.com

What is Broadband?

Broadband is a 'broad bandwidth' connection. It allows a large amount of data to travel through a medium at the same time. Broadband over Power Line (BPL) is a technology that allows Internet data to be transmitted over utility power lines and allows for high-speed Internet access.

What is Mobile Broadband?

Mobile Broadband is a type of wireless internet access that differs from WiFi. Just as the cellular phone revolutionised voice telephony by freeing the user from wires and stationary constraints, mobile broadband is doing the same for high-speed data. Users are no longer confined to desks, no longer inconvenienced with wires, no longer restricted to a stationary environment. Mobile broadband is a step up from local wireless data applications like WiFi, which gets rid of the wire, but not the confinement. Mobile broadband technology provides wide area coverage and works in mobile and fixed environments.

What is Social Networking?

A 'social network site' is a category of websites with profiles, semi-persistent public commentary on the profile, and a traversable publicly articulated social network displayed in relation to the profile.
Source: **www.zephoria.org.**

Profile. A profile includes an identifiable handle (either the person's name or details), information about that person (e.g. age, sex, location, interests, etc.). Most profiles also include a photograph and information about last login. Profiles have unique URLs (registered links) that can be visited directly.

Traversable, publicly articulated social network. Participants have the ability to list other profiles as 'friends' or 'contacts' or some equivalent. This generates a social network graph which may be directed or undirected. This articulated social network is displayed on an individual's profile for all other users to view. Each node contains a link to the profile of the other person so that individuals can move through the network through friends of friends of friends.

Semi-persistent public comments. Participants can leave comments (or testimonials, guestbook messages, etc.) on others' profiles for everyone to see.

Some examples of social network Internet websites are MySpace, Facebook, Friendster, Bebo, Youtube, Cyworld, Mixi, Orkut, etc.

High-speed Internet access has allowed for faster image downloads, video downloads and faster message sending and receiving. Some social networking sites are used as a marketing tool.

Websites like www.watchyourspace.ie have been developed by the National Centre for Technology in Education (NCTE) to encourage social networking in an online educational environment. In Ireland the Communications Regulator (Comreg) can fine telecom operators if they are in breach of communications regulations (Communications Regulation (Amendment) Act 2007).

YouTube goes Completely Mobile

Forget the iPhone, here comes the YouTube phone. In an exclusive partnership with video sharing site YouTube, LG electronics is developing a handset designed specifically for YouTube functionality.

The new handset, to be launched later this year, will have a specific user interface for filming, viewing and uploading YouTube videos directly to www.youtube.com.

'For the first time, LG customers will be able to film, upload and view videos on YouTube using their mobile phones just as they would be able to from their home computer,' said Dr Skott Ahn, president and CEO of LG Electronics Mobile Communications Company.

Irish Independent, July 2007.

iPhone will be 3G-enabled when it launches in Europe

John Kennedy

Apple's latest departure into mobile, the iPhone, will more than likely be 3G-enabled by the time it launches in Europe later this year and could be timed to coincide with the opening of European iTunes video stores and a follow-up 3G device in the US.

Irish mobile content expert Stephen McCormack, CEO of Wild Wave, speculates that when the coveted iPhone comes to Europe before Christmas this year it would be a relatively simple matter for Apple to configure the device to handle 3G.

When the 3.5 inch device launched in the US last week it did so as a 2.75G device, capable of GPRS and EDGE data transmission. The omission of 3G led many in the mobile industry to speculate that it would have limited success in Europe, where 3G is now standard and operators are already providing 'over the air' music download services.

However, McCormack believes that Apple could have gone with 3G from day one and that it was of political necessity when the company was in negotiations with AT&T to go with the 2.75G option.

'It will be 3G by the time they launch the device in Europe,' he predicts. 'When buying the circuit boards in Asia, if buying an actual phone chip, most will offer 3G and Wi-Fi as standard. When Apple was doing the deal with AT&T it is possible it didn't want to deal with music over the air as it would have created a conflict with AT&T's existing music download services.

'It is likely the compromise was to allow for building in-side loading from iTunes via your PC or Mac rather than downloading via the mobile network.'

McCormack's Wild Wave Technologies has worked with the local mobile industry to repackage Irish film products for consumption over 3G networks and lately has branched into Asia. The company has been at the spearhead of putting products on the Joost internet TV platform, launched earlier this year by the founders of Skype and Kazaa.

There has been a lot of speculation as to which European operators are most likely to win the rights to distribute the device in Europe and the general consensus is that the most likely operators will be Vodafone and T-Mobile.

Germany's *Rheinsche Post* has reported that Deutsche Telekom is about to announce that its mobile carrier T-Mobile will exclusively offer the device in Germany.

'Without 3G it is like trying to buy a black and white TV,' says McCormack. 'The Wi-Fi is there already but on the firmware side it is just a matter of switching it on.

'As soon as Apple launches in Europe it is more than likely there will be a simultaneous 3G device launch in the US,' McCormack believes.

A spokesman for Apple in Ireland said the company does not comment on future product launches.

Irish Independent, July 2007

Social Networks to be used in Net Safety Campaign

Niall Byrne

Internet safety campaigns targeted at Irish schoolchildren are to incorporate peer-to-peer and social networking elements, the National Centre for Technology in Education (NCTE) has said.

The NCTE runs safety campaigns about online privacy issues using its www.webwise.ie and www.watchyourspace.ie sites.

'We're trying to develop a peer-to-peer element in the Watchyourspace.ie site where students are discussing things,' said Jerome Morrissey, director, NCTE. 'That's where it's at with the slightly older teens. The best way for them to get engaged with this topic is if they write about their own experiences and share observations.'

Morrissey said that this approach reflected where internet technology is developing. 'Young people are writing more and are hopping ideas off each other and getting their ideas honed down, challenged and maybe adjusted. This sharing of content and honing down of views

and attitudes online is fantastic. It's the future.'

Another element in preparing students for life online is training the teachers to prepare them. From September, teachers will be able to avail of specialist tutoring about internet safety and privacy issues.

'We've just trained the first batch of tutors who will be training out of 21 education centres around the country.' said Morrissey.

The idea is not to have a specialist module in schools for internet safety but to integrate awareness of technology into school life.

'Internet safety is a boring topic for kids unless it's contextualised. We integrate it with everything that happens in schools. Teachers will carry this with them as a discussion topic all the time to be taken care of during the ordinary day. That's the only way to handle it.'

A new subject — Social, Health and Environmental Studies — that replaces Civics will also

incorporate net awareness. 'It's dealing with life issues and technology will be included in this – cyberbullying and so on.

'We're trying to sensitise young people to be careful. What you put up there is up forever. Kids need to have a self-selecting process.

'We warn them that in the future somebody might use what you put up for sheer entertainment as a way of finding out about them in an employment context. It's a serious issue.'

Despite the worries about online privacy, internet technology should be viewed as a valuable asset, Morrissey said.

'The idea is not to scare anybody but to say that technology is wonderful. The amount of writing that's going on is fantastic. Kids are writing more in a week than we ever did with our English essays. The aim of these initiatives [is] to say to kids 'the internet is fantastic, but here are a few ground rules'.'

Irish Independent, August 2007

What is Second Life?

This is a three-dimensional virtual world on the Internet entirely built and owned by its residents, where citizens can buy property, make friends and trade in their own unique currency (Linden dollars). It was opened to the public in 2003 and now has nearly ten million residents from around the globe. Press conferences and meetings can be held in Second Life – a form of virtual video conferencing. Large multinational companies like Coca-Cola, IBM, Dell, Warner Brothers and Adidas are readily adopting this new virtual world, and all have 'islands' or representations of their offices in Second Life as a representation of their branding – with a view to future business development.

Universities have their own Second Life presence with a virtual library (modelled on the James Joyce Library in University College Dublin). Visitors can use a virtual PC and read e-books, watch Sky News and watch library presentations.

UCD opens Library on Second Life

Marie Boran

University College Dublin (UCD) recently opened the doors of its sixth library, which exists only in Second Life, a popular virtual world on the internet where citizens can buy property, make friends and trade in their own unique currency.

'I attended a conference in Second Life and decided to set up a branch in-world. In between the conference and the opening we also conducted a multi-purpose survey of our real-life clients and found that 30pc would like Second Life-type virtual reference desks. It is early days yet but we get about 40 visits a day,' said Cathal McCauley, project leader for UCD's Second Life Library.

This is one of around 40 libraries that are located on Second Life's Cybrary City Islands, which plays host to the virtual version of existing public and university libraries.

Prominent US universities Berkeley, Stanford and Harvard already have their own Second Life presence.

'We've had instant messaging and blogs for quite some time now so we thought that the virtual world might offer another useful complement to the provision of traditional library services,' said McCauley.

The virtual library is modelled on the James Joyce Library, UCD's main library on the Belfield campus, and was developed with help from the US, UK and Holland.

Although it won't be quite the same as visiting the actual campus library, visitors can use a virtual PC, watch Sky News, read various e-books and watch library presentations.

The aim is to eventually have a staff presence in the virtual library, helping visitors to avail of UCD library services.

Anyone, UCD student or not, can access the library but McCauley told Silicon Republic that depending on services developed in the future, some type of access control may have to be considered.

Irish Independent, July 2007

Can business get a Second Life?

John Kennedy

As a number of sober-suited executives assemble in a plush conference room, they do so safe in the knowledge that no one can eavesdrop on their conversation. This is no ordinary meeting. In reality the executive are sitting at different points around the globe: it is their avatars, internet versions of themselves that are meeting in a virtual world known as Second Life.

This is not a scene from an Arthur C. Clarke novel. This is now. The secure conference room they meet in is provided by a cutting-edge Dublin firm known as V Rising, which in recent months was awarded a grant to conduct a feasibility study into virtual worlds by Enterprise Ireland.

The Second Life phenomenon — a virtual world where people in the form of 'avatars' can go to virtual versions of Dublin, London or Amsterdam and communicate — is beginning to excite the interest of big brand names and entrepreneurs who sense opportunity.

Second Life debuted in 2003 and today boasts over 8.9 million accounts. The virtual world — there are over 30 of them out there — has its own currency known as Linden dollars and has a booming real estate economy. At present a small number of residents earn net incomes from this economy selling anything from apparel to islands and castles.

Big business names like IBM, Dell, Adidas and Warner Brothers have all established 'islands' or representations of their offices in Second Life as an exercise in branding but with an eye on drumming up future business opportunities.

In recent weeks Coca-Cola launched its latest ad campaign with executives attending a red carpet bash in Second Life. When 20th Century Fox unveiled the summer blockbuster *Die Hard 4.0,* it held its press conference in Second Life, actor Bruce Willis's avatar answered journalists' questions; possibly even from the full-time reporter Reuters employs in Second Life.

At the IBM campus in west Dublin where 3,200 people are employed, a team of five at the company's 460-strong IBM.com division works full-time to represent IBM's 'island' on Second Life. Throughout IBM worldwide, more than 3,000 people have Second Life avatars, explained the director of the IBM.com division in Dublin, Hugh O'Byrne.

'You'll find lots of companies up there experimenting,' explains O'Byrne. 'We think it has potential as a way of doing business. We're just experimenting with it ourselves but we see massive potential in the human interaction you can bring. It's a big browsing environment in many ways.'

O'Byrne explains that IBM uses the Second Life environment as a means of providing customer service. 'We have six to 12 people on tap worldwide who will act as concierges 24/7. Their job is to say "hello" to anyone who walks in and guide them through products.'

The IBM office in Second Life also functions as a library as well as an auditorium for seminars, explains David Lallement, of the IBM's Second Life concierge. "We treat it as a good meeting point but I think the real innovation will come when more people start using voice in Second Life,' he says.

'One customer has asked us to build him a secure meeting room in Second Life and we're going to do it,' adds Greg.

ICT and Online Banking

The term 'ICT' means Information and Communication Technologies. In the current information age, advances in world communication have helped to increase globalisation and to make the world a smaller, more accessible place. The main types of ICT that exist today include:

1. The Internet – a worldwide network of computers joined by telecommunication lines.
2. The email facility – both a computer and mobile phone medium allowing us to send and receive electronic information.
3. Video Conferencing – a mode of communication that cuts out the need to travel: a video link allows several people to communicate from different locations, e.g. the 'poshare' video conferencing program.
4. Video Phones – used extensively by journalists to relate news to a newsroom at the touch of a mobile phone button.

What is E-Business?

E-business refers to all business processes that take place across electronic networks. This includes everything from buying and selling goods and services through the World Wide Web to interactive television, to advertising on the net.

Examples are: e-research, e-security, e-property, e-travel and tourism, e-education, e-working (telecommuting – working from home using ICT), e-government, e-health, e-transport and **e-commerce** (an interchange of goods, services or property of any kind through an electronic medium which can be the Internet, or over intranets (websites that can only be accessed within a company or group of companies), using interactive kiosks, using telephones or mobile phones or WAP phones (WAP means Wireless Applications Protocol). The interchange of goods, services or property via WAP phones is known as m-commerce.

B2C Transactions (Business to Consumer)

Online shopping involves the selecting of products from a virtual shopping area and putting them into a virtual shopping basket, paying by credit card and conveniently availing of home delivery of the goods. The provision of new product information to existing and future customers through the electronic medium has indeed revolutionised business to customer transactions.

B2B Transactions (Business to Business)

E-business transactions **between businesses** include the sourcing of new partners and materials helping to open up new markets and provide better customer support.

E-payments and Transfers

What is Electronic Funds Transfer (EFT)?

This refers to the computer-based systems used to perform financial transactions electronically.

The term is used to describe different concepts, including:

- cardholder-initiated transactions, where a cardholder makes use of a payment card
- electronic payments by businesses, including salary payments
- electronic cheque clearing.

EFT takes place when a cardholder uses either a Credit Card or a Debit Card (a regular bank card).

It can take place at an ATM (Automated Teller Machine) or at the point of sale (Electronic Funds Transfer Point of Sale, or EFTPOS).

EFT can also be initiated by the cardholder for mail order, telephone orders or Internet purchases.

The quality standard ISO 8583 often accompanies EFT card-based transactions.

The following are the types of transaction that can be carried out by the cardholder:

- Sale – payment for goods or services.
- Refund.
- Withdrawal – from ATM.
- Deposit – lodging money into account via ATM.
- Cashback – with a laser card: pay for goods and get extra cash out of your account at the same time (available from shops and supermarkets).
- Inter-account transfer – transferring money from one account to another account held by the cardholder.
- Payment – transfer of funds to a third party.
- Inquiry – an instant account balance inquiry.
- Administrative – e.g. electronically changing the PIN and other instructions.

The seller can verify the cardholder's signature. The most convenient method of payment, which is commonplace in retail shops, is payment using either a credit card or laser debit card. The cardholder has to punch in a PIN (Personal Identification Number) (chip and pin). Other information on the card is used by the seller via the card issuer, to confirm that the details on the card are valid: for example, the magnetic stripe data, which is not visible to the cardholder, can be checked by the seller.

What is a Debit Card?

A Debit Card is an electronic card issued by a bank that allows bank clients access to their account to withdraw cash or pay for goods and services. It provides an alternative payment method to cash when making purchases. Funds are withdrawn immediately from a cardholder's account.

This removes the need for bank clients to go to the bank to take cash from their account: they can just go to an ATM or pay electronically at merchant locations. This type of card, as a form of payment, also removes the need for cheques, as the debit card immediately transfers money from the client's account to the business account.

They are convenient and secure and easier than writing cheques: you don't need to show ID or pay extra fees. Debit cards are also considered to be a safer form of payment than cheques because a code is required to access the account, whereas cheques can be easily stolen.

Many debit cards are Visa or Mastercard, but there are many other types of debit card, each accepted only within a particular country or region, for example Switch (now Maestro) and Solo in the UK, Carte Bleu in France, Laser in Ireland, EC Electronic Cash (formerly Eurocheque) in Germany, etc.

There are currently two ways in which debit card transactions are processed: Online Debit (also known as PIN Debit) and Offline Debit (also known as Signature Debit).

What is a Credit Card?

A Credit Card is a plastic card, with a magnetic strip, which is issued by a bank or business and which authorises the holder to buy goods or services *on credit*. A high level of interest is charged on these purchases and a statement is issued to the credit card holder every month. The card may be used repeatedly to buy goods and services, subject to a credit limit set by the institution that issued the card to the cardholder. Credit card bills can become very expensive if cardholders do not pay off the amount they owe every month. Interest payments can cause the debt to spiral and become difficult for cardholders to manage.

However, credit cards when used sensibly provide a very convenient way to make purchases and make bookings.

Online bookings of flights, hotel accommodation and car hire is regarded as standard nowadays. A secure PIN can be used at the point of sale terminal to pay for goods and services.

What is 24-hour Banking?

This is the facility available to bank account holders to access their bank account and activate transactions at any time of the day either by phone or online.

Chip and PIN

Chip and PIN is the name given to the initiative based on the EMV standard, which is a group effort between Europay, Mastercard and Visa to establish a compatible standard for secure payments.

In many countries, the use of PIN-validated transactions with EMV smartcard chip readers is being strongly encouraged by the banks as a method of reducing cloned-card fraud, to the extent that cardholder-present transactions will soon not be possible in these countries without knowledge of a PIN, and the POS terminal reading the smart card chip on the card.

What are SSL and S-HTTP?

SSL or Secure Sockets Layer is a cryptographic protocol that helps provide secure communications on the Internet.

It creates a secure connection between a client and a server, over which any amount of data can be sent securely. S-HTTP is designed to transmit individual messages securely. SSL and S-HTTP are therefore complementary rather than competing technologies. Both protocols have been approved by the Internet Engineering Task Force (IETF) as a standard.

What is Western Union?

Western Union is a fast and reliable way to transfer money worldwide in minutes. There are over 280,000 agent locations worldwide in more than 200 countries and territories and people use it to send and receive money.

Complete Online Transaction	Call to Confirm Transaction	Receive Money
Sign in or register	For your security, operator	Receive money at any
Enter the details of your	may need to speak with sender	participating agent
money transfer	to confirm the transaction	location worldwide.
Pay with your Visa or		
MasterCard credit card		

Using Western Union to *send* money from Ireland: for amounts of €1,000 or more, senders must present either one form of primary identification or two forms of non-primary identification, one verifying their name and the other verifying their address. All forms of identification must be current.

Using Western Union to *receive* money from Ireland: persons under 18 years old must have some form of ID (e.g. birth certificate, student ID) and must be accompanied by a guardian who has an acceptable documentary evidence of identity to receive a money transfer payout. The agent will pay on the 'test question' alone for amounts up to €450. The payee must present the correct Money Transfer Control Number (MTCN).

Physical delivery is available by registered mail to street addresses only. If received before 3pm, delivery will be the next day, excluding Saturdays and Sundays.

Receivers must present acceptable documentary evidence of identity.

Primary forms of identification verifying full name include:

1. passport
2. driver's licence
3. national identity card.
4. national age card.

Arranging travel tops the poll among internet users

Twenty-eight per cent of all online shopping in Ireland is related to travel, according to a new survey by market research company Taylor Nelson Sofres MRBI (TNS MRBI). It is the highest proportion of spending on travel in any of the 37 countries surveyed. The survey also found that 19% of internet users in Ireland have shopped online in the four weeks prior to the survey.

The research was part of TNS MRBI's third global e-commerce report, which involved interviews with 42,238 people in 37 countries earlier this year. The report found that 46% of Irish people have used the internet in the four weeks previous to the survey, an increase of 7% on last year's survey. That growth was mostly in home users as more home PCs are being bought and used for web surfing.

Globally, CDs and books are, as they have been in the past, the most popular online purchases. But in Ireland it was travel, and no country spent more, proportionately, on travel than the Irish.

'The growth in low cost airlines appears to be clearly represented in this survey,' said Luke Reaper, a director of TNS MRBI. Books and CDs came second (15% of purchases) while tickets, at third, made up 12% of purchases.

The survey discovered that the proportion of internet users doing shopping had stayed static but that the number of internet users had risen, increasing the actual number of shoppers. It also discovered a surprisingly high common spend on the web.

Online retailers will be encouraged by the average spend on the internet. In Ireland, the average amount spent was €364 in the four-week period, despite findings that security is still the main barrier for users.

If there is going to be an improvement in the numbers of online shoppers then they have to deal with security,' said Reaper. 'One in four users who didn't buy said it was because they didn't want to put their credit card on the internet.'

Also encouraging is the age profile of shoppers: 77% are under 20, meaning that internet shopping is likely to grow as that demographic grows up.

AN INTERNET BANKING DEMO

Online Banking/Transactions/Investment

Online banking today allows the customer:

1. To access his or her account, to view balances, to print out online statements – a 24-hour service.
2. To see transaction history.
3. To pay bills.
4. To search for or track a cheque.
5. To top up mobile phones online.
6. To make transfers of money from account to account or out and into an account.
7. To invest in stocks and shares online.
8. To apply for a loan, a mortgage or a credit card online or to get an insurance quote (life policies etc).
9. To avail of foreign exchange facilities online.
10. To establish an Internet merchant account in order to set up a credit card payment system on a customer's (businesses) web site – transferring credit card details between the bank and customer web site and providing a secure certificate to encrypt and protect the credit card details. (The bank and ISP – Internet service provider – will help determine the types of software needed to carry out secure transactions.)

PRACTICE QUESTIONS

1. What is an SSIA? List two benefits of SSIAs to the Irish economy.
2. What is Funds Administration?
3. Why have the Revenue Commissioners been described in recent years as 'draconian' in relation to tax evasion?
4. Give a brief history of the Internet.
5. What are Broadband and Mobile Broadband?
6. What is Social Networking?
7. What is Second Life and why is it good for business?
8. What is ICT? Distinguish between e-business and e-commerce.
9. What is EFT? Explain e-payments.
10. Write notes on:
    (i) debit cards
    (ii) credit cards
    (iii) 24-hour banking
    (iv) Chip and PIN
    (v) SSL and S-HTTP
    (vi) Western Union.

Foreign Exchange and Currency Conversion

EMU – European Monetary Union – has meant that Europeans can now travel within the European Community and exchange euros for euros. (Refer to the beginning of this chapter.) Member states that have signed up for EMU and have converted to the euro currency no longer have the inconvenience of watching changing foreign exchange rates in order to figure out different costs of living and value for money in exchange for goods and services. There is now a greater ease of movement of money in EMU countries in particular in relation to travel and among European holiday-makers.

However, the currencies listed in the foreign exchange paper clip are not part of EMU and are denominated against the euro e.g. 1 euro = .9665 dollars and 1 euro = .629 sterling. So for every euro the tourist would only get about 62 British pence.

FOREIGN EXCHANGE

Market euro (previous close in parentheses)		Tourist euro Country	Buying	Sellling
Dollar	0.9665 (0.9673)	UK	0.612	0.6505
Sterling	0.629 (0.625)	US	0.9405	0.9945
D Krone	7.4247 (7.4218)	Canada	1.501	1.563
Jap Yen	118.55 (118.2)	Sweden	8.915	9.255
Sw Franc	1.4713 (1.4666)	Denmark	7.265	7.695
Sw Krona	9.075 (9.1075)	Switzerland	1.4213	1.5513
Nor Krone	7.35 (7.329)	Malta	0.391	0.431
HK Dlr	7.538 (7.5425)	Cyprus	0.5575	0.5975
Can Dlr	1.528 (1.5271)	Australia	1.7077	1.8227
Aus Dlr	1.7627 (1.7635)	Japan	113.85	123.05
NZ Dlr	2.0533 (2.0515)	Norway	7.15	7.6
Sing Dlr	1.7205 (1.7211)	N Zealand	1.9783	2.1283
Czech Kr	30.401 (30.356)	S Africa	10.1791	10.6591
Pol Zl	4.0386 (4.0599)	Thailand	39.405	45.405
Hng For	242.85 (243.50)	Hong Kong	7.188	7.908
Turk Lira	1647378 (1641268)	Singapore	1.6405	1.9405

Financial Information **Ulster Bank**

COMMODITIES

Copper	$1495.5	($1501.5)	Nickel	$6550	($6770)
Lead	$417	($422)	Platinum	$547.5	($553)
Zinc	$769	($773)	Silver	$4.57	($4.57)
Tin	$3925	($3895)	Gold	$316.30	($316.25)
Aluminium	$3101.5	($1311)	Oil	$27.68	($28.28)

Factors Affecting the Value of a Currency

Many factors have an effect on the value of a country's currency.

1. Economic boom or recession – trade cycle – investors speculate and if there is an upswing in the economic performance of the economy, investors are attracted (together with government grant incentives) to set up and offer jobs. If this trend continues, it signals a rise in the value of the currency.

2. Rising interest rates make it more difficult for people to spend as much because their loans (like mortgages) are higher and they find it difficult to save. This leads to depressed demand for goods and services, closures and unemployment. Investors look unfavourably on this type of economy and the value of the currency falls.

3. Inflation: Sometimes governments find it necessary to devalue a currency when inflation (rising prices) and interest rates are unmanageably high.

Business Information in Graphical Form

1. Tables

Tabulation is the procedure used to organise raw data (unorganised data usually in note or prose form) into a table. In order to understand the data that is contained in a table, we must differentiate between data and statistics as well as primary and secondary forms of the latter.

(a) Primary Data: is data that has been collected by the investigator personally. He/she knows under what conditions the data was collected and its limitations, e.g. a spending pattern survey carried out by using a questionnaire in a busy street in Dublin.

(b) Secondary Data: is data that already exists and is used by someone else. The conditions under which it was collected or its limitations are not known.

(c) Primary Statistics: are figures that are put into a table and have been collected as part of primary data.

(d) Secondary Statistics: are simply percentages or averages that appear beside the primary statistics in the table – a useful way of analysing primary statistics.

PRACTICE TABULATION QUESTION

Employees in Marshall Company numbered 1,500. The company was organised into three departments, Production, Sales and Administration. 400 people were employed in Production and 630 in Administration. There were 460 young females, 200 young males and 420 senior females employed with the company.

Of those working in the Production Department, 130 were young males, 90 were young females and 100 were senior females. The remaining employees in the department were senior males.

Administration was made up of 220 senior males, 200 senior females and 40 young males, with the remainder young females.

Sales was made up of 120 senior males, 120 senior females and 30 young males, with the remainder young females.

1. Compile a suitable table of information from this raw data detailing
    (a) Primary statistics – the information above arranged in an organised fashion that is easy to read.
    (b) Secondary statistics to analyse the employment distribution.
2. Comment on your findings.

Steps to tabulate raw data:

1. Decide on the number of rows and columns and whether a total column is needed (not always).
2. The independent variables (males and females categorised) should appear vertically and the dependant variable should appear horizontally (the numbers of employees, categories in production, in sales and in administration, generally are categorised based on being dependant on whether they are male or female).

    Other examples are 'The Profits of Companies' – the companies categorised would be the Independent variables, and profits would be the Dependant variable.

    'Sales over time' – time (in years, months, weeks or days) would be the Independent variable, and sales would change over time (sales = Dependant variable).
3. Clarity and neatness is essential and headings and subheadings should be clearly labelled. A key should be used if wording is too extensive and it overloads and clutters the table.

SOLUTION TO PRACTICE QUESTION

1. Employee Details of Marshall Company

	Production		Sales		Administration		Total	
	No.	%	No.	%	No.	%	No.	%
Sen. F	100	25	120	26	200	32	420	28
Sen. M	80	20	120	26	220	35	420	28
Young M	130	32	30	6	40	6	200	13.3
Young F	90	23	200	42	170	27	460	30.7
	400	100	470	100	630	100	1,500	100

KEY:

Sen.   Senior
M   Males
F   Females

2. Comment

The same number of senior males are employed in the company as females. The largest concentration of senior males appears to be in Administration (35%) with 26% of senior males employed in Sales. The percentage numbers of young males and senior females in Production are 32% and 25% respectively. There is an unusually large number of young females employed in Sales, 42%. The small percentages of young males in Sales and Administration, 6% each, is also noteworthy.

It appears that young females are chosen to promote the business creating a young company image. Possibly the reason for a large number of young males in Production is extra physical strength or other factors such as qualifications. Senior staff are concentrated in all areas, Administration figuring largest in proportion.

More information on company background, products produced or services offered would be necessary to make an accurate comment on the statistics in the table.

Bar Charts

The most common bar charts are:

1. Component Bar Charts
   (a) They show the breakdown of the total amount into its component parts.
   (b) They show how components of a total change from year to year.
   (c) They isolate the component parts of each year's total.
2. Percentage Component Bar Charts
   (a) They are similar to pie charts but are in the shape of a bar.
   (b) The parts of the total are shown as a proportionate block of the bar.
   (c) The length (magnitude) of the bar is not relevant because each bar is 100 per cent high.
   (d) Variations only occur in relative proportional sizes of percentage parts of the bar.
3. Multiple Bar Charts
   (a) The parts of the component bar are displayed side by side rather than all in the one bar as is the case for a component bar chart.
   (b) No Grand Total is shown – all the individual parts would have to be added up.
   (c) Comparative heights of each part of the total can be seen at a glance.

Most information can be depicted in one form or another by bar charts.

PRACTICE QUESTION

Given the following information draw:
1. A Component Bar Chart
2. Three Percentage Component Bar Charts – one for each year.
3. A Multiple Bar Chart.
4. Explore the reasons why one might be more useful than another.

Note: graph paper should be used to ensure a high level of accuracy.

The breakdown of company X's staff numbers was as follows:

Year 1: Production staff = 180, Sales staff = 75, and Administration staff = 45.
Year 2: Production staff = 200, Sales staff = 80, and Administration staff = 60.
Year 3: Production staff = 150, Sales staff = 60, and Administration staff = 40.

Workings for Percentage Bar Chart, Company X

Year 1 P = 180/300 x 100 = 60%   S = 75/300 x 100 = 25%   A = 45/300 x 100 = 15%
Year 2 P = 200/340 x 100 = 58.8% S = 80/340 x 100 = 23.5%   A = 60/340 x 100 = 17.7%
Year 3 P = 150/250 x 100 = 60%   S = 60/250 x 100 = 24%   A = 40/250 x 100 = 16%

COMPONENT BAR CHART
STAFF BREAKDOWN
COMPANY X

MULTIPLE BAR CHART
STAFF BREAKDOWN
COMPANY X

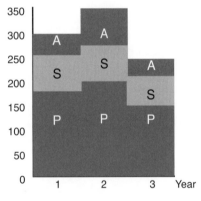

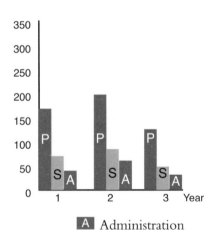

KEY    Production    Sales   Administration

% COMPONENT BAR
CHART COMPANY X

% COMPONENT BAR
CHART COMPANY X

% COMPONENT BAR
CHART COMPANY X

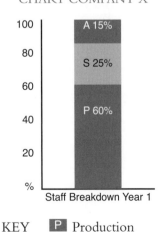
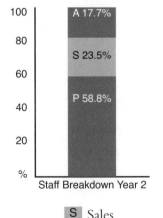
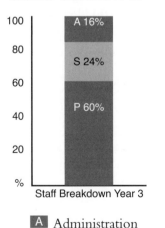

KEY   Production   Sales   Administration

Pie Charts

Circular diagrams used to show the relative sizes of component elements of a total.
- Use a compass to draw circle
- Use a protractor to draw the segments of the circle when estimated.

How to calculate measurements to obtain the sizes of the segments of the circle:

(a) If information is given in figures (rather than percentages) use the following formula to obtain the degrees of the circle:

$$\frac{\text{No. of degrees}}{\text{Total Cost or Sales figure}} \qquad \frac{360}{2,000 \text{ (say)}} = .18 \text{ (multiply this by each individual Cost or Sale value to obtain the degrees of the circle)}$$

(b) If information is given in percentages use the following formula to obtain the degrees of the circle:

$$\frac{\text{No. of degrees}}{\text{Total percentage}} \qquad \frac{360}{100\%} = 3.6 \text{ (multiply this by each percentage value to obtain the degrees of the circle).}$$

(c) To get back from degrees of a circle to percentages, divide each degree figure by 3.6.

- Once the pie chart is drawn, percentages are usually indicated in each separate segment of the circle.
- Pie charts are similar to percentage component bar charts in content. However, it is usually easier to see differences in component parts of a pie chart than in a bar chart.

PRACTICE QUESTION
(a) Look at the practice question on bar charts. For part 2 depict the information in the form of three pie charts – one for each year.
(b) Why are these three pie charts not readily comparable?

WORKINGS

To get the degrees of the circle

$$\frac{360°}{300} \quad = \quad 1.2 \quad \text{(multiply this by each part for year 1)}$$

$$1.2 \times 180 \quad = \quad 216°$$

$$1.2 \times 75 \quad = \quad 90°$$

$$1.2 \times 45 \quad = \quad \underline{54°}$$

$$\overline{360°}$$

$$\frac{360°}{340} \quad = \quad 1.06 \quad \text{(multiply this by each part for year 2)}$$

$$1.06 \times 200 \quad = \quad 212°$$

$$1.06 \times 80 \quad = \quad 85°$$

$$1.06 \times 60 \quad = \quad \underline{63°}$$

$$\overline{360°}$$

$$\frac{360}{250} \quad = \quad 1.44 \quad \text{(multiply this by each part for year 3)}$$

$$1.44 \times 150 \quad = \quad 216°$$

$$1.44 \times 60 \quad = \quad 86°$$

$$1.44 \times 40 \quad = \quad \underline{58°}$$

$$\overline{360°}$$

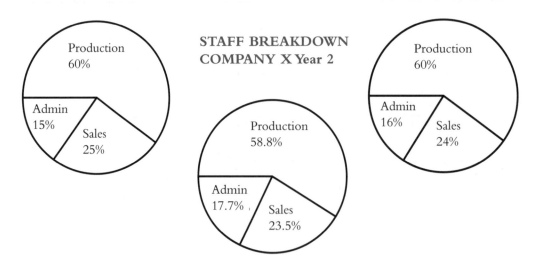

STAFF BREAKDOWN COMPANY X Year 1

Production 60%
Admin 15%
Sales 25%

STAFF BREAKDOWN COMPANY X Year 2

Production 58.8%
Admin 17.7%
Sales 23.5%

STAFF BREAKDOWN COMPANY X Year 3

Production 60%
Admin 16%
Sales 24%

Line Graphs

Many businesses wish to keep track of sales or costs and find the use of a line graph a suitable way of doing this. The following example depicts sales over six months. Line graphs can be linked with Gantt charts (discussed under 'Functions of Management' in Chapter 1). They both depict either sales or cost changes over time. If a target level of sales is anticipated, one can see at a glance whether this level has been reached or not.

Visual display instruments like tables, bar charts, pie charts and line graphs are regularly used by, for example, survey agencies like MRBI or Irish Marketing Surveys to show results of opinion polls or voting trends at election time. Business television programmes and television news use them to show results of information that viewers find easy to interpret at a glance.

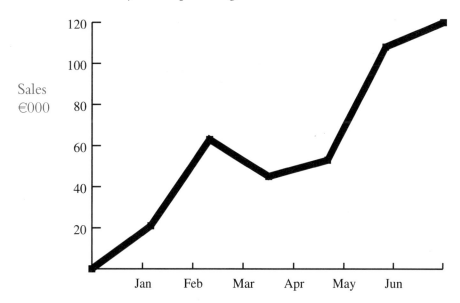

PRACTICE QUESTIONS

1. What is Tabulation?
2. How is Raw Data defined?
3. How do Primary Data and Primary Statistics differ?
4. How do Secondary Data and Secondary Statistics differ?
5. What steps are involved in drawing a table?
6. How do the *three* types of Bar Charts differ?
7. Which Bar Chart is similar in content (but not in shape) to a Pie Chart?
8. The Breakdown of Company Y's Staff numbers was as follows:

Year	Sales Dept	Production Dept	Administration Dept
Year 1	200	600	150

Year 2	210	500	120
Year 3	205	480	105

You are required to draw:

(a) A Component Bar Chart of the total information.

(b) A Pie Chart for Year 2 only. Show full workings.

(c) A Multiple Bar Chart of the total information.

Business Administration

Portfolio of Coursework (Sample Assignment)

Subjects taken by the students at St Margaret's College are as follows:

Subject	No. of Students 2009
LANGUAGES	
French	850
German	240
Spanish	200
	1,290
INFORMATION TECHNOLOGY	
Comp. Programme	300
Computer Applications	250
	550
PROFESSIONAL	
Management	380
Banking	120
Accountancy	190
	690
ACADEMIC	
Leaving Cert	150
Junior Cert	80
Transition Year	31
	261
Total no. students	**2,791**

1. Depict the above data in the following forms:
   (a) A Pie Chart – show full workings
   (b) A Multiple Bar Chart.
2. Comment on each visual display instrument used to display the data and the trend in the data.

Insurance Against Common Business Risks

The Irish Insurance Federation is the umbrella organisation for the insurance industry and is used by insurers (insurance companies) to check on the credit rating and solvency of brokers and intermediaries (**www.iif.ie**).

Insurance companies and brokers must register with the Irish Brokers' Association (IBA) (**www.iba.ie**) before they are allowed to operate. Registering with the Irish Insurance Compliance Bureau allows them to be fully bonded and recognised. A brokerage cast outside the IBA fold could not operate unless it was registered with the bureau. Insurance companies are obliged to operate in accordance with the provisions of the Insurance Act 1989 and the regulations that are attached to the Act. Matters relating to non-disclosure of commercial fees and inappropriate business activities can lead to expulsion from the IBA.

An insurer can be an insurance company or a financial institution or a broker that charges a fee called a Premium to insure private individuals and businesses against the risk of accident or theft. Insurers also offer life policies (life assurance) to protect against the risk of serious injury, disability and death.

A Broker is an individual or group of individuals such as the Automobile Association (AA) whose business it is to search around for the best available quote – in this case for motor insurance – and they take a portion of the premium that they quote for themselves (like a middleman).

The Insured, the person or business being insured, can get the value of the lost item back and replace it. A life policy will provide the insurer with peace of mind and will compensate his or her dependants in the case of his or her death. (*Note*: Life policies differ in value.)

An Insurance Policy is the agreement drawn up between the Insurer and the Insured that is presented by the Insurer (e.g. AXA) in the form of a document listing the conditions underpinning the agreement.

Underwriting a Risk is the guarantee given by the insurer to pay compensation to the insured (the extent of compensation is limited by the Principle of Indemnity – discussed later).

The most common insurance policies are

1. Motor insurance
2. House and contents insurance
3. Business insurance
4. Health insurance

5. Travel insurance
6. Life assurance
7. Other miscellaneous insurances

Motor insurance is compulsory by law (Road Traffic Act 1933) and is broken down into

(a) Third Party: The insurance company only pays out compensation for the damage to the other vehicle and/or person, but not for damage to your own vehicle.
(b) Third Party, Fire and Theft: Compensation is paid out for third party damage and for burn damage or theft of the vehicle and other appropriate compensation.
(c) Fully Comprehensive: The insurance company will pay compensation for the repair of all vehicles involved in any accident, including your own, as well as personal compensation. If you buy an expensive car, it is likely that parts for it will be expensive and it is best to avail of this type of insurance in this case.

- *Note*: The premiums – payments for motor insurance – will be higher if the driver is younger and regarded as being more risky. Premiums will also be 'loaded' (increased) for larger vehicles and if previous claims have been made.

No Claims Bonus: If a driver continues driving and is lucky enough never to have had an accident, he/she is rewarded with a no claims bonus which rises every subsequent year that the driver has a clear record.

- *Note*: Most insurances have increased substantially due to the high incidence of claims in recent times.

HOUSE AND CONTENTS INSURANCE

Usually when someone decides to buy a house, the house and contents insurance premium is included in the amount repayable to the financial institution with which they take out their mortgage (house loan). People also have the option of insuring their house and contents with separate insurance companies if they prefer. The insurance is usually in case of burglary, fire, etc.

BUSINESS INSURANCE

The most common insurance that businesses in general avail of is Full Public Liability Insurance. This covers them for accidents occurring on or in the vicinity of their premises. Crèches might have high premiums to pay due to the higher risk of children having accidents. Businesses involved in deliveries of any sort, where drivers are frequently parked in busy public areas, are also subject to large premiums.

HEALTH INSURANCE

The Voluntary Health Insurance Company (VHI) and Quinn Direct (formerly BUPA) are the two main health insurance companies operating in Ireland. Up to the time BUPA established itself in Ireland, the VHI had a virtual monopoly (dominating the market). There are different Health Plans – Plan A, Plan B, Plan C, etc. – that people avail of in case of accident or illness, or to cover maternity needs, etc. so that the cost of care is covered by the insurance.

Public hospital services themselves are free (doctors and nurses' services). In some cases there are public charges for emergency services and for hospital accommodation, but maternity accommodation in a public ward of a maternity hospital is free.

TRAVEL INSURANCE

Usually tour operators and travel agencies organise baggage and medical insurance for people going abroad on holiday. Banks now provide insurance that covers these types of risk, which cover holiday cancellation, medical and hospital expenses, personal accident, legal expenses, lost baggage, or the cost of getting a person home in case of emergency. Other cover might include winter sports equipment, twenty-four hour emergency medical assistance, missed departure/connection, and loss of passport.

EMU IMPLICATIONS FOR TRAVEL INSURANCE – WHAT TO DO IF YOU NEED HELP IN ANOTHER EU COUNTRY

Before leaving the country get an E1 11 (E one eleven) form from your local Social Welfare office, Health Board or doctor.

Emergency Care: In case of emergency only (defined by the doctor) it avoids the need to pay up front. The Social Welfare Department will pay the bill under its own system of payment. This is accepted throughout most of the European Economic Area.

Non-emergency Care: Complications arise for care that is not urgent. The traveller may have to pay for the cost of care abroad but can later claim this money back through the Social Welfare system. Get informed before you go!

LIFE ASSURANCE

This insures a person and his/her family in the event of his/her death or serious injury and it can also provide life savings if the person is willing to pay a higher premium for this provision. A lump sum of money will be paid out to dependants in the event of a person's death.

Many different policies are offered by different insurance companies and brokers and people in general usually avail of the type of policy that suits their own needs.

OTHER MISCELLANEOUS INSURANCES

Most business people who deal in assets will insure their equipment. For example, a hardware equipment hire business would have invested a lot of capital in the assets (equipment) and will insure them because they are the basis of their livelihood, e.g. lawnmowers or diggers for hire etc. Car hire is another business that would probably pay large premiums. Farmers insure their stocks and animals against fire and theft, employers insure their premises against the risk of employee theft or dishonesty (Fidelity Guarantee). Examples would be banks, post offices etc. Marine insurance covers losses which might be suffered while transporting goods by sea.

INSURANCE PROTECTIONS AND RISK

- Most insurance policies are concerned with the risk of fire, theft, illness or death, and flooding in some cases.
- *Note*: **It is important to enquire into the exact amount of cover that a policy stipulates. In some cases the small print reads 'cover except when loss is due to war or natural disaster' etc.**
- Insurance means that there is a possibility that loss will be incurred and compensation is for the value of that amount only.
- Assurance means a guarantee of a lump sum of money on the death or confirmation of terminal injury of the insured or the maturity of a savings policy after a set number of years.
- Premiums rise as the perceived risks rise. Young people are particularly penalised in the case of motor insurance for drivers under 25 years. Public liability insurance for crèches is high and drivers involved in deliveries also have high insurance premiums to pay.

Principles of Insurance

The Principles of Insurance are concerned with the conditions that create the need to insure, allow for items to be insured and allow for appropriate compensation to be gained, having placed a claim with the insurer.

1. INSURABLE INTEREST

You wouldn't insure something unless you had an interest in doing so! The insured must benefit from the existence of what he/she is getting insured and must suffer if it is lost. In short, a value is attached to whatever is being insured. Legal ownership is a prerequisite to this principle.

2. UTMOST GOOD FAITH

Trust must exist between the insurer and the insured. If all facts are not disclosed it would lead to a void contract of insurance.

3. INDEMNITY (SUBROGATION, CONTRIBUTION AND PROXIMATE CLAUSE ARE FOLLOW-ON CONDITIONS TO INDEMNITY).

Only the loss incurred is compensated – no more. The insured is no better off (no profit gained) than they were prior to the incident that triggered the claim. Life assurance is an exception to this principle.

4. SUBROGATION

After the insurance company has paid out the compensation to the insured, the company is entitled to claim against any third party and can take legal action against the person who was responsible (inbuilt in the policy – the insured gives the company permission to do this by signature).

5. CONTRIBUTION

If two different insurance companies are employed, i.e. if the insured is overinsured, the principle of indemnity still applies, and the insured only gets back the loss and no more. A loss is calculated as follows:

Hibernian Insurance and GRE (Guardian Royal Exchange) are both insuring stock in a premises. Hibernian insures €12,000 worth of stock and GRE insures €6,000 worth of stock. €4,000 worth of stock is taken in a burglary.

Hibernian pay out $\dfrac{12,000}{18,000}$ x 4,000 = €2,667

GRE pay out $\dfrac{6,000}{18,000}$ x 4,000 = €1,333

TOTAL €4,000

6. PROXIMATE CLAUSE

This refers to the nature of the risk that an item is being insured against. The insurance company always checks the policy to make sure that the risk was insured against before they pay out the compensation.

PRACTICE QUESTIONS

1. Write notes on
   (a) The Irish Insurance Federation.
   (b) The IBA.
   (c) The Irish Compliance Bureau.
2. In accordance with which legal Act are Insurance Companies and Brokers obliged to operate?
3. What is 'Underwriting a Risk'?
4. (a) What is a Premium and what factors will dictate how high or low it is?
   (b) What businesses have to pay higher insurance premiums and why?
5. What are the most common types of insurance policies?
6. With regard to Motor Insurance differentiate between third party, third party fire and theft, and fully comprehensive insurance.
7. What is a No Claims Bonus?
8. What is Public Liability Insurance and who avails of it?
9. Who are the VHI and do they still maintain a monopoly in Ireland?
10. (a) Who provides travel insurance?
    (b) What are the EMU implications for Travel Insurance?
11. (a) What is the difference between Insurance and Assurance?
    (b) What is Life Assurance and why is it so important?
12. What is Fidelity Guarantee?
13. List the Principles of Insurance and explain them briefly and clearly.

Insurance Proposal Form

Request a Quote

If you are an existing policyholder click here.

Household quotation details required:

Title   Mr ▼

Full Name: [   ]

Full Postal Address: [   ]

Full Address of property to be insured: [   ]

Is this your permanent residence?   Yes ⦿ No ○

If no please state details:

[   ]

Telephone Numbers:

Daytime: [   ]

Evening: [   ]

Your e-mail address: [   ]

Your Date of Birth: [   ]

What is your occupation: (including part time occupations)   [   ]

Please select which type of cover you need: Buildings Only ▼

What is your buildings value?   [   ]

What is your contents value?   [   ]

Do you want accidental damage cover?   Yes ○ No ⦿

Do you require cover for your personal belongings and valuables outside your home?

Yes ○ No ◉

If yes please state the sum insured and include details of any individual items worth more than €1,270 (£1,000)

```
┌──────────────────────────────────────────┐
│                                          ▲ │
│                                          █ │
│                                          █ │
│                                          ▼ │
└──────────────────────────────────────────┘
```

Do you need cover for pedal cycles? *(please tell us how many and the total value)*

```
┌──────────────────────────────┐
│                              │
└──────────────────────────────┘
```

Do you have any of the following:

☐ Approved alarm to IŞ 199 standards

☐ Do you have any mortice locks on your outside doors

☐ Do you have smoke detectors fitted?

☐ Are you in a neighbourhood watch area?

Previous claims/losses during the last 5 years:

Date of claim:
```
┌──────────────────────────────┐
│                              │
└──────────────────────────────┘
```

Full description of claim/loss:

```
┌──────────────────────────────────────────┐
│                                          ▲ │
│                                          █ │
│                                          █ │
│                                          ▼ │
└──────────────────────────────────────────┘
```

What is the amount of the payments made to date:

```
┌──────────────────────────────┐
│                              │
└──────────────────────────────┘
```

Is the claim settled?   Yes ○ No ◉

If there are any other details you feel are relevant, please fill in the following section:

```
┌──────────────────────────────────────────┐
│                                          ▲ │
│                                          █ │
│                                          █ │
│                                          ▼ │
└──────────────────────────────────────────┘
```

Your home is a Private Residence of standard construction and you have been free of convictions for the last 5 years.

Thank you for taking the time to complete this form, we will reply to you by e-mail with a quotation.

☐ Please tick here if you wish us to post a quotation out to you.

Accident Claim Form

Damage to Both Yours and Another Vehicle

Your Details:

Your Insurance Policy
Number:

Your Name:

E Mail address:

If you are registered for VAT please enter your VAT number here:

Home telephone Number:

Work telephone Number:

Your Vehicle Details:

Registration Number:

Make & Model :
e.g. Ford Escort 1.31

Is the vehicle registered in
your name?

Yes: ⦿

No: ○

Name of any financial institution or hire purchase company with an
interest in the vehicle?

Vehicle Damage...Inspection & Repair Instruction

Please check our approved repairer list before continuing.

Contact name and number to arrange a vehicle inspection:

What is the estimated cost of
repair?

Driver or person last in charge of vehicle

Full name:

Address:

E Mail address:

Date of Birth:

Home telephone Number:

Work telephone Number:

Driving Licence:

Full: ○

Provisional: ◉

Category of Licence:

Did the driver have your permission to drive the vehicle:

Yes: ◉

No: ○

Has the driver ever been convicted of a motoring offence or had any previous accidents?

Yes: ◉

No: ○

Accident details:

In what location did the accident happen:

Please enter the date and time of the accident:

In your view, how did the accident happen:

By how much do you consider yourself to blame?

Select one ▾

Please enter the name/s of any persons (including yourself) who admitted liability verbally or in writing at the scene of the accident:

Name of Garda and station to whom the incident was reported to or investigated by:

Has notice of intention to prosecute been given or summons received?

Yes: ○

No: ●

If 'yes' give details:

Witness details:

Name:

Address:

Approximate age:

Phone Number:

Witness category:　Select one ▼

Details of other vehicles/property involved:

Name of owner:

Name of driver:

Address:

Registration Number of vehicle:

Vehicle Make/Model:
e.g. Ford Escort 1.31

Please describe the damage to this vehicle:

Name of other person's Insurance Company:

Other Person's Policy Number:

SUBMIT

Sample Assignment Briefs

QUESTION 1.

Choose a Bank or Financial Institution and examine the following aspects of the Institution:

1. The types of loans offered categorised as Short-, Medium-, Long-term.
2. The procedure for getting a loan.
3. The most common services offered and charges incurred relating to personal customers.
4. The most common services offered and charges incurred relating to business customers.

QUESTION 2.

Choose an Insurance Company or Broker and do an analysis of the business, examining a range of the following aspects of the organisation:

1. Brief history and organisational structure
2. The types of insurance policies and cover offered and charges categorised with reference to the section on insurance in this chapter.
3. How the Principles of Insurance tie in with the policies offered.
4. How a claim is handled by the business – process of claim from point of receipt to point of payment.
   - Include in your assignment
     (a) An Insurance Claim form
     (b) An Insurance Proposal form.

4. Human Resources

Human Resource Management or Personnel Management is concerned with recruiting employees, looking after existing staff needs, dealing with employee grievances and disciplining or dismissing employees if the need arises. This management is also obliged to inform employees of their statutory rights regarding their employment in the organisation and is responsible for drawing up and maintaining documents (attendance records, personnel files and contracts of employment) in the Human Resources Department.

Workforce Planning

This involves forecasting future labour requirements and is based on the estimated 'Workforce Gap' expected to occur. A workforce gap is the difference between current employee numbers and future requirements. Workforce planning is also referred to as 'Human Resource Planning'. The likely availability of a suitable Labour Supply will dictate whether the workforce gap is bridged.

SHORT-TERM WORKFORCE GAP (UNDER ONE YEAR)

If a female employee has informed her superior that she will be taking maternity leave from a certain date, immediate workforce planning is required. The future temporary worker requirement must be matched by a 'suitable substitute'. This will be based on a suitable future supply of appropriately skilled labour to fill the temporary vacancy. Employee sickness also requires short-term workforce planning. This type of workforce gap can be difficult to bridge because of short notice.

MEDIUM-TERM WORKFORCE GAP (ONE TO FIVE YEARS)

If an employee decides to take a career break (his/her position can be held for a maximum of five years in many state employments), the position must be filled in a temporary capacity. If a company undertakes an assignment or project, it will interview interested and suitably qualified candidates and appoint them for the period of the contract.

LONG-TERM WORKFORCE GAP (OVER 5 YEARS)

The interviewers would carefully assess any position that would be foreseen as long term. Senior management positions are often (not always) long-term appointments. The suitability of the successful candidate is paramount in the mind of the interviewers. Permanent state jobs tend to fall into this category. Another example would be secondments (explained later in this chapter under the heading 'Internal Sources of Labour').

How to Assess the Workforce Gap

Management normally carries out an 'Employee Assessment or Audit'. This involves analysing the current workforce, taking into account the total number of employees and how they are categorised in terms of their posts of responsibility and their seniority. The diverse skills of each employee should be listed, as well as their qualifications. The future requirements should then be weighed up. Natural wastage (retirement, redundancy and unexpected disability) must be taken into account and the cost of training (if applicable) must be estimated. Some businesses must look carefully at the cost of overtime and the willingness of employees to work overtime. If employee turnover or absenteeism is high, a panel of part-time employees should be available to management to cover requirements.

The Importance of Good Workforce Planning:

It is important that managers have the appropriate back-up facilities to cover short-term labour shortfalls. Otherwise the business profile might be damaged and it could affect customer loyalty and/or sales. All workforce planning is difficult and is based on the following factors:

1. Social Factors – people matters – considerations such as whether people's home situations might reduce work effort and contribute to absenteeism.
2. Technological Factors – skills, the need for retraining and the question of whether more labour or less labour is needed based on more modern high-tech equipment being used in the business.
3. Demographic Factors – considerations such as whether an applicant would need to relocate in order to take up the job and the expenses connected with this decision.
4. Political Factors – qualifications and job specification to match with job description as advertised; the recruitment option – open competition and equal opportunity legislation considerations (discussed in the next section).

New Challenge of the New Irish

Shane Hickey

Recent statistics have indicated that the immigrant population now stands at 10pc of those living in the Republic.

With the number of immigrants working in SMEs constantly on the increase, firms have now had their attention drawn to the different employment environment that exists.

In the recent edition of the Irish Management Institute's (IMI) 'Management Focus', Dr Mary Hogan said companies now face more challenges.

'The Irish workplace has changed and changed utterly in the past 10 years. Formerly a relatively homogenous place, it is now increasingly culturally diverse,' said Dr Hogan, who works with the IMI BizLab on cultural diversity.

'Irish management is very capable of managing complex multicultural situations.

'It is also very apparent that the situation is evolving and changing constantly, placing an onus on the leaders of Irish organisations to harness the advantage of these changing circumstances.

'What is reassuring, however, is that there is already a wealth of experience and knowledge. But these need to be shared so that everyone can benefit fully from our cultural diversity.'

David Pierce, president of Chambers Ireland and head of inward investment at Ulster Bank, said that there need to be significant moves made in language training for the 'new Irish'.

'People come here and they don't have language training. We need to help them at their point of entry and when they come in here,' he said.

Companies need to welcome in foreign workers, according to Mr Pierce, and encourage the new work force.

Such is the lack of knowledge about foreign qualifications, many workplaces are now employing doctors and accountants in jobs for which they are completely overqualified. As a result, work needs to be done on a broader scale to understand what people are qualified for, according to Mr Pierce.

'There are doctors who need to come in and have to work at a lot lower levels because their qualifications have not been accepted,' he said.

'We need to do a lot more investigating of overseas qualifications and investigating what has been involved and then accept and adjust them and use their experience, rather than putting them into these jobs that we have them in at the moment.

'We need to train ourselves in understanding them and their background and culture, where they have come from, rather than our expectation.

'Communication has to be both ways. As an employer, we have got to have them speaking English because that is our national language and that is something we have to work towards.

'We need to give a small company the satisfaction of someone and their background and their qualification.

'They can see physically what they are doing, so the trades are pretty visible — but if you go into something where there is academia like the medical profession or business accounting, we need the professional bodies to be able to say to the potential employer that their qualification is recognised.'

When hiring, companies need to check the background of all workers, said Mr Pierce.

'A lot of companies here, regardless of whether you are Irish or a foreign national, need to do credit runs,' he said.

'In the bank, we have a whole system of a history of where you have worked and criminal records checked.

'Most people in the medical profession have to have police clearance, so it has become the norm for everyone, with terrorism worldwide.'

Irish Independent, 23 August 2007

Recruitment Options

The methods used to hire labour and to make appointments. Both Internal (recruiting from within the organisation) and External (recruiting from outside the organisation) sources of labour are discussed below.

External Sources of Labour

OPEN COMPETITION

Advertising in newspapers is the most common method used by companies in order to be seen to comply with 'Open Competition' requirements for hiring staff. The advertisement will generally consist of:

1. *THE JOB DESCRIPTION:* This consists of the job title, location, duties attached to the post and any other special features connected with the post.

2. *THE JOB SPECIFICATION:* This refers to the special qualities, qualifications and skills that are sought by the company.

   The companies in question will usually refer to their 'policy of equal opportunity' and a closing date for receipt of applications. They will also refer to competitive interviews assessed by interview boards based on appropriate qualifications and applicable work experience. They will state that applications will be treated in strict confidence (complying with the Freedom of Information Act and the Data Protection Act 1988) and in some cases will draw up a set of criteria to shortlist candidates. The statement 'Canvassing will disqualify' may also appear. This type of selection procedure is seen to be fair and non-discriminatory.

STAGES TO BE FOLLOWED IN RECRUITING THROUGH OPEN COMPETITION:

Stage 1: Design of application form for job vacancy.

Stage 2: Evaluation of selection procedure by selection board and management.

Stage 3: Newspaper advertisement.

Stage 4: Application forms are sent to interested parties.

Stage 5: Candidates are shortlisted on the basis of their application, qualifications, suitability and the number of vacancies. References are verified at this stage.

Stage 6: Selected candidates are invited to attend a preliminary interview and/or other qualifying tests (e.g. psychometric tests). The aim is to assess the merits of each candidate. (This does not always apply.)

Stage 7: Subsequent final interviews might be arranged.

Stage 8: Job offers and contracts of employment (which include regulations and conditions of service) are sent to successful candidates. They must sign and return the documents by a set date, if they decide to accept the job offer. The offer is normally subject to the candidate's successful medical examination.

Stage 9: In the case of state jobs the appointments must be sanctioned by the particular government department that the position is connected with.

STAFFING/MANAGEMENT CONSULTANTS

Executive search agencies are often employed by companies to search for and locate suitably qualified candidates for different positions where vacancies arise. It is usually when businesses are head hunting or searching for top-class management candidates that they employ consultants to do the groundwork for them. Head hunting usually involves a business offering the person a more attractive remuneration (wage) than he/she is currently earning. The cost of employing search agencies is usually very high. The recruitment company Marlborough is an example of a company that offers indigenous (within the economy) and multinational clients a range of personnel for their requirements.

EMPLOYMENT AGENCIES

1. Private agencies: are usually relatively expensive to employ but many companies utilise their services.
2. State or semi-state agencies: Foras Áiseanna Saothair (FÁS) is the main government agency providing training and employment services in the country. One of its functions is the provision of a placement service. There is no cost for the service. FÁS grants are often given to businesses if they undertake to recruit FÁS employees for periods of at least thirty-nine weeks.

Internal Sources of Labour

INTERNAL PROMOTIONS

These types of opening are usually advertised on notice boards within the particular establishment where the promotion is due. The criteria to award the promotion are usually based on suitability and merit (the ability and qualifications to do the job), as well as seniority and length of service in the particular area of promotion.

INTERNAL DEMOTIONS

When a person gives up or loses a post of responsibility, the vacancy remaining creates the need for more labour. Usually positions like these are filled from the internal source of labour on the existing staff.

CAREER BREAKS AND SECONDMENTS

When employees take a career break (maximum five years) or if they are granted a secondment away from their usual line of work, this creates temporary vacancies. These vacancies would be, if possible, filled in a temporary capacity by existing part-time staff.

An employee may look for a secondment if they are full-time and permanent employees in state jobs and their aim is to work for another government-run body or for the same government body in a different section. The work must be connected with their main employment and the work experience that is gained from it must be seen to contribute directly to their main employment.

REDEPLOYMENT OR TRANSFERS

Redeployment is the unavoidable transfer of staff to a different location or branch due to closure.

Voluntary Transfer happens when an employee requests a transfer to a different branch. The managers in the section that they wish to work in usually request the transfer. Their main employment position is held open (a temporary substitute is recruited) for them while they are on secondment.

Recruiting Options (Informal Methods)

These methods can range from existing staff recommending their friends or relatives as suitable candidates for positions, to sending unrequested CVs, career guidance officer recommendations and media or paper/magazine advertisements to prospective employers.

PRACTICE QUESTIONS

1. Define 'Human Resource Planning'.
2. How does the term 'Human Resource Planning' differ from the term 'Workforce Gap'?
3. Give *one* example each of a short-term, a medium-term, and a long-term Workforce Gap.
4. Define the following terms:
   (a) Employee Audit.
   (b) Natural Wastage.
   (c) Employee Turnover.
5. Why is Workforce Planning so important to managers?
6. How does the term 'External Source of Labour' differ from the term 'Internal Source of Labour'?
7. Make a clear distinction between 'Job Description' and 'Job Specification'. Give *one* example.

8. What do the following terms mean?
    (a) Head Hunting
    (b) Remuneration
    (c) Promotion and Demotion
    (d) Career Break
    (e) Secondment
    (f) Redeployment
    (g) Voluntary Transfer.
9. List the Formal and Informal methods used to recruit staff.

Functions of the Human Resources Department

The term 'Personnel Management' is now generally referred to as Human Resource Management. It can be defined as 'all those who have responsibilities for people matters'. Its purpose is to ensure that the employee has good working conditions. This in the long run helps towards job satisfaction and a pleasant working environment. Human resource management represents the formal recognition of the need for specialist individuals to deal with people management issues.

The Role of the Human Resources Department

The Human Resources Manager or the Personnel Manager's responsibilities include:

1. STAFF WELFARE:

The human resource department provides the employee with information on statutory and voluntary employee benefits, and entitlements relating to wages, salaries, hourly and piecework pay rates and temporary/permanent employment.

Statutory benefits: employee benefits underpinned by law. Entitlements and obligatory contributions:

    Maternity leave
    Holidays and holiday pay
    Employment pension schemes
    Sick pay
    Company cars (if applicable).

Voluntary benefits:

    Sports and recreation facilities connected with employment
    Child care facilities
    Health insurance
    Career breaks and secondments
    Option of extra pension subscriptions.

2. STAFF DEVELOPMENT

The 'human factor' determines levels of productivity (efficiency and speed of work). The impact of work conditions on performance has encouraged companies to set up staff seminars and staff development groups made up of a varied staff group to investigate the levels of satisfaction or dissatisfaction with the work environment. This development is an important mechanism that is encouraged by the Human Resource Department in order to keep staff happy. It also gives staff the opportunity to suggest improvements to existing working conditions.

3. STAFF MOTIVATION

Motivation means a stimulus to work hard to achieve objectives and targets. In 1943 Maslow, a clinical psychologist, analysed human needs in an effort to understand human drives and enthusiasm. His studies became the building blocks of subsequent research on staff motivation, career counselling and the understanding of the human condition. Maslow's Pyramid of Hierarchy of Needs describes how all behaviour is driven by needs. The basic physiological needs are food, shelter and security. Humans must experience security on the lower steps of the ladder to progress to the next step. The need for love, acceptance and recognition is experienced at this stage. The top two steps of the ladder, self-esteem and self-actualisation, are experienced as a result of a positive response, i.e. acceptance, respect, recognition, appreciation and praise.

MASLOW'S PYRAMID OF HIERARCHY OF NEEDS

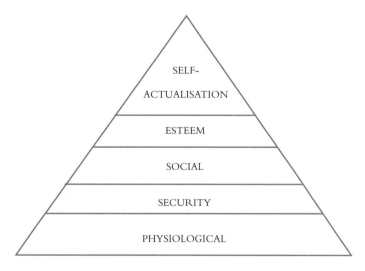

The understanding of human needs is directly applicable to the analysis of employee behaviour. Appropriate understanding of people and their behaviour within their work environment leads to good worker–manager relations and therefore avoids industrial relations problems, strikes and working to rule (deliberate slow-downs in the workplace).

The key terms in describing Maslow's hierarchy with regard to employees might be:

1. Recognition for work done.
2. Appreciation for work done.
3. Respect for employees.
4. Praise.

I have attempted here to interpret each step of the hierarchy in a 'staff needs' context as follows:

1. Physiological needs: Maslow's pyramid shows how staff members have material and personal needs.
   - Material needs are those physical things like equipment and room space which employees feel they have a right to or ownership of.
   - Personal needs, like the manager or superior creating a sense of well-being in the employee – a feeling that needs are being met, their efforts are valued, and that they matter to the organisation.
2. Security: When the manager or superior is meeting material and personal needs, it gives the employee a sense of security and well-being.
3. Social: This refers to the effective communication flow between the manager and the employee (superior and subordinate).
4. Esteem: When employees experience esteem, they realise they are appreciated and respected by their superior, resulting from effective communication flow and praise.
5. Self-actualisation: The employee will respond eagerly to positive signs and, in turn, will respond to the manager's or superior's needs. Their self worth will be fully realised, creating greater work effort and stimulating motivation.

Ultimately, the recognition of employees as people, not just as 'work machinery', is the key to good employer-employee relationships.

HERZBERG'S OBSERVATIONS

Frederick Herzberg (1966) observed that:

(a) Highly motivated workers characteristically
   (i) enjoyed the challenge of the work
   (ii) were involved in the decision-making process
   (iii) gained recognition and were given the opportunity to advance their careers or gain promotion.

(b) Workers with low motivation characteristically
   (i) were governed by too many rules – oversupervised
   (ii) had a bad relationship with senior staff and superiors
   (iii) were frustrated by workplace attitudes or bullying
   (iv) had a bad relationship with colleagues, leading to low self-esteem
   (v) had a cynical or divisive outlook
   (vi) had poor working conditions.

4. CAREER COUNSELLING

In most organisations induction seminars, in-service courses and training are provided to guide and advise employees how they should approach their jobs. These sessions are organised by the Human Resources Department, which will also readily provide information regarding promotional posts, secondments (already defined) and any other paths that might lead to career advancements if so requested by employees. Performance Appraisals (feedback on performance) are also offered by the HR department; and Training and Development may be offered, depending on the needs of the organisation.

5. DISCIPLINARY PROCEDURES AND DISMISSAL

Employees have to adhere to the organisation's rules and regulations regarding behaviour, absenteeism, punctuality etc. If they do not, then the disciplinary procedures laid down will involve:

1. A verbal warning from the employee's immediate superior for an occasional lapse in behaviour or work standards, e.g. being frequently late or swearing at a superior.
2. A formal written warning from the manager following an investigation into the case, if the employee re-offends in the same way, having taken no notice of the verbal warning and where more serious offences have taken place. Usually a copy of this written warning will be sent to the Human Resources Department.
3. A further written warning that dismissal is the next step. This subsequent disciplinary action is based on the unwillingness of the employee to adhere to previous warnings.
4. Management investigating and hearing the employee's case, followed by final warning.
5. Suspension or dismissal.

When employees are hired, they are given a copy of their conditions of employment and this would include a Code of Conduct which they are expected to follow.

What is Training and Development?

Organisations provide three main types of training:

1. in-service training
2. on-the-job training
3. off-the-job training.

Usually there are two division dealing with training and development in organisations:
* whole-school requirements, e.g. fire training and first aid
* professional development — upskilling of staff in specific areas of specialisation.

HR managers may decide to do a skills audit to determine the training needs of the staff.

What is Performance Appraisal?

This is when HR managers decide to review the work, skills and qualifications of each staff member one by one by carrying out interviews with them. This is referred to as a Performance Appraisal exercise.

Why Training Courses, Professional Development and Performance Appraisals are Good for Staff Morale and Motivation

- If an employeee upskills, he or she has the potential to diversify his or her work in an organisation to make the work more interesting.
- Employees who improve their skills have a better chance of being in line for promotion.
- Better skills can speed up the work and improve motivation.
- Performance appraisals give feedback to an employee on how efficiently they are working and each session can provide a forum for employees to alert the manager to their needs and wants regarding training and their employment as a whole. This encourages greater self-esteem in the employee.

Women to overtake men by 2012

Better exam results will catapult them to top at work

John Walshe — Friday 3 August 2007

Women are poised to take over the majority of top jobs in business, law, finance and the sciences within the next five years. And it's all because they are sstaying in education longer and gatting better results than men.

The projections are made in a joint report from FÁS and the Economic and Social Research Institute which looks at the likely share-out of jobs by 2012.

Just over a quarter of females will have degrees by then compared with only a fifth of men. A further 15.4pc of females are expected to have attained diploma/certificate level compared with only 9.5pc of men.

By contrast, nearly a fifth of men (18.9pc) will drop out of school with only a Junior Certificate. Just 11.4 of

women, however, will drop out at Junior Certificate level.

Women tend to concentrate in clusters of occupations while men are in a greater range of jobs, some of which face uncertainty.

The most obvious is construction where most workers are male.

And the report, written by Dr Pete Lunn, Prof Gerry Hughes and Ms Nicola Doyle, suggests male workers would be more exposed if there were negative shocks to the housing market and the construction sector in general.

It predicts that, in the medium term, overall jobs growth will be greatest in occupations that require third-level qualifications and high skill levels.

Professional, associate professional

and managerial occupations are expected to grow by more than 20pc relative to 2005 figures.

Outside of these high-skill occupations, some personal services occupations, including caring occupations such as childcare, are likely to experience similar expansion.

Highest growth is expected in business, financial and the legal professions, where numbers are predicted to rise by nearly 50pc. Other occupations forecast to expand are managers and highly qualified workers in health, education and science.

The report expects that two-thirds of the health and education professions will be populated by female workers in 2012 — in fact

8.5pc of all female workers will be in one or other of these areas.

At present, around half of business, legal and other professionals such as psychologists, actors and information officers are women but the report predicts that their share will increase to 55pc in the next five years.

In the case of science professionals, the report expects that women will account for 58.5pc by 2012 compared with 41.5pc in 1998. The category includes chemists, physicists and pharmacists.

However, the proportion of women engineers, including software engineers, is expected to drop. This reflects the recent decline in numbers of females entering related courses.

And area where women seem to be heading towards equality with men is management.

In 1998, a third of managers were women but this is expected to reach 46.9pc in five years.

However, Dr Lunn stressed this did not necessarily mean women were breaking through the 'glass ceiling' to the board room — it could simply be that more were being appointed to middle management and supervisory levels.
Source:
www.independent.ie/education

PRACTICE QUESTIONS

1. What is the meaning of the term 'Human Resource Management'?
2. Name the functions of the 'Human Resources Department'.
3. What are the differences between Statutory and Voluntary Benefits with regard to Staff Welfare?
4. What is Productivity and why is it so important?
5. What is the meaning of the term 'Motivation'?
6. How are performance appraisal techniques and training and development used to help improve motivation in an organisation?
7. Explain how Maslow's Pyramid of Hierarchy of Needs is applied to staff.
8. What steps are taken by the Human Resources Department regarding the following issues?
   (a) Career Counselling in employment
   (b) Disciplinary Procedures in employment.
   (c) Training and Development.
   (d) Performance Appraisals.

Purpose of Maintaining Documents in the Human Resources Department

The basic functions of the Human Resources Department that have already been discussed include: the selection, recruitment, training and deployment of suitable types and numbers of employees, as well as staff welfare, staff development, staff motivation, career counselling, staff discipline, staff dismissal and interacting with union representatives to discuss and hopefully solve disputes.

Documents such as employee statistics and personnel files, attendance records (including sick leave taken — both self-certified and medically certified), wage records and job specifications must be kept on record in the Human Resources

Department for future reference. Safety and welfare procedures, codes of conduct and disciplinary procedures are also recorded in the department.

1. An employee who leaves the employment will require a job reference and a P45 termination of employment form containing details of pay to take to the next employer.
2. Employee pension rights and payments may need to be reviewed or estimated.
3. Appointment (converting an employee's status from part time to full time) or promotional suitability (an employee's future potential) might need to be reviewed based on qualifications that are kept on record in the department. The manager can assess previous work done by employees and by choosing a suitable candidate can achieve and sustain high job performance to ensure the survival and success of the business (performance appraisal).

    A manager can assess an employee's potential to take on wider responsibilities by referring to their employment records held in the Human Resources Department.
4. An employee's attendance is monitored (with the help of attendance records and time sheets) and the level of absenteeism is noted. It could be a deciding factor with regard to future promotional prospects.

DATE	DAY	TIME	
13/07	Monday	9.00	IN
		13.00	OUT
13/07	Monday	14.00	IN
		17.00	OUT
14/07	Tuesday	–	IN
		–	OUT
14/07	Tuesday	14.00	IN
		17.00	OUT
15/07	Wednesday	9.00	IN
		13.00	OUT
15/07	Wednesday	14.00	IN
		17.00	OUT
15/07	Wednesday	17.45	IN
		19.45	OUT
16/07	Thursday	–	IN
		–	OUT
16/07	Thursday	–	IN
		–	OUT
17/07	Friday	9.00	IN
		13.00	OUT
17/07	Friday	14.00	IN
		17.00	OUT
17/07	Friday	17.30	IN
		21.00	OUT

CLOCK CARD/TIME SHEET

TOTAL BASIC HOURS   BASIC PAY

TOTAL OVERTIME   O/T PAY

TOTAL HOURS   TOTAL GROSS PAY

Managing vital resources

Organisations are increasingly looking
for better ways to manage their
human resources.

Barry McCall

Walk into almost any organisation's premises and you will find massive investments in IT geared towards managing productivity, costs, assets and so on. A manufacturing concern will be able to tell you to the nearest gram its output on any given day; you will also be able to find out exactly how much stationery it consumes in a month, how much coffee was drunk last year, and the age and value of every car in the company fleet. All at the touch of a few buttons on a PC.

The efficiency gains of organisations – both commercial and otherwise – during the 1990s was largely attributed to the IT revolution. Companies installed hugely sophisticated enterprise resource planning (ERP) systems which could track almost every aspect of the organisation's activities and ensure that tight controls were kept on costs while productivity was maximised through sophisticated JIT purchasing and manufacturing techniques.

However, against this background of heavy investment in business automation one area remained almost untouched, and that area was usually responsible for the heaviest cost burden – human resources. Human resource departments were still manually recording all employee details from hours worked through holiday entitlements to pension arrangements. Massive amounts of data were created and stored although little of it was turned into actual information.

For example, to make a simply query such as the amount of employees that took two weeks holidays during the

month of August would usually require either a manual search of holiday records or, at the very least, the writing of a macro to run on the holiday date spreadsheet.

And all the while the amount of data required to be kept was growing. For example, the EU Working Time Directive means that employers have to keep accurate records of the hours worked by its employees to ensure that they are in compliance with the law. Health & Safety Regulations mean that manufacturing companies have to keep huge volumes of data on file relating to safety training, the times of rest breaks, and so on. Furthermore, with employment legislation becoming increasingly complex detailed records of an employee's work performance and disciplinary record must be kept.

And this is just the straightforward stuff. Organisations which offer employees flexitime or other flexible working arrangements need to keep track of a whole variety of different data while other companies which have flexible reward packages which allow the trade off of holidays for pay, pension, insurance or other entitlements again have to have the means of recording all of these items for hundreds of employees.

There is also the relatively simple matter of pay. When a person gets promoted their pay and other conditions have to be improved. In many organisations this still requires a veritable flurry of paperwork with one department telling the HR department of the changes in the person's role, the

HR department telling the accounts department and so on and so on.

For this reason many companies began to view their HR departments as pen pushing operations rather than strategic resources – simply because they were overwhelmed by the amount of data required to be recorded and processed. They were unable to make a strategic input into the management of the organisation because they were too deeply involved in the day to day management of data.

With the increased focus on human resources over the past few years, largely prompted by skills shortages in some key areas, has come a realisation that the HR function needs to be automated and integrated into the rest of the business in much the same way as the accounts or purchasing operations are. Automated HR systems are no longer seen as a 'like to have' by many organisations, they have become a 'must have'.

This has seen a relative upsurge in the uptake of such systems over the past two years. 'As people did the whole ERP thing a few years ago HR wasn't seen as that important,' says John Caulfield, pre sales manager with Oracle Ireland whose customers in the HR area include Aer Rianta, Bord na Mona and Dublin City Council. 'They got away with doing it manually up to a point. But HR departments were doing too much paper pushing and not making the strategic input which they were capable of. Take employee appraisals for example. To ensure that they are fair and reasonable a lot of details about an employee's history has to be kept on file. Then there are the basic things like attendance details, holidays and so on.

And on top of that you can have organisations which operate what is known as total compensation management where employees can choose to have shorter holidays in favour of better pensions, or better life assurance and not such a high level of health insurance and so on. This not only means that every employee is potentially on a different package but that the company has to ensure that it has the right life assurance package to cope with this or that it is getting the best possible deal from the health insurer.

Due to these factors Oracle has seen a major increase in the sales of HR systems over the past two years. We have been seeing a huge increase over the past two years,' says Caulfield. 'Up until then we would have sold a lot of ERP systems but since then we have been selling lots of ERP systems with HR systems built in or indeed HR systems on their own.'

He also points out that the systems are more than simply about managing data efficiently. 'It's about the smooth running of the organisation,' he says. 'Take the issue of expenses claims. Everyone operates in some sort of approvals hierarchy for expenses. I need someone to approve mine before they will be paid. They are then apportioned to one budget or another and set off as a cost against a particular part of the business. But what happens if I move department or division? I will not only require a different person to approve my expenses but the cost centre to which they are attributed might well change as well. With a good HR system these changes can be implemented quickly and in a matter of seconds – but with the old manual systems it could take days or weeks of memo writing to sort out.'

Competence management is another important area.

'In large companies you need to be able to analyse your requirements for skills and competencies and measure that against what you have,' says Caulfield. 'After that you can make decisions on training or recruitment or whatever. And you need to stay constantly up-to-date with the skills and competencies of staff to ensure that they are utilised to the best advantage. This would be almost impossible without a good HR system in place.'

'HR departments are now using the internet and corporate intranets to deliver information and services to employees more efficiently and effectively than ever before,' says Dianne Flood, HR analyst with Softworks Computing. 'After initial fears that web applications would take the 'human' out of human resources, HR departments have embraced the web to re-engineer their processes. An idea that was initially spawned in the US, the implementation of web self-service applications for checking benefits, updating employee information and posting job requisitions has now expanded to include employee time and attendance information.'

Established in 1990, Bray-based Softworks Computing,is Ireland's largest supplier and developer of client server and web-based time and attendance /flexitime solutions and has been recognised as the fastest growing Technology Company in its field in Europe in the recent Deloitte Touch Tohmatsu European Fast 50 awards. 'We have concentrated on time management and the management of labour resources since our foundation,' says Dianne Flood. 'We have proven our ability to increase productivity and decrease costs, through improved management of human resources in our many customer sites. Our qualified and experienced staff are committed to meeting any unique requirements a customer may have through our project management,

customisation, implementation, training and support services.'

The company's 'Wise' software suite can be used for all aspects of time management, from the basic recording of hours/flexitime, overtime, and absenteeism, to extremely advanced but user-friendly management reporting capabilities. The integral report writer can produce any number of user-definable reports, providing information on absenteeism, lateness, overtime etc. by frequency, reason, percentage and cost to the company. It enables an organisation to identify any potential problems before they become serious, and thus manage and control them accordingly.

'Our customers, including companies such as Mercer, Coyle Hamilton, EMC, and Ordnance survey Ireland, as well as various Government departments, have realised that leveraging the power of the internet is critical to streamlining performance and enhancing employee job satisfaction and productivity,' says Flood. 'By embracing a web-enabled employee self-service portal, these companies have given their employees 'the keys to the car', when it comes to getting information about their holiday balances, entering absences and checking hours or flexitime earned. Tasks that once required layers of approvals and piles of paperwork are being automated, if not eliminated. Not only can employees book their holidays on line but an email notification is automatically routed to the relevant manager, who then decides whether to approve it or not. At the click of a button, management can approve or deny requests or applications.'

With a range of software and systems available to suit any company, regardless of size, and the growing use of the self-service option it looks as if HR departments will at last be freed from the relative drudgery of masses of paperwork…

(Sunday Tribune, August 2002)

Equality and Health and Safety Issues in the Workplace

What is Health, Safety and Welfare in the Workplace?

The Health and Safety Authority (HSA) is a state-sponsored body under the Department of Enterprise, Trade and Employment and has the overall responsibility for the administration and enforcement of health and safety at work in Ireland. It monitors compliance with legislation in the workplace and can take enforcement action, including prosecutions. The health and safety of people at work and of the public affected by work activities is protected by law in the Safety, Health and Welfare at Work Act 1989 (see below).

Employers have an obligation to their employees to ensure a safe work environment with no risks to health. Specific requirements regarding buildings are usually documented in a 'Safety Statement', which must be made available on request to health and safety inspectors and to employees.

Workplace bullying is also a health and safety issue that can be challenged under the Safety, Health and Welfare at Work Act 1989.

What is Employment Equality?

This is defined as the right, which all workers in the country have, to be treated equally and not to be the subject of employment discrimination.

The Equality Authority is an independent state body in Ireland. It was set up in 1999 to replace the Employment Equality Agency. It provides information to the public on equality legislation and it can, at its discretion, provide legal assistance to people who wish to bring claims to the Equality Tribunal. The Circuit Court deals with claims about gender discrimination.

There are two main pieces of legislation in place in Ireland that set out important rights for citizens and outlaw discrimination when it occurs. They are the Employment Equality Act 1998 (amended 2004) and the Equal Status Act 2000, as amended by the Equality Act 2004. (These Acts are explained below.)

Anyone providing employment opportunities, services or agencies where the public have access must not discriminate on any of nine distinct grounds:

- gender
- marital status
- family status
- sexual orientation
- religion
- age (does not apply to a person under 16)
- disability

- race
- membership of the Traveller community.

Equality Issues/Definitions

What is Positive Action?

Employers have in recent years been encouraged to establish policies and procedures to show that they are taking reasonable steps to demonstrate their commitment to equality and to avoid discrimination in the work environment. Usually these policies and procedures are documented in the form of an equal opportunities policy and grievance procedures (employee complaints procedures) in an employees' handbook, which is usually available from an organisation's human resources department.

Many employers promote 'positive action' by organising anti-racism, anti-harassment and anti-bullying training for staff. The aim is to comply with equality legislation and to avoid discrimination.

Definitions of Equality and Ethnicity, Racism and Cultural Diversity

An **ethnic group** is defined by a common identity, kinship, ancestry, culture, history or tradition. The Traveller community is still Ireland's largest ethnic minority, though in recent years immigration has created a multi-ethnic Ireland. Ethnic groups can sometimes be defined on the basis of having a common religion or language, e.g. Protestants and Catholics in Northern Ireland.

Ethnicity describes the membership of a particular racial, national or cultural group and observance of that group's customs, beliefs and language. Ethnic groups can co-exist comfortably with other ethnic groups, e.g. the Chinese community in New York.

Racial and religious equality means promoting equality between different races and people of different religious beliefs, and respecting and understanding cultural diversity, religion and customs.

Gender equality means promoting equality between the sexes.

Age equality means promoting equality for the over-50s.

Disability equality means promoting equality for the disabled.

Sexual orientation equality means promoting equality for non-heterosexual workers (gays, lesbians, bisexuals and transgendered people).

Equality regarding marital and family status means promoting equality for men, women and children in the home.

Workplace Bullying and Sexual Harassment

Sexual harassment is defined as 'unwanted conduct of a sexual nature or other conduct based on sex affecting the dignity of women and men at work'.

Bullying means verbal, physical or psychological aggression engaged in by an employer against employees or by an employee or a group of employees against another employee. It can take the form of intimidation, isolation, victimisation, exclusion, shouting, abusive behaviour, constant criticism or nagging, verbal threats, physical threats, humiliation, excessive controlling behaviour, unreasonable behaviour or task assignment, or posters, banners, emails and emblems that cause offence.

Union Representation in the Workplace

A union is a group of workers who make representations for common work entitlements regarding pay and conditions in the workplace. There are three main types of union:

1. Craft unions – skilled workers, e.g. the Irish Print Union.
2. White collar unions – professional, office and service occupations, e.g. the Teachers' Union of Ireland (TUI).
3. General unions – semi-skilled and unskilled workers, e.g. Services, Industrial, Professional and Technical Union (SIPTU).

The Irish Congress of Trade Unions (ICTU) is the umbrella organisation for most of the bigger unions in Ireland and it represents employees at the social partnership talks. These are talks between government representatives, employer representatives (e.g. IBEC and SFA) and other interested groups, such as the Combat Poverty agency. Pay structures and work conditions are recommended and negotiated and usually a National Wage Agreement (e.g. Partnership 2000) is secured for workers. Public sector workers such as nurses and civil servants are promised incremental pay increases.

Minimum Wage

This is the minimum a worker can legally be paid (usually per hour), in contrast to wages that are determined by the forces of supply and demand in a free market. In most cases, the minimum wage acts as a price floor. Each country sets its own minimum wage laws and regulations, and many countries have no minimum wage. The current minimum wage in Ireland is €8.65 per hour.

Equal Opportunities in Employment

Employers are legally obliged to adhere to the existing equality legislation when hiring and employing staff, whether they are full-time or part-time. When you are an employee or a prospective candidate your employer **cannot discriminate** against you in any of the following ways:

- **Recruitment procedure**: A discriminatory manner or discriminatory questions during the interview. (You have a right to information through an equality officer if you suspect discrimination has or is taking place.)
- **Access to Employment**: By having different entry requirements for you and for other applicants.
- **Conditions of Employment**: Unequal terms of employment and work conditions, overtime, shift work, transfers or dismissals (except remuneration).
- **Training, Work Experience**: Your employer must provide the same opportunities or facilities for employment counselling and training and work experience as those offered to other employees in similar circumstances.
- **Promotion or Re-grading**: The same access to promotional opportunities must be allowed by your employer as is allowed to similarly qualified or other candidates.

Rights and Responsibilities of Employees and Employers' Obligations and Responsibilities

The main duties of the employee are:
- To be available for work and provide a good service.
- To obey orders from superiors/employers.
- To exercise their work duties with diligence and an acceptable level of efficiency.
- To maintain confidentiality regarding company information.
- To be willing to compensate the employer for any damage caused or wrongful act committed.

The main duties of the employer are:
- To recognise equality issues – equal opportunities related to the workplace, i.e. gender, age, sexual orientation, ethnicity, race, marital status, etc.
- To ensure employees are treated appropriately in the workplace. (Most businesses are covered by full public liability insurance.)
- To adhere to the safety, health and welfare legislation.
- To respect employees' representation by their trade unions.
- To pay employees at an appropriate wage level as agreed by the social partners in national agreements such as Partnership 2000. The social partners include the Government, the Irish Congress of Trade Unions (ICTU), the Irish Business and Employers Confederation (IBEC), the Irish Tourist Industry Confederation (ITIC), the Small Firms Association (SFA), etc.

- To inform workers of their rights regarding their terms of employment by providing employees with a written statement of these terms.
- To provide workers with appropriate minimum notice before the termination of a contract of employment.

Employment Law Update (1993–2007)

If you have been out of the workforce in Ireland for some time, you will need to update yourself on changes that have occurred in the field of employment protection. The last decade has seen substantial changes and acquainting yourself with these developments will help you to maximise your rights.

Employment protection developments 1993–2007

The following is a summary of the legislation that has been introduced in this period concerning employment protection:

- *Employment Permits Act 2006.* This Act updates the Employment Permits Act 2003, introducing the Green Card permit and revising the legislation on work permits and spousal permits.
- *Employees (Provision of Information and Consulation) Act 2006.* This legislation sets established minimum requirements for employees' right to information and consultation about the development of their employment's structure and activities. From 4 September 2006 it applies to employers with at least 150 employees, from 23 March 2007 to those with 100 employees and from 23 March 2008 to those with at least 50 employees.
- *Safety, Health and Welfare at Work Act 2005.* This legislation replaced the provisions of the Safety, Health and Welfare Act 1989 when it came into operation on 1 September 2005. It consolidates and updates the existing health and safety law. Changes include the provision for higher fines for breaches of safety legislation.
- *Maternity Protection (Amendment) Act 2004.* This legislation made significant improvements to previous maternity protection legislation including new provisions relating to ante-natal classes, additional maternity leave, breastfeeding, reduction in compulsory period of pre-birth confinement, etc.
- *Equality Act 2004.* This legislation makes significant amendments to the Employment Equality Act 1998 such as providing for extension of the age provisions of that Act to people under the school leaving age (from 16) and those over 65 years. It also amends the Equal Status Act 2000 to extend the definition of sexual harassment and shift the burden of proof from the complianant to the respondent.
- *Protection of Employees on Transfer of Undertakings Regulations 2003.* This legislation applies to any transfer of an undertaking, business or part of a business from one employer to another employer as a result of a legal transfer (including the

assignment or forfeiture of a lease) or merger. Employees' rights and entitlements are protected during this transfer.

- *Protection of Employees (Fixed Term Work) Act 2003.* This legislation protects fixed-term employees by ensuring that they cannot be treated less favourably than comparable permanent workers and that employers cannot continually renew fixed term contracts. Under the Act employees can only work on one or more fixed term contracts for a continuous period of four years. After this the employee is considered to have a contract of indefinite duration (e.g. a permanent contract).

- *Organisation of Working Time (Records) (Prescribed Form and Exemptions) Regulations 2001.* The main purpose of this EU Regulation is the requirement by employers to keep a record of the number of hours worked by employees on a daily and weekly basis, to keep records of leave granted to employees in each week as annual leave or as public holidays and details of the payments in respect of this leave. Employers must also keep weekly records of starting and finishing times of employees.

- *Protection of Employees (Part-Time Work) Act 2001* – this replaces the Worker Protection (Regular Part-Time Employees) Act 1991. It provides for the removal of discrimination against part-time workers where such exists. It aims to improve the quality of part-time work, to facilitate the development of part-time work on a voluntary basis and to contribute to the flexible organisation of working time in a manner that takes account of the needs of employers and workers. It guarantees that part-time workers may not be treated less favourably than full-time workers.

- *Carer's Leave Act 2001* – this provides for an entitlement for employees to avail of temporary unpaid carer's leave to enable them to care personally for persons who require full-time care and attention.

- *National Minimum Wage Act 2000* – introduces an enforceable national minimum wage.

- Employment Equality Act 1998 – prohibits discrimination in a range of employment-related areas. The prohibited grounds of discrimination are gender, marital status, family status, age, race, religious belief, disability, sexual orientation and membership of the Traveller community. The Act also prohibits sexual and other harassment.

- *Parental Leave Act 1998* – provides for a period of unpaid parental leave for parents to care for their children and for a limited right to paid leave in circumstances of serious family illness (force majeure).

- *Organisation of Working Time Act 1997* – regulates a variety of employment conditions including maximum working hours, night work, annual and public holiday leave.

- *Protection of Young Persons (Employment) Act 1996* – replaced previous legislation dating from 1977 and regulates the employment and working conditions of children and young persons.

- *Adoptive Leave Act 1995* – provides for adoptive leave from employment principally by the adoptive mother and for her right to return to work following such leave.
- *Terms of Employment (Information) Act 1994* – updated previous legislation relating to the provision by employers to employees of information on such matters as job description, rate of pay and hours of work.
- *Maternity Protection Act 1994* – replaced previous legislation and covers matters such as maternity leave, the right to return to work after such leave and health/safety during and immediately after the pregnancy.
- *Unfair Dismissals Act 1993* – updates unfair dismissals law and amends previous legislation dating from 1977.

Complaints/Breach of Rights

Employment law in Ireland provides strong protection for employees who feel their rights have been breached. Complaints, disputes and grievances are heard before a Rights Commissioner who will listen to both sides before completing an investigation of the complaint and issuing a recommendation. Recommendations issued by the Rights Commissioner can be binding or non-binding, depending on the type of law under which the case is heard.

Claims under equality legislation are brought to the Equality Tribunal.

Often, disputes between employers and employees can be resolved using mediation. Mediation means that the Labour Relations Commission is contacted and appoints an independent person to meet with both parties and listen to both sides. This free service is available to all employees and employers (except members of the Gardaí, Defence Forces and Prison Services). Meetings are held privately and all discussions are confidential.

How to apply

Requests for mediation services should be made to the Workplace Mediation Service at the Labour Relations Commission.

Complaints, disputes or grievances regarding breaches of employment rights under certain legislation can be heard before a Rights Commissioner. Before you apply to have your complaint heard, you must notify you employer of your intention to contact the Rights Commissioner service. Where legal entitlements are involved, you should try and resolve the matter locally before referring to the Rights Commissioner service.

The following application forms must be completed and forwarded to the Labour Relations Commission in advance of a hearing before a Rights Commissioner.

Source: www.citizensinformation.ie

The C and A Machinery

This refers to the processes of Conciliation and Arbitration.

Conciliation is the attempt by a third party to help in the settlement of an industrial dispute by hearing all sides of the dispute and suggesting terms for settlement. The Labour Relations Commission provides a conciliation service.

Arbitration is a way of settling a dispute when both parties to the dispute request a third party to make a decision that they both agree to accept. This would come under the auspices of the Labour Court. Most disputes are settled by conciliation and there is a general unwillingness to refer disputes to arbitration.

The state provides the following specific institutions (all of which have various responsibilities for matters concerning employee relations) that are underpinned by current legislation. Employees can seek help with the appropriate institution to resolve problems that occur in connection with their workplace and/or in connection with alleged discrimination by management against employees in their workplace.

1. The Labour Relations Commission

The commission's functions are derived from the Industrial Relations Act 1990 (sections 24 and 25). Its aim is to promote good industrial relations by embodying employer, trade union (employee representation) and independent representation. The services it provides aim to prevent disputes and if this is not possible to resolve existing disputes.

Services

(a) Advisory body: It is an industrial relations advisory body. It helps and advises Labour Committees and Industrial Councils to carry out their functions.

(b) Resolution of disputes: The commission provides a conciliation service (involving negotiation and dialogue), taking steps to resolve employee industrial relations disputes before they require full Labour Court investigation. It reviews and monitors these developments. The success rate has to date been high. Basic pay claims, special pay increases and conditions of employment are the usual issues dealt with as part of this service.

(c) Prevention of disputes: The commission provides an advisory service to help identify and prevent situations that might eventually cause industrial relations problems (employee relations difficulties). It strives to provide this service by encouraging good industrial relations policies. It advises on and develops acceptable codes of practice for organisations and it analyses and researches problematic areas involving union/management agreements for both the private sector (firms and companies privately owned and operated) and the public sector (government and semi-state organisations). It helps government, employers and trade unions to co-operate and work together to everybody's satisfaction.

(d) Equality: It is responsible for ensuring that an equality service is provided in organisations and it is also responsible for the appointment of Equality Officers. The selection and nomination of persons for appointment as Rights Commissioners is also within its brief.

The Rights Commissioner

The Minister for Labour (underpinned by the Industrial Relations Act 1969) appoints the Rights Commissioner after suitable persons for the job have been recommended by the Labour Relations Commission. Rights Commissioners work as part of the Labour Relations Commission and investigate disputes relating to individual employees concerning industrial relations matters, unfair dismissals (1977 Act), maternity protection (1981 Act) and the Payment of Wages Act 1991. They only investigate a dispute if the Labour Court is not already handling it, only if it concerns an individual, not a group, and if there is no valid objection by any party in writing. Objections to pending investigations into disputes and to recommendations by the Rights Commissioner following an investigation must be made within three and six weeks respectively.

Equality Officers

Equality Officers work as part of the Labour Relations Commission but perform their duties independently. They investigate and make recommendations on issues in relation to claims for equal basic rates of pay (alleged sex discrimination), or marital status (allowances and maintenance), redundancy payments, overtime entitlements that are covered under the Anti-Discrimination Pay Act 1974 and alleged discrimination in relation to access to employment, conditions of employment and working hours, alleged sexual harassment, and promotion, that are covered under the Employment Equality Act 1977.

If the parties involved are not happy with the recommendations made by the Equality Officer, they are allowed to make an application to the Labour Court within forty-two days of the recommendation. The Labour Court's judgment on the case will then be legally binding.

Refer to **www.lrc.ie** for further information.

2. The Labour Court

The functions of the Labour Court are also derived from the Industrial Relations Act 1990. It is also underpinned by section 20 of the Industrial Relations Act 1969. If the Labour Relations Commission fails to resolve a dispute, the parties involved can ask the Labour Court to hear their case.

The dispute must be referred to the Labour Court by:

(a) The Labour Relations Commission (via written and oral reports through the chairperson of the Commission, a Rights Commissioner or an Equality Officer).
(b) The Minister for Enterprise, Trade and Employment.

The hearing usually involves a trade union representative, an employer, and an independent chairperson. The representatives are cross-examined and written and oral submissions are presented.

The Labour Court, on hearing the case, will issue a recommendation that is not legally binding but that employers and trade unions are encouraged to put in place.

3. The Employment Appeals Tribunal

The Tribunal operates under the Unfair Dismissals Act 1977. The decisions it makes are decided by reference to this Act as well as the Unfair Dismissals (Amendment) Act 1993, the Maternity (Protection of Employees) Act 1981, the Terms of Employment Act 1994 (covering minimum notice etc.) and the Redundancy Payments Acts 1967–89.

As suggested by the Acts above, the Tribunal hears cases that concern unfair dismissals, maternity protection of employees, the protection of employees following employer closure and liquidation, and regular part-time worker protection, minimum notice and terms of employment, and redundancy payments.

PRACTICE QUESTIONS

1. Name and briefly explain the main legal Acts that protect employee rights under current legislation.
2. Name the *three* institutional frameworks from which employees can seek help when problems occur in connection with their workplace.
3. What are the functions of the Labour Relations Commission?
4. What are the functions of the Rights Commissioner?
5. How is the right to equality protected under current legislation?
6. What are the functions of the Labour Court?
7. What are the functions of the Employment Appeals Tribunal?

A Brief History of the Trade Union Movement

The concept of trade unionism established itself in the mid-nineteenth century. In Ireland James Larkin founded the ITGWU (Irish Transport and General Workers' Union) in 1909. Employees were poor and dissatisfied with their wages and conditions of employment. Larkin called for a strike in the Dublin Tramways Company in August 1913. Employers locked all ITGWU members out of their places of work. By September 1913, 25,000 people were locked out in Dublin, aptly named the '1913 Lock-out'. This incident marked the beginning of the trade union movement in Ireland.

The Role of a Trade Union in the Workplace at Branch and National Level

A trade union is defined as 'a continuous association of wage earners with the objective of improving or maintaining conditions of employment'. Trade unions fall into three broad groups: employee associations (e.g. SIPTU), employer associations (e.g. IBEC) and trade associations (e.g. the Irish Nurses Organisation, INO).

Employee trade unions are further categorised into three main types in Ireland: Craft unions, General unions, and White Collar unions.

CRAFT UNIONS: are trade unions that protect workers that are in the 'skilled' category. Workers must have a period of apprenticeship appropriate to their work before they will be accepted into the union. Examples of Craft unions are the Electrical Trade Union and the Irish Print Union.

GENERAL UNIONS: are trade unions that cater for semi-skilled and unskilled workers and attract members from different industries. The main general union is the Services, Industrial, Professional and Technical Union (SIPTU), discussed below.

WHITE COLLAR UNIONS: are trade unions catering for professional, office and service occupations. Examples of these unions are the Teachers' Union of Ireland (TUI), Association of Secondary Teachers of Ireland (ASTI), Irish National Teachers' Organisation (INTO) and the National Union of Journalists (NUJ).

The main objectives of trade unions are:

1. To unite employees who have common interests.
2. To secure improvements in members' conditions of employment and rates of pay through negotiation with employers and the government. (Refer to 'Social Partners and Collective Bargaining' discussed below.)
3. To maintain agreed conditions of employment, which include making sure that promises of any pay increases are honoured.
4. To negotiate on behalf of members when disputes arise.
5. To protect their members and strive to ensure security of their jobs.
6. To provide a mechanism allowing members to express any job dissatisfaction and to highlight any developments at local level that might conflict with their job specification and job description (defined earlier).
7. To minimise exploitation of workers.
8. To control activities of members and discipline them if necessary.
9. To provide members with other services like information services regarding pension rights, car insurance schemes and advice regarding any areas of doubt concerning union directives.
10. Training courses for union representatives.

Social Partners and Collective Bargaining

The Social Partners, that is, the unions (on behalf of employees), employers and government representatives collectively discuss and negotiate issues concerning conditions of employment and pay revisions. This is referred to as Collective Bargaining. It replaces individual bargaining, which is generally not very effective and would fail to secure agreement with management on many issues. The conflicts of interest that usually exist between management and workers are best ironed out using the collective bargaining mechanism.

There is no constitutional provision for trade union recognition. This means that employers that are not part of any union themselves are not obliged to recognise employee grievances that are highlighted via the employee trade union.

Why should employers recognise trade unions?

The employee's right to be represented by the union will:

1. Be beneficial for the employee, providing a good degree of security that will lead to better work effort and job satisfaction.
2. Be beneficial for the employee, as it is possible to have proper negotiations over pay and working conditions.
3. Be beneficial for the employer, placing management into a good position to influence union attitudes. There is the possibility for management to create a good atmosphere in the firm by being seen to be fair with regard to decision-making.
4. Be good for the business itself, as a framework exists that can be used to sort out disputes.
5. Minimise the risk of strikes and the occurrences of work-to-rule situations.
6. Be good for all parties, as it imposes certain defined conditions on the conduct of business activities.

Organisations Representing Employees, Employers and the Unemployed

IRISH BUSINESS AND EMPLOYERS' FEDERATION (IBEC)

The Federation of Irish Employers (FIE) and the Confederation of Irish Industry decided to amalgamate in 1993 to form IBEC, the largest employer association in Ireland.

Functions:

1. It represents employers when the Social Partners (unions, employers and government) meet to discuss economic issues and employee/employer disagreements and disputes.

2. IBEC representatives attend important conferences which deal with issues that directly affect employers, and report back to their members who number over 4,000.
3. Economic and Social Policy (involving grant-aid for investment) is a main area of interest and IBEC represents Ireland when representatives take part in meetings of the Union of Industry and Employer Confederations in Europe (UNICE) and at meetings of the European Trade Union Confederation (ETUC) on behalf of its members.
4. It carries out research on behalf of employers.
5. It provides a consultancy service and advises employers on issues like health and safety.
6. It produces publications and provides training for employers.

IRISH SMALL AND MEDIUM ENTERPRISES ASSOCIATION (ISME)

ISME is the main small business lobby group (privately funded) in Ireland that has an input into Social Partner discussions (e.g. National Wage Agreements, Partnership 2000, Towards 2016). It discusses economic issues and other issues that might affect small and medium-sized businesses with the managers of those businesses and with the other Social Partners. It keeps its members up to date with newsletters.

ISME works in close co-operation with the Minister and with 'Enterprise Ireland' the body set up by the Minister, which aims to further promote small and medium-sized indigenous (home) industry.

SMALL FIRMS ASSOCIATION (SFA)

The Small Firms Association represents and provides economic, commercial, employee relations and social affairs advice and assistance to small and medium enterprises (SMEs). There are 7,000 member companies. Information packs on health and safety requirements in the workplace, management training and development, discount schemes, IT management, business and economic trends and employee relations are available to meet the needs of small and medium companies.

Employees are also entitled to be members of an affiliated trade union that represents the employees of that organisation. Employees can make their grievances known through their trade union representatives and can pursue matters until satisfactory resolutions are found.

SERVICES, INDUSTRIAL, PROFESSIONAL AND TECHNICAL UNION (SIPTU)

The beginning of the 1990s saw the birth of a new union, SIPTU, when on 1 January 1990 the amalgamation of the ITGWU and FWUI took place. SIPTU is by far the largest trade union in Ireland. Members of the Irish Transport and General Workers' Union (ITGWU) and the Federated Workers' Union of Ireland (FWUI) were balloted in November 1989 and the amalgamation was the result of the ballot. Other membership groups have been accommodated within the SIPTU structure without difficulty, retaining their distinctive characters, while at the same time benefiting from the additional resources, services and protection that the SIPTU umbrella provides. Groups accommodated in this way were:

- Federation of Rural Workers
- Irish Advertising and Design Associates
- Irish Agricultural Advisory Organisation
- Irish National Painters' and Decorators' Trade Union
- Local Authority Professional Officers
- Medical Laboratory Technologists' Association
- National Association of Transport Employees
- Racing Board Tote Staff Association.

Many other groups of employees are affiliated to and represented by the trade union:

- Association of Artists Ireland
- Association of Irish Composers
- Irish Actors Equity
- Society of Irish Playwrights
- Employees in banking, clerical, administrative, supervisory, sales, hotel/catering and many other occupations.

IRISH NATIONAL ORGANISATION FOR THE UNEMPLOYED (INOU)

This is the lobby group that represents the interests of both the short-term and the long-term unemployed in Ireland. It has significant input into Social Partner discussions and national wage agreements like Partnership 2000. Changing economic circumstances like decisions taken by both the private sector (firms and businesses) and the public sector (government) are the concern of the INOU if they are seen to be a future cause of unemployment. The privatisation of companies (decisions to sell government-owned companies to private firms) can be a major cause of unemployment, as can the proposed withdrawal of foreign companies (e.g. Digital) from the country. In recent years the INOU has had a greater input into decisions that have been made, in particular in relation to Partnership agreements.

Note: **Refer to the section on Trade Union Operations at National Level under 'Features of Grievance Procedures' in the next section of this chapter for information on Partnership Agreements.**

The Irish Congress of Trade Unions (ICTU)

This is the co-ordinating umbrella body to which many individual trade unions are affiliated. The congress itself is not a trade union, so it has no legal status.

Functions:

1. It provides a framework to co-ordinate the activities of trade unions in Ireland.
2. It consults with government on matters affecting industrial relations – wage agreements etc.
3. It represents collectively the trade union movement with regard to industrial relations, and legislative and administrative matters.
4. At the request of affiliated unions, it may negotiate at national level with employers' organisations on policy and principles relating to pay and conditions of employment.
5. It promotes unity within the trade union movement as a whole.
6. It aims to reconcile views and relationships of unions that have similar classes of workers in their membership.
7. It aims to encourage (in some situations) amalgamation of similar unions to help strengthen their structures.
8. It provides affiliated trade unions with advice and information such as legal advice and educational information and facilities.

Note: **Some trade unions are registered with the Registrar of Friendly Societies (now under the control of IFSRA, the Financial Regulator). Some trade unions are registered with both the ICTU and the Registrar.**

SAMPLE LIST

Trade Unions affiliated with the ICTU **(Source: The Irish Congress of Trade Unions)**	Trade Unions Registered with the Registrar of Friendly Societies **(Source: The report on the Registry of Friendly Societies, Government Publications Office)**
Amalgamated Engineering and Electrical Union	
Prison Officers' Association	The Association of Electrical Contractors (Ire)
Association of Secondary Teachers Ireland (ASTI)	Irish Hairdressers' Federation
Bakery and Food Workers' Amalgamated Union	Irish Airline Pilots' Association
	Irish Bank Officials' Association
Irish National Teachers' Association (INTO)	Irish Postmasters' Union
Mandate (The Union of Retail, Bar & Admin. Workers)	Irish Printing Federation
Irish Nurses' Organisation	Irish Taxi and Hackney Owners' Association
National Union of Journalists	Irish Veterinary Union
Teachers' Union of Ireland (TUI)	Licensed Vintners' Association
SIPTU	National Bus and Rail Union
National League of the Blind of Ireland	Retail Jewellers of Ireland

- Many more organisations are listed in the source documents mentioned above.

Features of Grievance Procedures

Some trade unions operate at three different levels – workplace level, branch level and national level.

If an employee feels that he/she has been badly treated by colleagues, superiors or 'the system', he/she would:

(a) Bring the grievance to the attention of the workplace union representative/s.

(b) Arrange a meeting with the workplace manager/s.

(c) If a satisfactory resolution is not achieved at this stage the workplace representatives would bring the matter to the attention of the branch union representatives who would request a meeting with the manager/s.

(d) If a satisfactory agreement is not reached at this stage and if a head office governs the workplace, the branch-union representatives would request a meeting with the chief executive or executives based in the head office. (Note: Sometimes this stage structure does not apply depending on the type of organisational structure that exists.)

(e) Having found no resolution the branch representatives would then either:

1. put a strike action motion to the union branch committee that must be voted on; or

2. recommend that the employee refer the matter on to the Labour Relations Commission, which might refer it on to the Labour Court.

TRADE UNION OPERATIONS AT WORKPLACE LEVEL

Workplace union representatives are usually called Shop Stewards. They are elected by fellow staff union members. Their representation involves:

1. Posting union business and information received in the mail on the union bulletin board to keep members informed on current events within the union.

2. Providing staff that wish to join the union with application forms and information regarding subscriptions and collecting subscriptions when applicable. (Many union subs are collected using the DAS method, which means Deduction at Source. The subscriptions are taken directly from their wages, with their approval.)

3. Attending branch meetings approximately once a month and whenever other emergency or special meetings occur. Shop stewards are not paid to attend these meetings on behalf of members.

4. Liaising with union head office.

5. Negotiating with management and representing fellow members when disciplinary and grievance issues arise.

TRADE UNION OPERATIONS AT BRANCH LEVEL

Branch representatives are usually part of the Branch Committee, which includes the Branch Secretary, the Branch Treasurer, and the Equality Officer. These members are elected at the union's AGM (Annual General Meeting). They are made up of employees from different organisations who are employed by the same body located in the same geographical area.

The business of the branch is:

1. To negotiate better terms and conditions for all branch members (all branches). This involves formally meeting with managers of different branches of the organisation to help negotiate fair and better conditions and to help resolve disputes that arise between individual members and management.
2. To manage the internal affairs of the union.
3. To make representations (put forward motions to improve members' pay and conditions) at the Annual Congress held once a year. Delegates who are to attend the Congress are elected at the AGM.

TRADE UNION OPERATIONS AT NATIONAL LEVEL:

Union officers are elected at the Annual Conference. The conference itself is the national forum where motions are put forward, resolutions are passed and union policy is determined. The union's National Executive is the body responsible for ensuring that decisions made at the conference each year are implemented. The people who head the union are full-time employees of the union – called General Officers. They are the President of the union, the Vice-President, the General Secretary, and the Union Treasurer.

The National Union Meeting:

This is a meeting of all the members of the union in the country and is referred to as a Congress or an Annual Conference. A specific number of delegates are put forward and elected from individual branches to attend the Congress and speak on (debate) motions in a public arena before a vote is taken to pass or reject these motions. The motions passed then become resolutions that are later discussed with the other Social Partners, i.e. employer representatives (IBEC, Irish Business and Employers' Confederation), and government representatives. Wage agreements like the Programme for National Recovery 1987, the Programme for Economic and Social Progress (PESP) 1991, and the Programme for Competitiveness and Work (PCW) 1994, were negotiated based on resolutions that were reached at Congress and the Annual Conferences.

Essential Ingredients of a Contract of Employment

A Contract of Employment is an offer in writing of:

(a) Temporary Employment – usually a fixed-term employment contract – usually a maximum commitment of three years or less; or

(b) Permanent Employment.

A temporary contract will contain a statement of the terms and conditions of employment broken down into:

(a) Nature of post of employment – temporary

(b) Duration of employment – annual fixed-term employment (or otherwise)

(c) Duties and extra duties required from time to time

(d) Working hours

(e) Salary

(f) Travel and subsistence allowances (if applicable)

(g) Holiday entitlements – also referred to as annual leave

(h) Special leave – e.g. compassionate leave or exceptional circumstances

(i) Sick leave entitlements

(j) Notice of termination of employment

(k) Maternity procedures and entitlements

(l) Grievance and disciplinary procedures

(m) Medical examinations (if applicable)

(n) Declaration and signatures – employee and employer (counter signature)

A Permanent Contract will contain a statement including most of the terms and conditions mentioned above, but will usually also include Probation requirements.

What is the difference between piece-work payment and flat-rate payment?

Piece-work payment means the employee is paid according to the colum or amount of work he or she completes.

Flat-rate payment is payment per hour, per day, per week or per month. It is usually a salary-based type of payment.

A Sample Contract of Employment

Dear

We have a temporary vacancy in . . . . and I have pleasure in offering you temporary employment in this post.

A statement of your Terms and Conditions of Employment is enclosed. I should be grateful if you would signify your acceptance of the offer by signing the attached copy of this letter and <u>returning it to</u> . . . .

Your employment is temporary, commencing on Monday 19 June 2XXX and terminating on Friday 28 July 2XXX. The Unfair Dismissals Act 1977–1991 shall not apply to a termination consisting only of the expiry of this term without its being renewed.

Please report for work to . . . . at 9.00 a.m. on . . . . You should bring with you your Income Tax Form P45. As you will see from the attached Terms and Conditions, your salary will be paid monthly, one month in arrears. This payment will be made on the second Friday of each month for any employment with us during the previous month – therefore, you may be with us 6/7 weeks before you receive any payment. If this is likely to cause you any difficulty you should approach your Assistant Manager concerning the arrangement of advance payment of some of your salary.

If you are unable to start on that date, please contact me without delay. If you require further information or clarification on any aspect of this correspondence, please get in touch with myself at ext. . . . .

I would like to take this opportunity to wish you every success and happiness during your period of temporary employment with us.

Yours sincerely,

I accept the temporary position as offered. I acknowledge receipt of a statement of the general terms and conditions of my employment and Staff Rules. I have read these and I accept them as the terms and conditions of my contract of employment with . . . . . . I shall report for duty as requested.

SIGNED: _____   DATE _____

STATEMENT OF TERMS AND CONDITIONS OF EMPLOYMENT – REPUBLIC

1. NATURE OF EMPLOYMENT

You will be employed on a temporary basis.

2. SECRECY

You are required to treat all information gained as a result of your employment with . . . . . as strictly confidential, both during and after your employment with . . . . For this purpose you will be required to sign a Declaration of Secrecy Form.

3. WORKING HOURS

The normal working week is from Monday to Friday inclusive.

The normal working day may vary, but overtime is calculated on a daily basis in respect of each completed quarter-hour worked in excess of 7.25 hours (exclusive of one hour's lunch-break).

Your normal starting and finishing times will be advised to you by your Manager/Head of Department.

Payment for overtime work will be at such rates as are in force from time to time, and is based on completed quarter hours worked in excess of the normal day.

(Details of eligibility and current overtime rates are available from Managers/Heads of Departments).

4. SALARY

Your salary will be at the rate of . . . . . . per week payable monthly. In addition, overtime is payable at the current agreed rates, at present . . . . . per hour.

5. HOLIDAYS

Provided you have worked at least 120 hours in a calendar month, you will be entitled to holidays at the rate of one and three quarters working days per month worked, this leave to be taken by agreement with your Manager/Head of Department but before six months continuous employment has elapsed.

If you have worked less than 120 hours in a calendar month you will be entitled to 6 hours paid leave for every 100 hours worked and to proportionately less for periods of less than 100 hours worked provided:

- you are normally expected to work at least 8 hours per day.
- you have at least 13 weeks continuous service. These 13 weeks are not included when calculating annual leave entitlements.

Holiday pay and payment in lieu of accrued holidays on termination of employment will be paid at the rate of . . . . . per day.

You will be entitled to the same Bank/Public Holidays as permanent Officials, details of which are available from your Manager/Head of Department (if you have worked 120 hours in the 5 weeks preceding the holiday or have 13 weeks continuous employment and are normally expected to work more than 8 hours a week).

6. BENEFITS NOT APPLYING TO THIS EMPLOYMENT

You will not have entitlement to benefits applicable to permanent employees,

e.g.
- club subscriptions
- pension benefits
- staff loan facilities, etc.

7. SICK LEAVE

If you are unable to attend work because of illness, your Manager/Head of Department should be notified as early as possible on the first day.

Where you have cumulative service of one year or more you become entitled to paid certified sick leave up to a maximum of four weeks in any one year. However there will be no pay for absence due to sick leave during the first year of employment. You may be required to see the company doctors or a doctor nominated by the Bank at any stage during your employment. You will be entitled to see any medical report made at the request of the Bank and said report shall not be used by . . . . except for lawful purposes.

8. NOTICE OF TERMINATION OF EMPLOYMENT

The Minimum Notice and Terms of Employment Act 1973 will apply to notice of termination by . . . . or by you of your employment. The statutory minimum notice which must be given is one week. . . . . . . reserves the right to give payment in lieu of notice.

9. MATERNITY

The Maternity Protection of Employees Act 1981 shall apply to female temporary staff regarding maternity leave and the right to return to work. The requirements in each of sub sections (1) and (2) of Section 22 of the Act are mandatory. (Details available from Personnel Manager.)

10. GRIEVANCE AND DISCIPLINARY PROCEDURES

A listing of the principal staff rules is attached. Detailed Grievance and Disciplinary Procedures have been devised to ensure that fair and prompt arrangements exist for dealing with grievance or disciplinary matters. Grievance and Disciplinary Procedures will be provided on request.

11. ALTERATIONS IN TERMS AND CONDITIONS

Alterations in your Terms and Conditions of Employment will be advised, normally by general Circular or Memorandum to Branches/Departments, as they occur from time to time.

12. GENERAL

It is understood that you will perform, to the best of your ability, all duties assigned to you and will at all times obey all reasonable instructions given to you.

Data Protection Act 1988

The following individuals, firms and other bodies who keep personal information on computer are required to register:

- Public authorities and other public sector bodies
- Financial institutions, insurance companies and individuals or firms whose business consists wholly or mainly in direct marketing or direct mailing, providing credit references or collecting debts
- Any others who keep personal information on computer relating to racial origin, political opinions, religious or other beliefs, sexual life, criminal convictions or health (other than health information on employees kept in the ordinary course of personnel administration and not used or disclosed for any other purpose)
- Those whose business consists wholly or partly in processing personal data on behalf of others.

It is an offence for anyone who is required to register but has not done so to keep personal information on computer.

Note: All those who keep personal information on computer, whether or not they are required to register, must comply with the data protection provisions of the Act from that date.

Application forms for registration, notes on how to register and a Guide to the Act may be obtained from the Office of the Data Protection Commissioner, 74 St Stephen's Green, Dublin 2

TERRITORIAL APPLICATION OF THE DATA PROTECTION ACT

1. If a data controller is **based outside Ireland** and does not use any equipment for data processing (the processing of personal data) in Ireland and does not have any branches or agencies acting on its behalf in Ireland, the data controller is not subject to the Act.
2. If a data controller is **based in Ireland**, then the Act applies.
3. In unclear cases where headquarters are not in Ireland or are in Ireland but carry on all of their activities in other countries, the new European Communities (Data Protection) Regulations, 2001 allows for the replacement of section 23 of the Data Protection Act. In general the regulations apply only to data controllers established 'in the state' – where equipment is used in Ireland. This does not include Northern Ireland.
4. In general, data controllers in EEA (European Economic Area) countries are subject to data protection laws in the EEA country in which they use equipment to process personal data and in which they are based.

The Services of the Irish Ombudsman

The Ombudsman deals with complaints against government departments, local authorities, the HSE and An Post. The first Ombudsman was appointed in 1984. Ombudsman is a Swedish word meaning 'representative of the people'.

The basis for the services provided by the Ombudsman is the Ombudsman Act 1980. Important features of the Act are as follows:

1. The appointment is made by the President, and the office is held for six years.
2. The Ombudsman can be removed from office by the President due to misbehaviour, incapacity or bankruptcy and must vacate the office on reaching the age of 67 years.
3. The Ombudsman is empowered to make recommendations only – his or her findings are not binding and these recommendations are dealt with in private in the first instance to allow the body concerned to make their own representations.
4. He/she must report on the response of the body complained against and if a response to one of his/her recommendations is not satisfactory he/she may make a special report to the Oireachtas.
5. Excluded from investigation are:
   (a) Cases where the matter is before the courts or where a court decision is being appealed against.
   (b) Cases relating to recruitment or terms and conditions of employment (dealt with by LRC – Labour Relations Commission).
   (c) Cases relating to aliens or naturalisation (emigration).
   (d) Cases relating to prison pardons or sentences or court penalties.
   (e) Cases relating to the administration of prisons.
6. A minister of the government can request that a particular case not be investigated. The Ombudsman must cease his investigation immediately.

The European Ombudsman

The institution of the European Ombudsman was created by the Maastricht Treaty in 1992. The European Parliament elected the first European Ombudsman, Mr Jacob Soderman from Finland, in 1995.

The European Ombudsman investigates and reports on maladministration in the institutions and bodies of the European Community, such as the European Commission, the Council of the European Union and European Parliament based only on complaints made. Only the Court of Justice and the Court of First Instance do not fall within his jurisdiction. Any citizen of the European Union or resident in a member state can lodge a complaint. If an attempt at conciliation fails, the Ombudsman can make recommendations to solve the case. If a problem arises he/she can make a special report to the European Parliament.

Many complaints made to the European Ombudsman concern:

* Administrative delay, lack of transparency or refusal of access to information.
* Work relations between the institutions and their agents, recruitment of staff and the running of competitions.
* Contractual relations between the institutions and private firms, for example in case of abrupt termination of contract.

The European Ombudsman produces an Annual Report to the European Parliament and this is translated into all the official languages of the European Union. He also visits all member states.

Practice Questions

1. Define the term 'Trade Union'.
2. There are *three* different types of employee unions. What are they?
3. What is the purpose of an employer association?
4. List *five* main objectives of trade unions.
5. Who are the Social Partners and how are they connected with Collective Bargaining?
6. List *three* benefits to employers of recognising trade unions.
7. What is ICTU? List *four* of its functions.
8. Explain the basic differences between the *three* levels at which Trade Unions operate.
9. Write notes on:
   (a) Shop Stewards
   (b) DAS.
10. A Trade Union's Annual Conference displays how it operates formally at National Level. Why is this meeting so important?
11. Give *five* reasons why documents are kept on file in the Human Resources Department.
12. What are the essential ingredients of a Contract of Employment?
13. What is the substance of the Data Protection Act 1998?
14. Write notes on the Ombudsman.

Ombudsman Publishes Case Reports

Date released: 10 January 2008

The Ombudsman, Emily O'Reilly, has today published details on her website of three complaints she has successfully resolved. The Ombudsman periodically publishes case reports on her website in order to further increase public awareness of the wide ranging work of her Office. These case reports will be of interest to public representatives and organisations which provide advice and support to the general public and will encourage them to bring the services of the Office of the Ombudsman to the attention of members of the public who need them.

The three cases now being published relate to the following:

A County Meath pensioner received backdated pension arrears of over €18,000 following a complaint to the Ombudsman. The man complained about the decision of the Department of Social and Family Affairs to award him a reduced pension (75% rate) due to an outstanding unpaid liability for self-employed insurance from 1988 to the date on which he qualified for a State Pension (Contributory). Having examined the Department's file, the Ombudsman did not find a basis to question the Department's decision. However, she noticed from the file that there were gaps in the complainant's social insurance record in the late 1960s. She got additional information from the complainant about his employment record at the time and then asked the Department to investigate whether replacement social insurance contributions were due to him. It turned out that he was due replacement contributions and this resulted in the payment of backdated pension arrears in excess of €18,000 to the man.

A farmer from County Meath will be €60,000 better off as a result of the Ombudsman's intervention in his complaint against the then Department of Agriculture and Food about his application to be accepted as a New Entrant for the Single Farm Payment scheme. In doing so, he asked the Department to exclude the reference years 2000 and 2001 as he would have gained financially if those years were not used for calculating his entitlements.

The Department declined to exclude the reference years in question as it deemed the applicant to be engaged in 'farming activity' during the period but the Ombudsman concluded that the Department had erred in its decision. As a result, the Department agreed to accept him as a New Entrant and excluded the years 2000–2001. The financial difference was very significant. He was granted an annual entitlement of €10,000 for the duration of the scheme (2005–2112). Provided he stays farming, the Ombudsman's intervention will mean a difference of approximately €60,000 to him over the period in question.

A fall of snow was the critical factor in the Ombudsman deciding that a complainant should not have been fined for parking on a yellow box in a car park. The complainant's car was ticketed in a Castlebar Town Council car park. She appealed the decision to the Council but was not successful. The complainant acknowledged that she may not have been parked in a designated parking space but maintained that on the day in question it was snowing and when she arrived at the car park the ground was covered with snow and there was no way of knowing the exact location of the designated parking spaces. Following the Ombudsman's examination of the facts she concluded that a refund should be granted and the Council agreed.

Source: www.ombudsman.gov.ie.

A Sample Student Trade Union Assignment

The Association of Secondary Teachers of Ireland (ASTI)
Compiled by Shane Creedon, Computer Applications and Business student in
Crumlin College 2006–2007

History of Trade Unionism and ASTI

In 1889, the first effort to organise unskilled workers into unions began. Craft unions
had been in place for 150 years before. By 1890, only 7,500 people had been
members of a union. It was slow to grow as owners were opposed to trade unions.
In Ireland, the Irish were concerned with the Land Question, so the rights of
individuals in towns and cities were ignored. People were slow to join, for fear of
being fired. In 1900, the union had more than 60,000 members who were involved
in strikes in Dublin, Cork, Belfast and Wexford.

In the twentieth century, wages were low and there was a lot of unemployment.
People knew that strikes could bring about change. The ITGWU was growing in
size and strikes brought about wage increases. The most notable strike was the 1913
Lock-out.

Trade unions were eventually accepted in the workplace. The membership was
growing, and a number of new, individual unions were being formed in the
workplace in the 1930s. This caused problems both for the workforce and
employers. Different unions wanted to strike for different reasons. There was great
rivalry between unions. A new body of trade unions was set up, the ICTU. This was
because, at a meeting of trade unions in London the ITGWU did not want to
breach Ireland's neutrality. So the ICTU was set up in 1959.

In the 1960s, there was economic growth, and white-collar unions were
beginning to grow. New companies were coming to Ireland and trade unions were
eventually accepted.

In the 1970s, all-out strikes were used to pursue demands. Also, national pay
agreements were introduced. This meant that unions could negotiate with employers.

The ASTI was founded in 1909. It was set up to achieve a system of registration,
an adequate salary scale, reasonable security of tenure and good service pensions. To
meet their demands, they launched a sophisticated lobbying campaign. In 1912,
parliament gave a grant for lay secondary school teachers' salaries of £40,000.
Registration and security provisions were made.

The Molony Committee recommended changes in administration financing.
They wanted wages increased from £180 to £450 per annum. The final offer was
a £40 increase for men and a £30 increase for women. In 1920 the ASTI had their
first strike. In 1923 the first annual delegation took place. In 1924 the Department
of Education was set up, and in 1929 the secondary school superannuation scheme
was set up. The union eventually succeeded in getting a registration of teachers, and
an eight to twelve per cent salary increase. Membership has grown to 14,236 in 1994
and there is now job security for teachers.

ASTI Union Structure

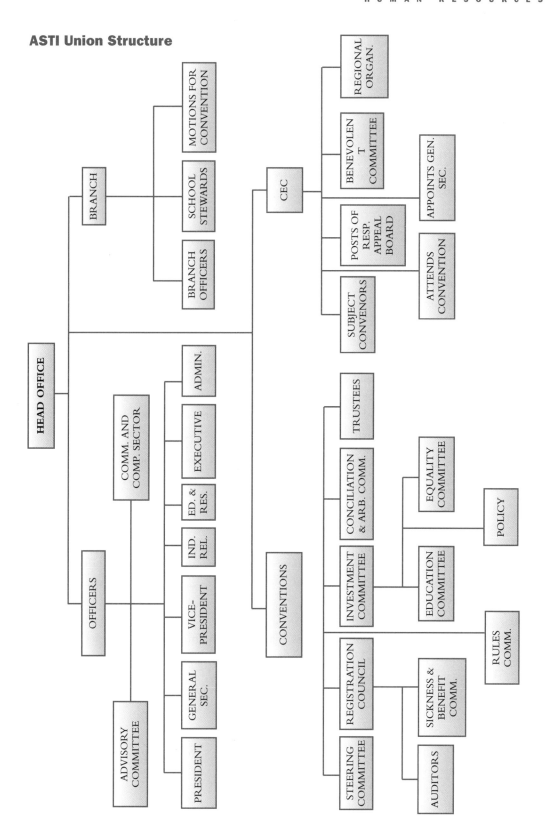

Election Procedures for ASTI

The ASTI is organised in branches of schools in geographical regions. Each school is affiliated to a branch. Members of branches elect a number of their members to the Central Executive Council. Each branch also elects members as delegates to the Annual Convention.

A standing committee of twenty-three members manages the business of the association. A president is elected at the Annual Convention. The term of office runs from 1 August to 31 July. (He/she is the president-elect for the period running from the Annual Convention to 31 July.)

The Honorary National Organiser and regional organisers are elected by the CEC. A school steward is elected to liaise with the local branch, CEC members and Head Office.

Election of School Stewards

The election of school stewards should take place annually. Each branch arranges that a school steward is elected by the ASTI members of the staff of every school within its area which has more than once teacher who is a member of the association. This election takes place on 1 May of each year. The newly elected school steward, as soon as possible, notifies Head Office using the appropriate form, the Regional Organiser, the Honourable Secretary of his/her branch, and the Hon. secretaries of the branches concerned, of his/her election. The General Secretary informs each school manager of his/her branch, concerning the school steward they elected after 15 May.

Membership of ASTI

There are four classes of membership in the ASTI
- Full membership (for serving lay teachers with the relevant qualifications)
- Associate membership (for lay Higher Diploma or final year college students)
- Emeritus membership (for members who retire on reaching retirement age)
- Honorary life membership (conferred only in recognition of outstanding service to the association).

ELIGIBILITY FOR FULL MEMBERSHIP
- All lay serving assistant teachers who hold qualifications for registration as a secondary teacher
- If they hold a primary university degree
- If they are entitled to become a member.

ELIGIBILITY FOR ASSOCIATE MEMBERSHIP
- H.Dip. in Ed. lay students in their final year or when they have qualified are eligible for associate membership.

ELIGIBILITY FOR EMERITUS MEMBERSHIP

All serving teachers who have retired on reaching the required age, or due to medical grounds, can become an Emeritus member.

APPLICATION FOR MEMBERSHIP

- Fill in the correct application form agreeing to the rules.
- Agree deductions from salary.
- Be proposed and seconded by branch members.
- Pay one-quarter annual subscription for full membership, if not deducted from salary.

INELIGIBLE FOR MEMBERSHIP

- A branch may refuse membership where there is a valid objection by standing committee or CEC.
- Principal teachers with sole power to appoint or dismiss teaching staff are not eligible for membership.
- The decision of the Central Executive Council to accept or reject is final.

Roles and Services of the ASTI

The role of the ASTI is to promote increases in funding for education, and improvements in facilities. It is directly involved in curriculum content and reform. It has direct representation on the National Council for Curriculum and Assessment, Syllabus Committees, the Registration Council, on the Public Services Committee of the ICTU and Posts of Responsibility Appeals Board.

It also represents its members at meetings with the Department of Education, the government and the political parties. Through press releases, conferences and the media, it seeks to improve the teachers' working environment.

At local level, it gives advice on rationalisation, contracts, adequate staffing levels, redeployment and leave entitlements. School stewards, CEC, branch officers and Head Office give advice and information on trade union and professional matters.

ASTI Services:

1. It is represented on
   - School authorities and boards
   - Managerial bodies
   - Government departments
   - Media and general public.
2. It negotiates to
   - Increase salaries and hourly pay
   - Improve and protect working conditions
   - Secure jobs
   - Develop curriculum

3. It advises on
   - Career and professional matters
   - Access to information
   - School stewards availability in schools
   - Branch representatives
4. It gives legal assistance on
   - Urgent legal counselling
   - Legal expenses
5. It gives benevolent funds to
   - Members retiring through illness
   - Dependants of deceased members
6. It gives sickness benefit
   - Illness-related expenses
   - Optical and dental benefits
   - Prescribed hearing aid benefits
7. It gives seminars and training on
   - Equal opportunities
   - Child abuse
   - Adult education/training
   - Annual Education Conference
   - European Social Fund for schools
   - Training for school stewards and branch officers
   - Health and safety
   - School libraries
8. It has a contingency fund
   - For financial benefits for members during disputes
9. It has a salary protection scheme
10. It has car a insurance scheme for
    - Reduced car insurance costs
    - Open to spouses of members
11. It has publications
    - *ASTI* monthly journal
    - *Secondary School*, a quarterly educational journal
    - *Nuacht*, current affairs journal
    - *School Year Diary*
    - Regular publications and leaflets on education matters
12. It has library/information centre for
    - All members
    - Books and magazines on education
    - Computerised documents
    - Access to educational databases

- Comprehensive media file
- Education and research officer

13. It has other benefits
    - Rail vouchers
    - VHI group scheme
    - ASTI credit union.

The ASTI's main aim in 1909 when it started was to:

- Have a registry of teachers
- Adequate salaries
- Employment security
- A good pension scheme.

The ASTI has achieved for secondary school teachers the following.

1. A growth in membership.
2. Salary increases.
3. Job security (protecting employment and redeployment protection for teachers)
4. Pupil:teacher ratio improved
5. Provisions for disadvantaged students (guidance teachers)
6. Curriculum development (introduction of the Junior and Senior Certificates).
7. Career options (career breaks, job-sharing).

It has done this through successful lobbying, campaigns, public meetings and demonstrations and media publicity to bring about these changes.

Bibliography

ASTI, Members' Handbook.
ASTI, Membership Information.
ICTU, *Understanding Trade Unions: Past & Present.*

Human Resources Worksheet

Mini Case Study (Situational Analysis)

Mary Whelan is the young and newly appointed Human Resource Manager at RHS Clothing, a high fashion clothing firm based in Co. Cork. The firm has been expanding over recent years and currently employs a total of 65 staff.

Most of the staff members are semi-skilled machinists and factory floor workers. They make up over three-quarters of the staff. The rest of the staff are office-based, mainly managers and administration staff.

Despite Mary's easy and friendly manner, much suspicion and unease exists among staff regarding piece-work payment and new performance appraisal systems that Mary wants to introduce. Mary believes that these changes will ultimately benefit staff motivation and increase productivity.

Mary aims to create a more employee-centred organisation. Her job will not be easy as a number of what could be viewed as negative features have manifested themselves in the course of time.

- Several layers of supervision have grown.
- A large growth in technical specialists and support staff has occurred.
- A growth in the number of procedures and rules has lead to a good deal of inflexibility.
- A weakening of general decision-making with relatively little input from employees.
- A fall off in the level of innovation.
- Poor communication and duplication of certain activities.

Questions on Case Study

QUESTION 1

a) Give two reasons why Mary's plans to introduce piece-work payment has caused suspicion and unease. List two benefits of piece-work payment for the employees.

b) What is a performance appraisal system and how are staff members assessed using this system? List two ways it could benefit staff.

c) Give two other ways in which Mary could motivate her staff.

QUESTION 2

a) Analyse the negative features listed in the case study and give three reasons why they may have developed.

b) List three ways in which Mary could try to turn the negative features into positive ones.

c) List two ways Mary could solve existing communications problems and indicate why you consider them to be good HR practice.

SECOND SECTION

QUESTION 3

a) Distinguish between a short-term, medium-term and long-term workforce gap, giving one example of each.

b) List three external and three internal sources of labour.

c) Explain the main stages to be followed in recruiting through open competition. Refer in your answer to the difference between a job description and a job specification.

QUESTION 4

a) List two reasons why staff motivation is key to the successful operation of an organisation.

b) Explain Maslow's theory of hierarchy of needs and list two reasons why it is central to HR training and practice. Illustrate your answer appropriately.

c) List three types of training used as part of training and development and explain two ways in which training can motivate staff.

See the Gill & Macmillan website for the suggested solution.

Sample Assignment Briefs – Human Resources/Trade Unions

1. Carry out a brief profile of an Irish Trade Union using the following headings as a guide:
   (a) History, size and membership and general purpose of the union.
   (b) Mission Statement.
   (c) Organisational Chart of some aspect of the Trade Union (can be the complete chart, a breakdown of head-office staff or a branch profile or equivalent, e.g. general secretary, vice president of the union, etc.)
   (d) Functions of members mentioned on Organisational Chart(s) explained.
   (e) Union Meetings.
   (f) Grievance Procedures.

2. Analyse the workings of any Human Resources Department using the following headings as a guide:
   (a) History, size and ownership of the business.
   (b) Size and layout of the HR Department (with visuals, staff numbers etc.)
   (c) Organisational Chart of the HR Department and HR staff functions explained.
   (d) Filing methods and general HR Department day-to-day functions/duties.
   (e) Recruitment Procedures.
   (f) Disciplinary Procedures.

3. The student brief is as follows:
Select and cut out *four* advertisements for various types of jobs from the newspaper. For each advertisement:
(a) Identify what type of Company or Organisation is advertising.
(b) Identify at what level in the organisation the person will work.
(c) Identify what type of Recruitment Option is being used.
(d) Identify who the applicant will be responsible to and what is the extent of his/her job specification (some imagination and knowledge of the world of work should be evident).
(e) Identify what type of person (qualifications, attributes, skills, experience etc.) is required.
(f) Outline any available information about remuneration with reference to 'flat rate', bonuses, overtime, or other incentives.

Note: The Examiner marking the assignment will take variety of advertisements, clarity of analysis, extent of knowledge, imagination in interpretation and neatness of presentation into consideration.

Sample Questions for Student Research on 'A Trade Union'

1. Could you give me some information on the history of the Trade Union?
2. What is its Mission Statement?
3. Where are the Trade Union offices located, i.e. head office, branches?
4. Is the Trade Union affiliated to the ICTU (Irish Congress of Trade Unions)?
5. How many and what categories of members does the Union have?
6. Could you provide me with an Organisational Chart of the Trade Union? (E.g. President, General Secretary, Assistant General Secretary, etc.)
7. What are their functions?
8. What is the structure in place with regard to union meetings?
9. What grievance procedures can members avail of?

Sample Questions for Student Research on 'The HR Department'

1. When did the business become established? Did it relocate?
2. How many branches/departments are there?
3. What products or services does it offer?
4. What type of ownership is there (e.g. sole trader, partnership, private, public company etc.)?
5. Who owns the business (shareholding)?
6. Could you provide me with an Organisational Chart of staff in the HR Department? If not, can you help me to compile one?
7. Can you explain the basic functions of the staff in the HR Department?
8. What filing systems are used in the HR Department, e.g. alphabetical, numerical, historical, mixture?
9. What are the recruitment procedures of the business, e.g. open competition, agencies used, word of mouth, etc.?
10. Could you provide me with a copy of a sample newspaper advert, letters of reply or contracts of employment to include in my project?
11. How do you discipline staff, e.g. reminders (memos), verbal, written warnings, suspensions, dismissals?
12. Do you hold staff development days? If yes, do you think they help to motivate staff and increase work effort?
13. How are the staff motivated – by career advancement/promotions etc.?

5. Preparing for Meetings

A meeting is a forum that allows for communication within a group of people.

Role of a Meeting within the Organisation

Meetings are designed to:

1. Allow immediate face-to-face oral exchange, feedback and presentation within a controlled framework, where a chairperson's job is to provide this control and regulation of activities.
2. Help enhance understanding and act as a forum for persuasion.
3. Humanise the context of the organisation's communication channels by opening the parties to personal contact and each other's direct scrutiny and by exposing the characteristics of individual personalities. Open and spontaneous communication is usually encouraged with constructive criticism being paramount to improvements and more satisfactory work arrangements.
4. Spread information quickly and efficiently with full advice on and explanations of business given to participants, to avoid misunderstandings.
5. Create possible decision-making forums usually with detailed discussion before decisions are arrived at, and where previous unfulfilled commitments can be discussed further and sometimes enforced.
6. Iron out difficulties (problem-solving) and promote better 'people relationships' and co-operation.

Different Types of Meeting

Meetings are generally set up by posting a *Notice* informing people where and when the meeting is to be held, together with an *Agenda* briefly detailing what the meeting is about.

1. Informal meetings usually have a chairperson who regulates activities by keeping order and by encouraging contributions to the discussion when necessary. He/she informally guides the discussion along the lines set by the agenda.
2. Formal meetings differ from Informal meetings because as well as the requirements for a Notice to be posted or sent and an Agenda to be drawn up:
   (a) The participants are governed by legal requirements, where they have the right to have an item included on the agenda provided that they give due notice of it to the chairperson.

(b) A sufficient number of participants must be present at the meeting in order to form a *Quorum* (a required number of participants to vote).

(c) The participants usually sign an attendance book to prove that they were present at the meeting.

(d) The participants presiding over the meeting have formal titles like *chairperson* and *secretary*. When these people are not available 'Acting' participants take their places temporarily.

(e) Formal *Minutes* of the meeting (an accurate summary of proceedings) are taken usually by the secretary.

(f) A formal *Report* of the meeting is usually compiled by the secretary and sent to participants.

(g) The *room layout* of the meeting and the seating arrangements of the participants are sometimes sketched to provide further evidence of attendance and to show that formal procedures were followed.

(The terms written in italics will be discussed later.)

EXAMPLES OF DIFFERENT TYPES OF MEETING:

Types of meeting run from the Most Formal to Less Formal to Informal.

The Most Formal meetings are usually Annual General Meetings (AGMs), Annual General Conferences, Board Meetings, Extraordinary General Meetings (EGMs), Department Meetings, Union Meetings, Public Inquiries and Council Meetings.

Less Formal Meetings might be Staff meetings, Club committee meetings, Sub-committee meetings, Task groups and Quality Circle meetings.

Informal meetings might be staff development meetings, authors informally meeting with editors, inter-departmental meetings.

- Formal procedures involve thorough preparation by presiding participants with full written records, official rules of procedure, participant behaviour and rules of law governing the meeting being strictly adhered to.

- Informal arrangements involve informal notes (if any) being taken for reference, with no formal rules for participants and an unstructured procedure being apparent. MBWA, 'Management by walk around', is an informal technique that managers use – they regularly walk around about the workplace and have informal chats with subordinates. It is a deliberate means of stimulating motivation and can help to raise job satisfaction. On the other hand, employees can view it as an intimidating means of motivation.

Note: It is interesting to note that informal meetings can be the key to good organisation because many issues that are discussed informally gain universal agreement before the formal forum is set up. Also input from people who may not wish to voice their opinions or objections in a more public and formal setting can prove to be informative and useful to guide the final decision-making process. It ensures that everyone's needs are considered within the organisation. In short, everyone gets a look in. (Refer to Chapter 1 'The Organisation' where Formal and Informal Organisational Structure is discussed.)

The Functions of Specific Types of Meeting

1. THE AGM

The Annual General Meeting is held once a year by clubs, associations and companies that all shareholders or members are entitled to attend. An invitation is posted or sent to them. The Companies Act requires by law that companies hold an AGM. Officers (i.e. chairperson, vice-chairperson, secretary, treasurer and other typical posts such as publicity officer, equality officer, etc.) are elected or re-elected for the year ahead. Annual reports regarding issues and monies (the financial position of the business including profits/dividends) are dealt with and copies of these are made available to members or participants. Shareholders can question directors openly and satisfy themselves with regard to the current performance of and future plans for the business.

2. AN EGM

An Extraordinary General Meeting is held if a serious turn of events occurs like the possibility of the company going into liquidation. A good example where a meeting like this is required would be if a company merger was envisaged in the near future. This meeting that the board of directors or committee calls notifies all shareholders or members of an EGM to discuss the specific item of business.

3. BOARD MEETINGS

A Board Meeting or Committee Meeting is a meeting of a task force that heads the organisation. The members have delegated authority to make decisions, and can serve as people who can be consulted for the purpose of co-ordinating activities within the organisation. The board members have the authority to carry out the decisions arrived at by them at these meetings. This type of company meeting is underpinned by the Companies Act 1985.

An MPC is a Monetary Policy Committee meeting that a bank or financial institution might hold to review interest rates and the general financial policy of the institution. It is an example of a type of board meeting.

4. DEPARTMENT MEETINGS

Organisations divide up labour into departments. Usually each department has a 'head of department' and he/she calls internal department meetings that only apply to people directly connected with the department in question. These meetings take place approximately once a month. A review of the past month's activities with regard to that department takes place. Participants make suggestions for change and engage in constructive discussion to allow for improvements within the department. Appropriate statistics and documentation are provided by the head of department to motivate and inform workers present at the meeting.

5. Union Meetings

The different types of Union Representatives are discussed in detail in Chapter 4, 'Human Resources', in the section 'Features of Grievance Procedures'. The corresponding meetings that are presided over by these representatives are:

Workplace Union Meetings

The staff union representative posts a notice and an agenda of the intended meeting on the union notice board. A satisfactory period of notice, usually a week, should be given to staff. Sometimes it is necessary to call an emergency meeting when it is not possible to give this amount of notice to members.

The functions of these meeting are:

1. To keep members informed on current events within the union.
2. To discuss grievances that members wish to raise and to suggest ways that solutions may be found.
3. To decide by majority vote to strike or operate a work to rule in order to gain management's attention, which might result in better pay and conditions of employment.
4. To decide whether disputes at local level should be brought to the attention of the branch representatives.
5. To decide whether disputes might be resolved more quickly by taking the legal route (via the Labour Relations Commission and the Labour Court – discussed in Chapter 4).

Branch Union Meetings

The union head office will send individual workplace union representatives notification of branch meetings which take place usually on a monthly basis. Notification is also given of special or emergency meetings from time to time. Usually the branch chairperson, the branch secretary, and from time to time other officers preside over the meeting. All the members of different branches are entitled to attend these meetings and to vote.

The functions of this type of meeting are:

1. To address and discuss grievances resulting in motions being put forward and agreed upon by 'the branch'. These motions must be sanctioned by the Union Executive Body and by the General Officers if they are to be presented as

motions that could be converted into resolutions and become union policy at national level (at the Annual Congress/Conference).

2. To address and discuss problems at local workplace level and decide on options to resolve these disputes to everyone's satisfaction.

3. To discuss issues regarding pay and conditions and discrimination and to put forward motions to deal with local problems in these areas.

4. Each branch holds its individual Annual General Meeting once a year (the functions of an AGM have been discussed previously).

THE NATIONAL UNION MEETING:

This is a meeting of all the members of the union in the country and is referred to as a Congress or an Annual Conference. A specific number of delegates are put forward and elected from individual branches to attend the Congress and speak on (debate) motions in a public arena before a vote is taken to pass or reject these motions. The motions that are passed then become resolutions that are later discussed with the other social partners, i.e. employer representatives (IBEC, Irish Business and Employers' Confederation) and government representatives. Wage agreements like the Programme for National Recovery 1987, the Programme for Economic and Social Progress, PESP (1991), the Programme for Competitiveness and Work, PCW (1994), Partnership 2000 and Toward 2016 (2006) were negotiated based on resolutions that were reached at Congress and the Annual Conferences.

6. PUBLIC MEETINGS

Certain European directives and case-law precedents affect the holding and conduct of some meetings. This would apply to public inquires and tribunals, which are types of public meeting. The legal Acts that underpin these types of meetings are the Public Meeting Act 1908, the Public Order Acts of 1936 and 1986, and the Representation of the People Act 1983.

Both the public sector (government, state and semi-state bodies) and the private sector (private companies and organisations) have meetings to regularise affairs within respective areas of authority. Together, the informal and formal organisational structure that also applies to meetings is the driving force that leads to good communication networks that in turn leads to effectiveness and efficiency.

Aer Lingus says EGM would breach law

31 August 2007

The board of Aer Lingus has rejected a request from Ryanair to hold an extraordinary general meeting of shareholders.

Ryanair, which owns 29% of Aer Lingus, had requested the meeting to discuss Aer Lingus's withdrawal of the Shannon-Heathrow service.

It wanted Aer Lingus to retain the route, and suggested that it switch its recently announced Dublin-Gatwick routes to Belfast. Aer Lingus and Ryanair would be competing on the Dublin-Gatwick route.

The board of Aer Lingus, in a letter to Ryanair, said the holding of an EGM would infringe Irish and EU competition law, in view of the European Commission's rejection of Ryanair's proposed takeover of Aer Lingus.

Aer Lingus said it was clear that Ryanair was 'attempting to influence and co-ordinate the strategic conduct of Aer Lingus, its closest competitor'.

A spokeswoman for Transport Minister Noel Dempsey said he would be making no comment on the Aer Lingus decision as he believed this was a matter for the board of Aer Lingus to decide.

Source: www.rte.ie./business

PRACTICE QUESTIONS

1. (a) Define the meaning of a 'Meeting'.
   (b) List *four* objectives of meetings.
2. What are the main differences between a Formal and an Informal Meeting?
3. Name *five* different types of meetings and explain how they differ.
4. What are the functions of a Workplace Union Meeting?
5. What are the functions of a Branch Union Meeting?
6. What are the functions of a National Union Meeting?
7. What legal Acts underpin public meetings like Tribunals of Inquiry?

Roles, Powers and Duties of Officers at a Meeting

THE CHAIRPERSON

A chairperson regulates activities at a meeting by keeping order and by encouraging contributions to the discussion when necessary. He/she guides the discussion along the lines set by the agenda (in the form of a sequence of business decided in advance). Anything that the chairperson has not been informed about in advance can be referred to under 'Any Other Business' (AOB) if time permits.

In formal meetings, the chairperson has more complex responsibilities and set rules will be applied by him/her.

1. The chairperson will make out a chairperson's agenda that directly corresponds with the main agenda, except personal notes will appear under each item on the main agenda. (A sample is given later.) It provides a personal reference to guide the chairperson when he/she is chairing the meeting. The chairperson's agenda will allow him/her to implement the correct procedure (points of order) that must be observed in convening and constituting the meeting and in the conduct of the debate.

2. In the event of queries or complaints regarding procedure (points of order) the chairperson must give an immediate ruling.

3. He/she must deal firmly and exercise courtesy when participants engage in irrelevancies, long-windedness, interruptions, show a lack of courtesy or use improper language.

4. He/she must regulate proceedings when participants are voting upon issues in order to arrive at a clear-cut decision agreed by a majority.

A well-led meeting can be very productive and effective for the purposes of planning, consultation, problem-solving and decision-making, relaying decisions and instructions, downward and upward briefing (to subordinates and superiors), inter-departmental and cross-departmental liaison.

THE SECRETARY

A Secretary would normally

1. Have 'before-meeting duties' like fixing the date and the time of the meeting and preparing, posting and/or sending out the Notice and the Agenda to interested parties.

2. Be responsible for choosing and preparing the location of the meeting, ensuring appropriate size of venue, good accessibility, appropriate facilities (overhead projectors etc.) and suitable seating arrangements.

3. Have 'during the meeting duties' like making notes and assisting the chairperson regarding clarification of statements made etc.

4. Have 'post-meeting duties' like preparing the Minutes of the meeting based on the notes taken at the meeting, and might be required to communicate decisions taken based on the discussion at the meeting and/or act on these decisions (this does not always apply).

THE TREASURER

The functions of the Treasurer are:

1. To receive and record subscriptions from members of a club or union and to send the new member a receipt acknowledging receipt of the money.

2. To lodge the money into the appropriate club or union bank account.

3. To pay all club or union bills.

4. To keep the accounts (financial transactions) of the club or union correct and up to date.

5. To prepare a yearly Financial Report for the club or union's AGM and make the report available to members.

Terms Associated with Meetings
(including regulations governing meetings)

1. Clear Days: refers to the time required to convene a meeting, not counting the day the notices are sent out and the day the meeting is held. (An organisation's rules may place a different definition on Clear Days depending on their requirements.)

2. In Camera: refers to a meeting that is held in private where the public or the press are not allowed to attend.

3. A Motion: is a proposal put to a meeting. For example, Motion No. 1 might be, 'I propose that Mary Smith be elected as Treasurer of this branch' (usually naming the branch of the organisation). There is usually a 'seconder' to back up the 'proposer'.

    Examples of Motions:

    'propose that the meeting postpone consideration of the subject';

    'propose that the debate be adjourned.'

Informational proposals can also be cast as motions, e.g. 'I propose to receive the report on the annual accounts given by the treasurer for the year ended . . .'

4. A Proposer: is a person who puts forward a motion at a meeting.

5. A Seconder: is a person who immediately supports the proposer's motion. A seconder usually signs the minutes of a meeting also.

6. A Resolution: If a motion is accepted, but has to be put to superiors or executives, it is referred to as being 'carried'. If, however, it is regarded as a decision, the motion then becomes a 'resolution'.

7. Standing Orders: are rules governing the conduct of meetings. A standing order might be invoked to move that a resolution be suspended. (This means that a decision is delayed pending certain conditions.)

8. An Amendment: is a proposal to change the wording of a motion, *before* it is put to a vote.

9. An Addendum: is the change that is made to the wording of a motion *after* a vote has taken place.

10. Substantive Motion or Resolution: When a motion is changed it becomes a substantive motion that must be voted on again. If carried, it becomes a decision, at which point it is a substantive resolution.

11. A Point of Order: To raise a point of order at a meeting might be to clarify a point that has already been raised or to disagree with it. The point of order should be dealt with immediately by a ruling from the chairperson. Points of Order are designed to ensure:

(a) that regulations are being observed.

(b) that the proceedings of the meeting are not later rendered invalid.

(c) that voting procedures are being adhered to (e.g. making sure that someone who is not entitled to vote does not vote – they are not allowed to manipulate proceedings).

12. An 'Ad Hoc' Committee: is one formed for a special purpose.

13. A Quorum: is like a quota – the minimum number of people who must be present at the meeting before the meeting can begin discussions. (Most organisations have rules concerning a quorum for meetings.)

14. A Proxy: is a 'stand-in' or the person authorised to act and vote on behalf of a shareholder at an organisation's AGM, with the shareholder's approval. At some company meetings proxies have the right to be present but not to speak.

15. A Scrutineer: is one who checks the validity of votes on behalf of interested parties, e.g. at elections.

16. A Teller: is a person who counts votes.

17. A Debate: is a representation of participants' opinions on an item that appears on the Agenda. In a larger forum such as a Conference (Fianna Fáil or Fine Gael Ard Fheis, Teachers' Conferences etc.), motions are debated by different delegates which are then voted on and, if carried, become resolutions. The chairperson is usually the president, vice-president or a prominent leader of the organisation.

18. Through the Chair: It is the chairperson's task to guide the meeting through the sequence of short debates. One speaker is allowed to speak at a time. Speakers who wish to interrupt or to argue with others are urged to 'address the chair'. This is a way of controlling interruptions, heckling, and arguments among the participants at the meeting.

19. An Adjournment: is an interruption in the proceedings of a meeting before they have been completed. It can take the form of an interruption or a postponement to a later date.

(a) If there is a problem regarding the holding of the meeting and the notice to convene has already been issued, the meeting cannot be postponed. The procedure is to hold the meeting, but to propose a motion for an adjournment before any business is done. The secretary may issue an advance notice to members that the adjournment will be proposed, so that they do not waste time coming to the meeting.

(b) If the quorum is a minimum of two people (or higher) and someone leaves, the meeting must be temporarily adjourned because the quorum is lost.

(c) If it is impossible to maintain order, the chairperson will decide to adjourn the meeting.

20. Casting Vote: When there is an equal number of votes 'for' and 'against', the chairperson has/may have a deciding vote.

21. Abstention: The free decision that all members have not to vote either for or against the motion.

22. 'Nem Con': This is a Latin phrase *nemine contradicente* meaning 'no one voted against the motion' but some members abstained.

23. Unanimously Carried: This means all members voted in favour of the motion.

24. *Sine Die*: This occurs when a meeting adjourns without fixing a date for the next meeting.

Procedures for Voting at Meetings

Voting is the mechanism used by members of an organisation, club or union to make decisions and to reach agreement regarding motions (proposals) and convey these decisions to members and to the chairperson.

It is often possible to reach agreement without voting at meetings. (Government mostly reach decisions without voting.) At many informal meetings it is not necessary to take a vote. However, when voting is necessary it is important that:

1. The motion (proposal), i.e. the matter for discussion and the point to be decided, be clearly explained and conveyed by the chairperson to the members voting. Voters should know exactly what is being proposed.

2. The regulations governing the meeting are strictly adhered to (discussed previously).

3. Those voting can confirm exactly what was decided.

HOW IS THE VOTE TAKEN?

1. By Acquiescence: This is the approval of the motion by the members clapping.

2. By Voice (or acclamation): If all those in favour of the motion say 'Aye' and all those against the motion say 'Nay'. The decision has usually been temporarily agreed upon beforehand.

3. Show of Hands: The chairperson invites the members to raise a hand, 'All those in favour?' The teller or chairperson counts the votes. Then the chairperson invites 'All those against?' to raise a hand and the chairperson or teller counts these votes. Then the result of the count is declared. This system is based on 'one person, one vote' or if it is allowable a member's proxy will vote on his or her behalf.

4. By Proxy: The member nominates a person to vote on his or her behalf (or gives the nominee voting instructions) only if the organisation's rules permit.

5. By Poll: After the result of the show of hands, the chairperson must decide whether a poll is required, when members request it. It must either be taken immediately or a date set in the near future. If it is decided to vote by poll, the result of the show of hands must be withdrawn. Individual members then must sign a form (voting paper) indicating their preference 'for or against the motion'. Companies generally vote by poll and in these cases because of shareholdings the system might not necessarily be based on 'one person, one vote'.

6. By Ballot: This is the voting procedure for general and local government elections. Voters tick their preference on a voting paper and place it in a special ballot box. This method of voting is a secret ballot.

7. By Division: Members voting walk into different rooms based on 'for' or 'against' preferences and tellers count the numbers and report back to the chairperson. Internal government voting is carried out in this way.

The chairperson declares the result and asks the secretary to include this detail in the minutes of the meeting. The item of business or the debate cannot be reopened for discussion during this meeting. It can, however, be agreed to reschedule it for another time.

Purpose of an Agenda

An Agenda (Latin for 'things to be done') is usually posted or sent out by the secretary, together with the notice, and is a brief description of what the meeting is about. It is usually drawn up in the form of a list of items to be discussed in order of importance.

It informs every participant about

1. The subject of items to be discussed. Speeches, arguments and questions can be prepared in advance.

2. The order of items to be discussed. This will allow members to attend only when items of interest to them are being discussed.

3. The limited time schedule: the chairperson must make members aware that there is a time limit for debate.

A Sample Combined Notice and Agenda of a Business

The following is the Agenda for the AGM of Maryville Football Club.

Notice of the Annual General Meeting of Maryville Football Club

Notice is hereby given that the sixth Annual General Meeting of Maryville Football Club will be held.

MARYVILLE FOOTBALL CLUB

ANNUAL GENERAL MEETING

Friday 12 November xxxx at 8 p.m.
In Glenstall Hotel, Maryville
AGENDA

1. Apologies for absence.
2. Minutes of the previous AGM.
3. Matters arising from the minutes.
4. Chairperson's Report.
5. Treasurer's Report.
6. Election of Officers.
7. Any Other Business (AOB)
8. Date of next meeting.

Signed:

_____

Frank James
Secretary

MARYVILLE FOOTBALL CLUB

CHAIRPERSON'S AGENDA   NOTES

For the AGM to be held in the Glenstall Hotel
on Friday 12 November xxxx at 8 p.m.

1. *Apologies for absence*
   Mr J. Downey and Ms A. Malone are unable to attend.

2. *Minutes of the previous AGM.*

3. *Matters arising from the minutes*
   Subscriptions: Refer to updated report on estimated
   expected rise in subscriptions and consequent revision
   needed in facilities on the premises.

4. *Chairperson's Report* (attached).

5. *Treasurer's Report* (copy attached).

6. *Election of Officers*
   Proposals for Ms Kathleen Johnson as next year's Secretary
   replacing Mr Harry Black. And Mr Seamus O'Connor
   replacing Regina White as Treasurer.

7. *Any Other Business*
   Item 4: Mr John McCarthy has officially issued his
   resignation as Senior Grounds Supervisor and Mr Frank
   Fahy has been officially appointed to the position.
   Reminder to thank Mr John McCarthy for his years of
   service and to welcome Mr Frank Fahy to the position.
   Item 6: Ms Mary Fox has agreed to organise events and
   presentations at the Club's Annual Dance this year.
   Reminder to thank her.

8. *Date of next meeting*
   Friday 2 February xxxx at Maryville Clubhouse at 8 p.m.
   (subject to agreement).

The Notice sometimes appears in the page preceding the Agenda:

<u>NOTICE</u>

**MARYVILLE FOOTBALL CLUB
ANNUAL GENERAL MEETING**

Friday 12 November xxxx

At
8 p.m.
in
Glenstall Hotel, Maryville.

Signed:
_____

Frank James
Secretary

Purpose of the Minutes of a Meeting

The minutes of a meeting are a written record of the meeting taken by the secretary (or another nominated person). They are usually taken in the form of shorthand notes and later written up in a formal structure (example given later). The minutes represent a form of reported speech and insignificant outbursts (or personality clashes) are sometimes edited out of the minutes.

The benefits of writing up the minutes of a meeting are:
1. They propose to serve as a complete and concise record of business and as a source of reference regarding details of information, commitments, agreements and disagreements uttered orally by participants.
2. They provide some evidence and back-up and can be referred to regarding conflicts of facts about the meeting, where participants might deliberately forget or distort the account of speeches made at the meeting.

Types of Minutes

1. Resolution Minutes

Strictly only the decisions that were taken (excluding the debate or objections) will be detailed. These minutes might be used to disguise conflicts of opinion and objections raised. For example 'It was resolved that Maryville Football Club AGM should be held on Friday, 12 November xxxx, at 8 p.m. in Glenstall Hotel, Maryville.'

2. Narrative Minutes

This is a concise written record of events and debate leading up to the resolutions (decisions) and the resolutions themselves. Participants' speeches, comments, contradictions, agreements and suggestions are noted and participants are held accountable for what they say. The aim is to give a thorough insight into the feelings of participants without unnecessary irrelevant details. For example, 'The Chairperson addressed the meeting and expressed her dissatisfaction that no compromise was reached regarding the formulation of a Company Mission Statement. She referred the meeting to Ms Moloney on this matter. Ms Moloney reported that since the last meeting in April, based on suggestions made to her, she had formulated two sample Mission Statements that she believed would be acceptable to staff. Mr Jones expressed dissatisfaction at not being consulted about the matter. The Chairwoman rejected Mr Jones's complaint out of hand and confirmed that every member of staff had been given detailed information on the requirements. The Chairwoman ordered that a vote be taken on the matter and then requested a show of hands to accept or reject the sample statements. *It was resolved* that sample Mission Statement 2 would serve as the Company Mission Statement for the foreseeable future and would appear in the next company prospectus and future brochures.'

3. Action Minutes

Following decisions (resolutions) taken, the chairperson sometimes has the authority to direct members' actions. This would be in the form of indicating what results are expected following the resolutions and who is responsible for each area. A separate column is often included on the right-hand side of the script to indicate the person who has been appointed to the specific area of authority or who volunteers to perform the duty.

An Example of Narrative Minutes

MARYVILLE FOOTBALL CLUB

Minutes

These are the minutes of the Maryville Football Club Annual General Meeting held on 12 November xxxx in Glenstall Hotel, Maryville.

Present: All Members accounted for and present.

The meeting commenced at 8 p.m. The Chairperson Ms Marie O'Donnell opened the meeting and expressed her satisfaction at the attendance at the meeting. She also spoke of the future envisaged success of the club and future involvements.

1. Apologies for absence.
2. Minutes of the last Annual General Meeting:
    The Secretary Mr Frank James read out the Minutes of the last AGM held on 11 November 1996. The Minutes were then approved and signed by the Chairperson, Ms Marie O'Donnell.
3. Matters arising from the Minutes of last year's AGM:
    The Chairperson referred to the updated report on estimated expected rise in subscriptions and consequent revision needed in facilities on the premises. With reference to the agreed proposal at last year's meetings she referred to the fact that work had already begun on extending the clubhouse and improving the pitch. A new bar and changing area for women would be incorporated in the plans. The cost of the work was detailed and distributed to members and the source of the funding was also detailed in this report.
4. Chairperson's Report:
    A copy of the report was circulated to members and the chairperson referred to the need to review security in the club due to theft of equipment and belongings in the recent past. The Chairperson proposed that 'a special meeting should be held in the club to discuss the matter on 30 November xxxx'. This proposal was seconded by Mr Frank James, Secretary.
5. Treasurer's Report:
    The Treasurer, Ms Regina White, distributed copies of last year's Treasurer's Report and she explained details of outgoing money and incoming money for the last year as well as new subscriptions.
6. Elections of Officers:
    The election of a new Secretary was held as follows:

    Kathleen Johnson was proposed by John Franklin.
    Seconded by Mary Smith.

The election of a new Treasurer was held as follows:

Seamus O'Connor was proposed by Darren Walters.
Seconded by Donnacha O'Neill.

Ms Marie O'Donnell agreed to remain in the position as Chairperson. This was proposed by Frank James and seconded by Seamus O'Connor.

Voting for the elections was by 'a show of hands' and in each case the motions were accepted unanimously.

7. Any Other Business:
The Chairperson Ms O'Donnell announced the recent resignation of Mr John McCarthy, the senior grounds supervisor. She thanked him for his years of service and she welcomed Mr Frank Fahy to the position. The Chairperson also thanked Ms Mary Fox for agreeing to organise the club's Annual Presentation Night and Dance which is to be held on 7 December xxxx starting at 8 p.m.

8. Date of Next Meeting
The Chairperson announced that the next regular club meeting would be held on 2 February xxxx at 8 p.m. at the Clubhouse.

Signed: Seconded by
         Marie O'Donnell
         Chairperson
Date: 12 November xxxx

Signed:
         Kathleen Johnson
         Secretary

There was no other business to be discussed and the meeting was brought to a close.

Note: Minutes are sometimes numbered in ascending order (going up) and continue from meeting to meeting. In this example, the last minute is numbered 8, therefore the first minute of the next meeting should be numbered 9.

Purpose of Writing a Report

Reports are generally compiled in response to a request for an investigation of an issue, usually following a meeting. The aim and objectives, as well as findings and recommendations, appear in the report. The aim is referred to as 'the terms of reference'.

A report could be regarded as a fact-finding document, with a lead person or group of experts responsible for compiling it.

DIGIFOTO LTD
Health and Safety Report

Name of Report Writer: Jim White, Health and Safety Officer

Date Report Compiled: 20 June XXXX

Terms of Reference:

To investigate the health and safety risks in the studio area of Digifoto Ltd and the adequacy of its health and safety procedures and to make appropriate recommendations.

Methodology:

* Checklist log kept of a five-week period.
* Manager interviewed.
* Three staff members interviewed.

Findings:

* There is no real health and safety awareness in the organisation. No risk assessment has ever been carried out, and there is no health and safety statement.
* Cables are not stored away – high risk of accident and injury to staff and customers, including floating liquids risk.
* No first aider on site: poorly stocked first aid kit.

Recommendations:

* A risk assessment should be carried out immediately.
* A policy on health and safety and a safety statement should be compiled.
* Liquids should be banned from the studio .
* First aid training should be provided to staff and a dedicated first-aider appointed.
* Fire training should be provided to staff and a fire officer appointed.
* Cables should be tidied carefully out of reach and sight of children where possible.
* General health and safety awareness should be emphasised by managment.

Follow-up meeting to be held on 2 August XXXX.

A Sample Student Summary of Meetings

Compiled by Jean Ryan
Computer Applications and Business student in Crumlin College 2007–2008

Meetings as a Form of Communication

Communication involves the exchange of information between people, and it successfully occurs when the receiver understands what the sender means to convey. In other words, communication is a two-way process which not only requires the message to be received, but also to be understood. Communication is an essential activity for any organisation. The communication process must be both effective and efficient. An effective method, used by organisations to communicate with their employees, is by the means of meetings.

A **meeting** may be defined as the grouping of two or more people to discuss business of common interest. Meetings are a form of oral communication and may be formal or informal. An effective meeting is a highly efficient tool of communication for organisations. It enables organisations to discuss and co-ordinate various activities, give briefs on particular issues, consult with each other, make decisions, solve problems and set future goals and objectives. Formal meetings are conducted under strict guidelines, whereas informal ones are less organised. There are different types of meetings, which may be classified as follows:

1. AGM – Annual General Meeting
2. EGM – Extraordinary General Meeting
3. Board meetings
4. Statutory meetings
5. Executive meetings
6. Consultative meetings
7. (a) Committee meetings
   (b) Sub-committee meetings
8. Review meetings
9. Ad-hoc meetings
10. Inaugural meetings
11. Ordinary meetings
12. Video Conferences

Functions of the Chairperson

- to plan in consultation with the Secretary, the dates and times of the meeting.
- to draw up the Agenda, again in consultation with the Secretary.
- to keep order and prevent disruption.

- to maintain the policies of the organisation.
- when a vote is tied, he/she must use a casting vote.

The Role of the Secretary

- to draw up the Agenda in consultation with the Chairperson.
- to set out the Notice of the Meeting.
- to circulate the Minutes from the previous Meeting (draft minutes).
- to write up the Minutes of a Meeting.
- to plan the next Meeting with the Chairperson.

The Duties of the Treasurer

- to receive yearly subscriptions from members.
- to issue receipts to members.
- to pay the bills on behalf of the organisation.
- to lodge all the organisation's money into bank accounts.
- to keep account books of all transactions made by the organisation.
- to prepare the Financial Report for the AGM.

Notices

NOTICE OF A MEETING

For meetings such as Committee Meetings, General Meetings, or Extraordinary General Meetings, written Notices must be prepared and sent to those entitled to attend. A Notice should contain details of the subject matter, the place, time and date of the meeting.

An Agenda

AN AGENDA OF A MEETING

The secretary, in consultation with the chairperson, is responsible for drawing up the Agenda of a meeting. An agenda is a list of subjects to be covered within the duration of the meeting. A meeting will be far more effective if those attending know in advance what is to be discussed. They will then be able to sort out their ideas, gather data, find out views of colleagues, and come well informed and ready to contribute. It also ensures that every item of importance will be reviewed, and no topic will be overlooked. This is known as meeting preparation, and is of vital importance in order for a meeting to be successful.

The list or programme of items to be discussed at a meeting is generally listed in order of priority, and is usually numbered for easy reference. On the right-hand side of an Agenda a space may be included for recording decisions taken on each item of business.

How to Plan for a Meeting

(A simple student account – in the capacity of secretary to the meeting)

1. Before the meeting, I consulted the Chairperson about the number of participants expected to attend the proposed meeting in order to choose a suitable room/venue.
2. I decided on the seating arrangement to suit the numbers attending and the general mood of the chairperson (negotiating style) – as this was a type of brainstorming session, where new ideas would be embraced!
    Note: Room layout styles are illustrated in the next section.
3. I made sure that OHP equipment (machine and pens) and Internet/computer facilities would be available to the group as one participant wished to use visual aids (Microsoft Powerpoint).
4. I placed a clip notepad, pen and mineral water at each participant's space.
5. I then checked with the chairperson about the date, time and agenda of the meeting before I posted the notice and agenda in a prominent place, well in advance of the meeting.
6. When everyone was seated and the meeting was about to commence, I put up a poster on the outside of the meeting room door 'Meeting in Progress, Please Do Not Disturb'.

Layout Plan of a Meeting

ROOM LAYOUT

The Secretary should always ensure that the meeting room is laid out properly. The chosen meeting room should be laid out in whatever style is appropriate for the size, degree of participation and formality of the meeting.

The way in which the furniture is arranged for meetings can have a big effect on the atmosphere and efficiency. For example, a meeting held round a boardroom table has a completely different atmosphere from one in which participants are free to place their chairs where they wish. The following are eight common arrangements and layouts of the meeting room:

1. Boardroom
2. Round table
3. Negotiating
4. Freestyle
5. Theatre style
6. Schoolroom
7. Horseshoe
8. Herring-bone

The following are eight arrangements of a meeting (note: X indicates where the Chairperson is seated).

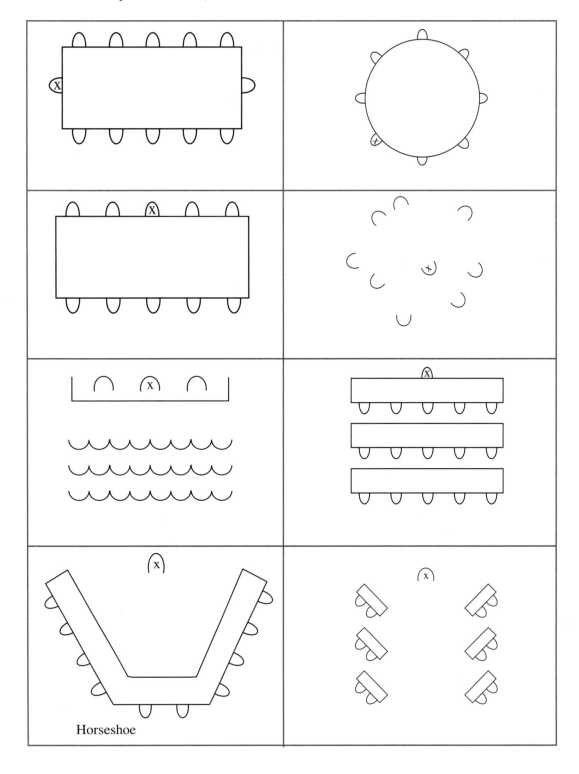

Horseshoe

When laying out the plan of the meeting, the following are some of the considerations required to be taken into account beforehand.

(a) The time and place of the meeting should be known well in advance.

(b) Agendas must be circulated well before the date of the meeting.

(c) Minutes must be written up as soon as possible after the meeting.

(d) In relation to the meeting room:

- inform reception
- put notice on the door notifying that a meeting is in progress
- have refreshments available if a long meeting is expected
- collect files, reports and attendance sheets
- remember spare agendas, paper and shorthand notebook
- have graphs and charts (if needed)
- redirect incoming calls
- locate tape recorder (if required)
- check cloakroom facilities available
- ensure adequate heating, lighting and ventilation.

In all formal meetings the following seating arrangement is a must. The Chairperson must sit in the middle with the Secretary sitting on his/her right-hand side, and the Treasurer seated on the left.

Minutes of a Meeting

THE MINUTES

After the closure of a meeting, the secretary has the responsibility of writing up the minutes of the meeting. The minutes of a meeting are a written account of what was discussed and what decisions were taken at a meeting. At a subsequent meeting the minutes should be read, proposed and seconded and then signed by the chairperson when adopted, thus ensuring accuracy. The minutes of a meeting are of extreme importance. If a dispute arises, the court can ask to see the minutes of a meeting. Therefore they must be accurate. With regard to the Companies Act 1963, all companies must keep the minutes of meetings held by directors and shareholders.

Information which should be included in the minutes of a meeting are:

- the type of meeting
- the date, time and place of meeting
- names in attendance
- names of absentees
- the approval of previous meeting Minutes, containing signature of chairperson showing/indicating approval

- summary on matters arising from Minutes
- the resolutions passed or motions rejected
- the adjournment, postponement until a later date, or conclusion of the meeting
- the date of the next meeting (if decided).

Reports

A Report is a summary, or an account, of what was investigated, what terms of reference were used and what findings resulted. A Report should be laid out and presented clearly to its readers. Reports are needed for many reasons such as:

- assessment or investigation of a situation
- recommending a course of action based on findings
- circulating new information or ideas or work needed to be undertaken
- keeping others informed of progress on particular projects.

The following are the rules which apply when writing up a Report.

Accuracy – the Report should be correct and exact.
Brevity – the Report should be of a reasonable length.
Clarity – the Report should be clear and understandable
Simplicity – the Report should be simple, not complicated.

Conclusion

When studying this topic 'Planning Meetings', it became obvious that an effective meeting is an extremely efficient tool in the communication of an organisation. Communication is of vital importance for an organisation in order for it to be successful and gain profits. Meetings inform those within a company of important issues, decisions, problems, goals, objectives and potential new developments. Meetings help to keep those within an organisation up to date with company activities, its financial position and how it compares with competitors.

Meetings – the Top 20

The following are guidelines which directors, chairpersons, managers and supervisors should follow in order to maintain an effective meeting at any hierarchical level.

Top 10 dos

Set clear objectives for every meeting
Circulate agenda and papers in advance
Complete thorough personal preparation
Choose a suitable room and lay it out carefully
Stick firmly to the agenda

Use visual aids as a help to control discussion
Time your contributions carefully
Use the skills and knowledge of all participants
Use time sensibly throughout.

TOP 10 DON'TS

Don't hold a meeting unless it is really necessary
Don't invite people who need not attend
Don't wait for latecomers unless there is a special reason to do so
Don't let personal feelings affect meeting behaviour
Don't mix creativity with criticism
Don't take part in more than one discussion at one time
Don't force a decision before adequate debate
Don't argue directly with other participants; debate through the Chair
Don't, when in the Chair, express your own views unless it is essential to do so.

PRACTICE QUESTIONS

1. Who are the main Officers at a meeting?
2. What are the functions of the Chairperson of a meeting?
3. What is a Chairperson's Agenda? Draft your own example.
4. What are the functions of the Secretary of a meeting?
5. What are the functions of the Treasurer of a meeting?
6. Explain the following terms:
   (a) Motion
   (b) Quorum
   (c) Point of Order
   (d) Through the Chair
   (e) Casting Vote
   (f) Unanimously Carried.
7. What *three* main unwritten rules govern most formal meetings?
8. In what different ways can a vote be taken?
9. What do the following terms mean with regard to meetings?
   (a) Notice
   (b) Agenda
   (c) Minutes.
10. Explain the *three* categories of Minutes of a meeting.
11. What are the reasons for compiling a Report? What headings are normally used?

Sample Assignment Brief – Meetings

1. You are the secretary at a meeting. Explain the plans that you put in place in advance of the meeting. Support your plans with illustrations as appropriate.

2. Having attended the meeting, please submit the following business documents:
   (a) Notice of the meeting.
   (b) Agenda of the meeting.
   (c) Minutes of the meeting (please attach written notes).

Please note – all formal documents should be formally presented, with particular attention paid to layout, spelling and punctuation.

Sample Student Assignment

1. Plans I put in place in advance of the meeting:

- I chose a suitable room that would suit about 15 people.
- I decided on a horseshoe room layout style having consulted with the chairperson.
- I made sure all participants had pen, pencil and paper at their station as well as mineral water.
- I checked with the chairperson regarding equipment that might be needed if any of the participants were giving a presentation (e.g. overhead projector, OHP pens, flipcharts and pens, computer for Powerpoint presentation, TV, video, DVD, CD players). However, none was needed.
- I checked with the chairperson regarding the agenda and the time and length of the proposed meeting and then posted the Notice and Agenda on the main notice board.
- On the day of the meeting, just before it started, I posted a notice on the outside of the meeting room door 'Meeting in Progress, Please Do Not Enter'.

LAYOUT AND SEATING PLAN

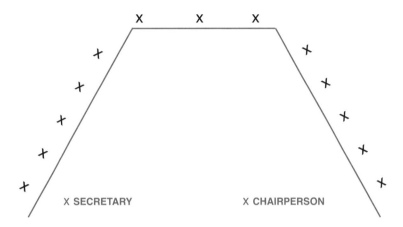

X SECRETARY   X CHAIRPERSON

2. a. Notice

NOTICE

A Meeting of the Limerick Senior College
Fashion Show Committee will take place

on

Thursday 18 October 20XX

at

9.30a.m.

in

Room 1, Top Floor
Limerick Senior College

2. b. Agenda

AGENDA

1. Apologies
2. Date, Time, Venue and Refreshments
3. Sponsors, Advertising and Tickets
4. Models and Clothes
5. A.O.B.
6. Date of next meeting

Sign

MEETING IN PROGRESS

PLEASE DO NOT ENTER

2. c. Minutes

Limerick Senior College

Fashion Show Committee

Minutes of Meeting

These are the minutes of the meeting of the LSC fashion show Committee that was held on Thursday 18 October 20XX at 9.30a.m. in Room 1, top floor, Limerick Senior College:

PRESENT
Ms Jane Fitzpatrick (Chairperson)
Ms Miriam Ryan (Secretary)
Ms Susan Browne
Ms Fiona White
Mr Joseph Black
Mr Frank Walshe
Ms Joan McCarthy
Ms Vera Lynn
Ms Jacinta Henderson
Ms Gemma McDonnell
Ms Roisin Wren
Mr David George

APOLOGIES
Ms Mary Ryan was unable to attend due to work-related matters.

DATE, TIME, VENUE AND REFRESHMENTS
It was agreed that the show should be staged on 5 December 20XX and that it will commence at 8p.m. with a 7.30p.m. wine and cheese reception. It was also agreed that the interval should happen at 9p.m. for a duration of 15 minutes.

Fiona suggested that the venue should be Jurys Hotel, based on a proposed discount offered by them. She also informed the meeting that she had checked the costs of ramp, host and lighting/music and all amounted to €500.

SPONSORS, ADVERTISING AND TICKETS

It was agreed that the chosen charity would be ISPCC Children's Charity.

Frank agreed to research sponsors by getting a list of existing suppliers to the college.

Susan proposed that an 'event publication' with different sized advertisements might be offered in return for contributions of money, services or goods on the night. Joan said that she would encourage Graphics students to help with the publication. Vera also said she had some desktop publishing skills that might be of use.

Joseph agreed to get the tickets printed for free by a printer he knows.

MODELS AND CLOTHES

It was agreed that there would be six male models and twelve female models, all of whom will be students of the college. Miriam and George agreed jointly to look after the clothes, where some previous student designs could be showcased as well as a good selection of shops. A selection of evening casual, sports and bridal wear could be organised.

Gemma agreed to train the students on Wednesday of each week commencing next week with auditions in the afternoon.

ANY OTHER BUSINESS

Susan agreed to deal with the raffle and to source prizes from different businesses in the city and from staff in the college.

NEXT MEETING

It was agreed that the next meeting will take place on Thursday 25 October at 9.30a.m.

_____

Secretary

_____

Chairperson

_____

Date

6. Processing Business Documents

Definitions and Explanations of Documents and Business Terms including Discounts and VAT

The different types of business organisation discussed in Chapter 1 must all involve themselves in paperwork in order to track transactions. The Documents that are part of everyday business are:

1. LETTERS OF ENQUIRY

The formal procedure for enquiring about a prospective supplier's prices and terms of trade is for the business that is enquiring to write a 'letter of enquiry' stating 'Please send me information on the following good, etc.' This form of enquiry has in recent times been replaced by simply telephoning and the subsequent receipt of a fax including the information asked for.

Email has also replaced the letter of enquiry. It is, however, important to be able to structure any enquiry using the appropriate letter presentation (sample given later).

2. PRICE LISTS AND QUOTATIONS

Customers who do not trade with the business on a regular basis usually ask for a Price List. Regular traders who aim to have future accounts with the business usually request a Quotation.

The Quotation is an important document as it is proof of the prices offered and any trade agreements made between traders that operate on a credit basis (i.e. who do not pay immediately – buyers who have accounts with different suppliers). Accounts are usually set up if the buyer is a regular customer and discounts are built into the transaction.

TERMS OF TRADE These are the trade agreements made between the supplier and the purchaser (seller and buyer) regarding Trade Discounts and Cash/Settlement Discounts, and these are indicated on the Quotation. Sixty days' Credit means that the Supplier allows the buyer approximately two months to pay the Invoice (Bill). Most Suppliers offer 30 days' (or net one month) credit to buyers.

Usually if a bill or invoice is dated 2 June and 60 days' credit is allowed, this means that the buyer does not *strictly* have to pay within 60 days. It does mean, however, that this invoice must be paid by 31 August. The same would apply if the invoice were dated 30 June. A longer payment period is gained if the invoice is dated at the beginning of the month.

The three types of discount that exist are:

(a) Trade Discount: given by suppliers to regular buyers on a long-term basis. This discount is a form of recognition for staying with the same supplier and ensuring them of your continued business. The percentage allowed is often 10%.
(b) Settlement Discount: given only if amounts due are paid within a specific time period (often 14 days); can be between two and five per cent.
(c) Cash Discount (COD): given if the buyer pays cash immediately over the counter (varies depending on the bill).

Most traders 'shop around' and try to get the best quotation possible, keeping an eye of course on quality.

3. PURCHASE ORDER

This is a letter sent from the buyer to the supplier to order a certain amount of goods. The buyer usually keeps one copy to check against the delivery docket and the invoice. Goods are more often ordered directly over the phone and the order is entered into an order book at both the buyer end and the supplier end. This is an important exercise because the volume of transactions in one day makes it impossible to keep a mental track of every order made. This order will subsequently be checked against the delivery docket when the goods arrive. Often Purchase Orders are faxed to the supplier and confirmation of receipt of the fax might be in the form of a return phone call.

4. DELIVERY DOCKETS

These are Dockets that arrive with the goods supplied. When the goods are dispatched (sent out), the warehouse supervisor who releases the goods checks them against the purchase order and retains the top copy of the Delivery Docket. The goods are usually dispatched by road, rail or air transport, and the person delivering the goods asks the person receiving the goods to sign the second copy which duplicates on to a third copy underneath it. The delivery person takes the second copy back to the suppliers' headquarters and this is verification that the goods were delivered. The third copy remains with the goods and the buyer.

5. INVOICES

An Invoice is a bill sent by the supplier to the buyer, charging him/her for the goods that were delivered. A reference Delivery Docket Number and Purchase Order Number (where required) appears on the invoice in order to make it easy to match the documents mentioned.

Pro-Forma Invoice (PFI): This document looks like an invoice but is only a sample. It gives details of what would appear on a valid invoice to inform the customer, in advance of deciding to purchase, about cost, carriage (transport costs) and VAT charges.

Cash Invoice: is an invoice given to a buyer if they pay over the counter immediately whether by cash, cheque or credit card.

Credit Invoice: is an invoice that the supplier sends to the buyer. The buyer is given one, two or three months to pay the bill.

VAT

VAT means value added tax. It appears on invoices. It is an indirect tax levied on goods and services by government. This means it is collected by different parties and paid to the government. The VAT rates that apply are 0, 12.5 and 21 per cent.

VAT is a regressive tax (it does not take account of the ability to pay). For example, a pensioner and a millionaire might want to buy furniture at a selling price that includes 21% VAT. This 21% will not be reduced for the pensioner.

DIFFERENCES BETWEEN ZERO-RATED *VAT* AND EXEMPT FROM *VAT*

Some sellers, such as those who sell goods for charity, are exempt from VAT. They are regarded as non-profit-making organisations and cannot claim VAT back on purchases made. Other sellers, like those selling bread, do not charge VAT because bread is regarded as a necessity. However, because these sellers are officially trading, they are allowed to claim VAT back on their purchases. They are therefore zero-rated suppliers/sellers. Some other zero-rated traders are funeral undertakers and sellers of books and periodicals.

Most goods have VAT levied on them at the point of sale. Goods are usually subject to 21% VAT, and services are usually subject to 12.5% VAT.

WHY BOTHER CROSS-CHECKING PURCHASE ORDERS, DELIVERY DOCKETS AND INVOICES?

Mistakes can sometimes be made, such as

- the wrong order being delivered (due to a mix-up/mistakes made by the clerk or dispatcher), or
- too few or too many goods are sent.

If discrepancies are undetected, a business can lose a lot of money, and cost effectiveness is one of the main objectives of successful firms.

Purchase invoices received are entered into the Purchases Book to keep an account of the volume and type of goods received.

Sales invoices that are compiled by businesses and sent to their customers are entered into the Sales Book to keep an account of the volume of sales, how many debtors there are, and how much each debtor owes.

WHAT TO DO WHEN DISCREPANCIES ARE DISCOVERED

Credit Notes

A Credit Note is sent by the supplier giving the buyer recognition of credit given for the return of goods due to:

1. The goods being damaged in transit (while being transported), flawed or faulty.
2. An overcharge, when too many goods were delivered and charged for on the invoice. (The delivery does not match the original Purchase Order.)
3. Wrong goods were delivered. (Possibly a mix-up with another customer's order.)

Debit Notes

If a buyer realises that he/she has been undercharged, human nature tells us that the likelihood that the buyer will run to the phone and inform the supplier is fairly slim!

If, however, the supplier detects the mistake, it will be brought to the attention of the buyer and a Debit Note will be sent to the customer to make up the difference, i.e. the undercharge.

A Debit Note is like another invoice that was forgotten about, except for the important difference that it is directly connected with a particular invoice that was sent previously. The reference invoice number will appear on the Debit Note. When the buyer receives the Debit Note, a copy of it can be clipped directly to the corresponding invoice.

Statements

This is a document that is sent to the buyer to inform him/her about how much is owed to the supplier. It is usually sent out by the supplier every month, listing all the invoices that have been sent out, any Credit Notes and Debit Notes sent out, and any payments made by the buyer.

PRACTICE QUESTIONS

1. What *nine* business documents do businesses send out and receive on a regular basis? Define *each* briefly.
2. Distinguish between a Price List and a Quotation.
3. What are Credit Terms?
4. Name *three* discounts that business people avail of and distinguish clearly between them.
5. What is the difference between a Credit Invoice and a Cash Invoice?
6. Explain in detail what VAT is.
7. What are the differences between 'Zero Rated VAT' and 'Exempt from VAT'?
8. Why is it necessary to match up documents?
9. In each of the following cases, what document is compiled to indicate
    (a) an undercharge
    (b) a return of goods
    (c) an overcharge
    (d) an omission from an invoice?

SAMPLE QUOTATION

No. 12212

NEERY FIREPLACES LTD
21 REDROSE INDUSTRIAL
PARK

KELLS
CO. MEATH

Customer Name: Mr Michael Walsh

Customer Address: Edenfoley Builders Ltd,
                      Athboy,
                      Co. Meath.

Telephone: (042) 431212

Date: 2/5/XX

The following are the terms of agreement that we wish to offer you with the view to doing business with you in the near future.

Terms: 60 Days' Credit
                      Trade Discount 12.5% on all orders
                      Cash/Settlement Discount 5% extra if paid Net one month
                      Carriage paid

• **Prices and the terms of agreement will be reviewed every six months and are subject to change. We ensure that we will give you due notice of any such planned changes.**

We hope that the terms that we are offering you are to your satisfaction and we anticipate trading with you soon.
We will be glad at any time to clarify any queries that you might have regarding our product range.

Yours faithfully

Mary Malone
Mary Malone
Sales Manager

Choosing Suppliers, Pricing and Assessing Quotations

When a person starts in business, he/she may decide to purchase raw materials from suppliers in the local area to minimise transport costs (Carriage).

Carriage Inwards: is a *trading cost* of transportation that suppliers put on bills when they invoice a buyer. The supplier has at this stage already paid the cost.

Carriage Outwards: is an *expense* to a supplier when he/she delivers goods to a buyer and bears the transportation cost.

Quality and Cost Minimisation (keeping costs at a minimum) are both difficult to weigh against each other. It is often said that you pay for what you get. However, it is worthwhile remembering that:

1. If you wish to follow the Economic Route the larger stores are able to sell at cheaper prices (because they buy in bulk and are able to avail of large trade discounts) and a lot of their products are of good quality. This is called an 'Economy of Scale' – one of the benefits of larger-scale operations
2. If you wish to specialise, specialist shops and outlets are relatively more expensive but their turnover is good in their own 'Niche Product Areas'.

It is only with some experience that businesses find suitable suppliers who charge prices that make it cost effective for the business that is buying to trade.

It must be remembered that a Mark-up on cost prices must be estimated and be worthwhile for the business. The cost price must be low enough for the business to sell their products or service successfully at a profit. Breakeven Analysis, discussed in Chapter 2, outlines how a breakeven price can be arrived at.

PRACTICE QUESTIONS
1. What is the difference between Carriage Inwards and Carriage Outwards?
2. Why is it difficult to reach a happy medium between maintaining Quality and keeping Costs down?
3. What is the meaning of the term 'Niche Product Area'?

Example 1: Purchase Order Cash Invoice Exercise and Suggested Solution

Ms Fitzpatrick was redecorating her house and she had previously visited and spoken with a sales consultant in All Weather Paints. She sent a Purchase Order by fax to Jim Smith of All Weather Paints, having written a Letter of Enquiry also addressed to him. Jim faxed the Price List to her and, having delivered the goods, he subsequently sent her the Invoice. Note how the Invoice figures are calculated by reference to the Price List and the Purchase Order.

- When compiling the Invoice it is important to remember that Discount is always subtracted before VAT is added.

LETTER OF ENQUIRY

12 The Lawns
Clonmel
Co. Tipperary
Tel: (0504) 22422
Fax: (0504) 22423

10/7/XX

Mr Jim Smith
All Weather Paints
Weatherfield
Thurles
Co. Tipperary

Dear Jim,

Following our phone conversation, kindly forward to me a current Price List of your products. I hope to purchase some of them in the near future.

Yours truly,

Jane Fitzpatrick

Jane Fitzpatrick

PRICE LIST OF PAINTING AND DECORATING PRODUCTS

ALL WEATHER PAINTS

PRODUCT CODES	DESCRIPTION OF PRODUCTS	VAT	PRICE (in euros)
P(IN) 75	Interior Matt 1 lt	B	7.50
P(IN) 50	Interior Gloss 1 lt	B	9.00
P(IN) 80	Interior Vinyl Silk 1 lt	B	7.50
P(IN) 100	Interior Eggshell (Alkyd) 1 lt	B	11.00
P(IN) 110	Interior Eggshell (Acrylic) 1 lt	B	8.50
P(Ex) 150	Exterior Matt 2.5 lt	B	12.00
P(Ex) 90	Exterior Matt 10 lt	B	37.00
P(Misc) 120	Scrumble Trans Oil Glaze 2.5 lt	B	45.00
Br200	Badger Softener	B	41.00
Br195	Stencil Brush	B	1.50
Br90	Sable Writer	B	7.00
Br12	Paint Brush 1.5 inch pure Bristle	B	6.00
Br14	Paint Brush 2 inch pure Bristle	B	10.00
Br16	Paint Brush 2.5 inch pure Bristle	B	12.00
Br18	Paint Brush 3 inch pure Bristle	B	15.00
Br20	Paint Brush 4 inch pure Bristle	B	25.00
Br22	Paint Brush 6 inch pure Bristle	B	30.00
Sp110	Sea Sponge (Synthetic)	B	7.50
Sp120	Marine Natural Sea Sponge (Lge)	B	40.00
Sp80	Marine Natural Sea Sponge (Sm)	B	30.00
Pap100	Wall Stripper	B	250.00
Pap120	Wallpaper Table	B	15.00
Pap130	Wallpaper Hanging Brush	B	20.00
Pap133	Seam Roller	B	4.50
Sc170	Scaffolding 4ft h x 3.5 ft w	B	72.50
WSp 12	White Spirit (Sm)	B	2.00
WSp 14	White Spirit (Lge)	B	4.75
Ro186	Roller (9 inch)	B	12.50
Ro120	Roller (6 inch)	B	6.50
Ro124	Roller Extension Poll	B	15.00
SERVICE	INTERIOR DESIGNER	A	QUOTE

Large Range of Paints and Wallpaper available

Wallpapers Prices from €10 to €150 per roll

Wallpaper Borders from €10 to €20 per roll

VAT CODES	A = 12.5%	B = 21%

WRITTEN PURCHASE ORDER

12 The Lawns
Clonmel
Co. Tipperary
Tel: (0503) 22422
Fax: (0503) 22423

Date: 15/7/XX

Mr Jim Smith
All Weather Paints
Weatherfield
Thurles
Co. Tipperary

Dear Jim,

Please supply me with the following goods as soon as is convenient.

CODE NUMBER	QUANTITY
P(IN) 80 (Rose Colour)	5 Lt
P(IN) 110 (Rose Colour)	1 Lt
Br195	2
Sp110	1
WSp12	1

Please include on the bill that you are sending to me an amount of €30 plus VAT that I owe your Interior Design Consultant.

When you deliver the goods I will pay cash on delivery. Please phone me in advance to arrange a time of delivery.

Yours truly,

Jane Fitzpatrick

Jane Fitzpatrick

Having received this written purchase order from the cash customer, All Weather Paints allocates an Order Number to it for reference purposes. The Order Number is 4567.

DELIVERY DOCKET

From: All Weather Paints
Weatherfield
Thurles
Co. Tipperary

No: 230
Date: 20/7/XX
Order No: 4567

GOODS:

5 lt Interior Vinyl Silk – Rose Colour	Ref: P(IN) 80
1 lt Interior Eggshell (Acrylic)	Ref: P(IN) 110
2 Stencil Brushes	Ref: Br 195
1 Sea Sponge (Synthetic)	Ref: Sp 110
1 Small Bottle White Spirit	Ref: WSp 12

Received the above goods:

Signed:

Jane Fitzpatrick

CASH SALES INVOICE
ALL WEATHER PAINTS

Weatherfield
Thurles
Co. Tipperary
Telephone: (0504) 21331
Fax: (0504) 21332
VAT No. IE 1234567 D
Purchase Order Number: 4567
Invoice Number: 1101

Ms Jane Fitzpatrick   Date: 20/7/XX
12 The Lawns
Clonmel
Co. Tipperary

Product Code	Q	Description of product	Price p. unit	Vat 12.5%	VAT 21%	Total
P(IN) 80	5 lt	Interior Vinyl Silk–Rose Colour	€7.50 p Lt		€37.50	
P(IN) 110	1 lt	Interior Eggshell (Acrylic)	€8.50 p Lt		€8.50	
Br 195	2 no.	Stencil Brushes	€1.50 ea.		€3.00	
Sp 110	1 no.	Sea Sponge (Synthetic)	€7.50 ea.		€7.50	
WSp 12	1 no.	White Spirit (Sm)	€2 ea.		€2.00	
SERVICE		Interior Design Service	€30	€30.00		
Totals				€30.00	€58.50	
		Less Cash Discount 5%		€1.50	€2.93	
				€28.50	€55.57	
		Add VAT		€3.56	€11.67	
				€32.06	€67.24	

Total   €99.30
Plus Carriage   €10.00
Total Invoice Price   €109.30

Since Ms Fitzpatrick has agreed to pay cash on receipt of the goods, the Cash Invoice serves as the Delivery Docket and she has been given a 5% Cash Discount because she is paying COD. This type of gesture by a business helps to give the business a competitive edge and entices the customer to return again to purchase goods – maintains consumer loyalty.

Example 2: Credit Invoice Exercise and Suggested Solution

QUESTION

Kelly and Sons Painting and Decorating Subcontractors have been trading regularly with All Weather Paints and can avail of an ongoing 10% Trade Discount which is deducted from every bill irrespective of when it is paid. This agreement was reached when the two parties began trading a long time ago. On 7/8/XX Kelly and Sons placed the following order for goods.

You are required to compile

1. The Purchase Order dated 7/8/XX
2. The Delivery Docket dated 8/8/XX
3. The Credit Invoice dated 10/8/XX

Code No.	Quantity
Br20	5
Sc170	1
P(EX) 150 Magnolia	2 tins
P(IN) 75 White	10 lt
P(IN) 50 White	10 lt
P(IN) 80 White	10 lt

SOLUTION

PURCHASE ORDER

No: 4898

Customer Name: Kelly and Sons Painters & Decorators
Customer Address: Randles Park
Clonmel
Co. Tipperary
Telephone: (0506) 31212

Date: 7/8/XX

TO: Mr Jim Smith
All Weather Paints
Weatherfield
Thurles
Co. Tipperary

Code Ref.	Quantity	Description	VAT Rate (%)	Unit Price
Br 20	5 no.	Paint Brush 4"	B	€25.00 ea.
Sc 170	1 no.	Scaffolding 4'h x 3.5'w	B	€72.50 ea.
P(Ex) 150 Magn	2 tins	Exterior Matt 2.5 lt	B	€12.00 p. lt
P(IN) 75 White	10 lt	Interior Matt 1 lt	B	€7.50 p. lt
P(IN) 50 White	10 lt	Interior Gloss 1 lt	B	€9.00 p. lt
P(IN) 80 White	10 lt	Interior Vinyl Silk 1 lt	B	€7.50 p. lt

Delivery Instructions: Delivery by transit van on 8/8/XX

Signed *Mick Kelly*

Purchasing Officer

DELIVERY DOCKET

From: All Weather Paints
     Weatherfield
     Thurles
     Co. Tipperary

No. 234
Date: 8/8/XX
Order No: 4898

GOODS:

5 no.	Paint Brush 4"	Ref: Br 20
1 no.	Scaffolding 4'h x 3.5'w	Ref: Sc 170
2 lt	Exterior Matt 2.5 lt	Ref: P(Ex) 150 Magn
10 lt	Interior Matt 1 lt	Ref: P(IN) 75 White
10 lt	Interior Gloss 1 lt	Ref: P(IN) 50 White
10 lt	Interior Vinyl Silk 1 lt	Ref: P(IN) 80 White

Received the above goods:

Signed: *Mick Kelly*

CREDIT INVOICE
ALL WEATHER PAINTS

Weatherfield
Thurles
Co. Tipperary

Telephone: (0504) 21331
Fax: (0504) 21332
VAT No. IE 1234567 D
Purchase Order Number: 4898
Invoice Number: 1102

Date 10/8/XX

Kelly and Sons
Painters & Decorators
Randles Park
Clonmel
Co. Tipperary

Product Code	Quantity	Description of Product	Price p. unit	VAT 12.5%	VAT 21%
Br20	5 no.	Paint Brush 4"	€25.00 ea.		€125.00
SC170	1 no.	Scaffolding 4'h x 3.5'w	€72.50 ea.		€72.50
P(Ex) 150 Magnol	2 lt	Exterior Matt 2.5 lt	€12.00 p. lt		€24.00
P(IN) 75 White	10 lt	Interior Matt 1 lt	€7.50 p. lt		€75.00
P(IN) 50 White	10 lt	Interior Gloss 1 lt	€9.00 p. lt		€90.00
P(IN) 80 White	10 lt	Interior Vinyl Silk 1 lt	€7.50 p. lt		€75.00
Total					**€461.50**
		Less Trade Discount 10%			€46.15
					€415.35
		Add VAT			€87.22
Total Invoice Price					**€502.57**

Terms of Trade: Net One Month; Trade Discount 10%, Cash Discount 5%, 14 days 2.5%

Example 3: Routing an Invoice – Student Exercise

This means sourcing an invoice or tracing its origin. It involves compiling the corresponding
1. Delivery Docket.
2. Purchase Order.
3. Quotation.
4. Letter of Enquiry.

Refer to the appropriate Practice Question at the end of the chapter.

Example 4: Identifying Discrepancies on Orders and Invoices

(includes a Credit Note and Debit Note):

Refer to the All Weather Paints Price List at the beginning of the section:

On 12/8/XX Mary Jones, Limerick Builders Ltd, Main Street, Limerick, telephoned the following order to All Weather Paints:

Quantity	Product Code
10	P(IN) 75 Burnt Sienna
3	Br 195
4	WSp 14

She received the correct goods and checked the Delivery Docket that arrived with the goods to verify this. On 14/8/XX Mary received the Invoice for the goods. However, when she checked the Purchase Order Form she realised that the Invoice stated P(IN) 50 in error. She immediately phoned All Weather Paints and they confirmed the mistake and forwarded the Credit Note to Mary a day later thereby acknowledging the overcharge.

Refer to the All Weather Paints Price List at the beginning of the section:

CREDIT NOTE
ALL WEATHER PAINTS   **No: C/N676**

Weatherfield
Thurles
Co. Tipperary
Telephone: (0504) 21331
Fax: (0504) 21332
VAT No. IE 1234567 D
Reference Purchase Order Number 2323
Reference Invoice Number 3424

Ms Mary Jones   Date: 15/8/XX
Limerick Builders Ltd, Main Street, Limerick

Date	Details	Price	Total
	Incorrect Product Code P(IN) 50 Burnt Sienna Should be P(IN) 75 Burnt Sienna Subsequent Overcharge	10 x €2.50	€25.00
	Add VAT @ 21%		5.25
	TOTAL CREDIT GIVEN		€30.25

Important Note:

As already mentioned, Credit Notes are also sent by suppliers when a buyer returns damaged goods or goods which were not ordered.

Example 5: Debit Note – Question and Solution

Refer to the All Weather Paints Price List at the beginning of the section:

On 20/8/XX Mary Jones, Limerick Builders Ltd, Main Street, Limerick, telephoned the following order to All Weather Paints:

Quantity	Product Code
14	P(EX) 90 Magnolia
1	P(EX) 150 Magnolia

She received the goods the day after she phoned and she checked the Delivery Docket to verify that she had received all the goods she had ordered. She received the Invoice for the goods the next day and realised that Product Code P(EX) 150 had not been charged for. She received a phone call from Jim Smith, All Weather Paints, that day to inform her of the error. He said that he would send on a Debit Note to rectify the undercharge, and this arrived two days later.

DEBIT NOTE

ALL WEATHER PAINTS   No: D/N389

Weatherfield
Thurles
Co. Tipperary

Telephone:(0504) 21331
Fax: (0504) 21332
VAT No. IE 1234567 D
Reference Purchase Order Number 2848
Reference Invoice Number 3797

Date: 24/8/XX

Ms Mary Jones
Limerick Builders Ltd
Main Street
Limerick

Date	Details	Price	Total
	Item omitted from Invoice No. 3797		
	P(EX) 150 – undercharge	1 x €12.00	€12.00
	Add VAT @ 21%		€2.52
	TOTAL		€14.52

Important Notes:

Once an Invoice is sent out it cannot be changed. This is why Credit Notes and Debit Notes play such an important part in the correction of errors when traders are engaged in transactions.

• In the last two examples, Trade Discount was not allowed to Limerick Builders.

Payment Methods

Money is Legal Tender, that is, a means of payment that must be accepted by law in return for payment of a debt. The most common payment methods to date are payments by:

1. Cheque (Cheque Card Validation)

A Cheque Card is given to all creditworthy current account holders. It is nearly always requested by the shop or outlet to verify the authenticity of the cheque – to ensure that the cheque will not 'bounce' (not enough money in the account to meet it). If there is a shortfall in the account the bank will allow the account to go into debt (the red) because they trust the customer to restore the balance in the account to a credit balance (money in the account) as soon as possible. So if you have a cheque card to accompany cheques, any embarrassment will be avoided.

2. Credit Card

Payment using a credit card is immediately validated by computer (e.g. in super-markets) or with card number via phone or Internet.

Credit cards are generally given to creditworthy customers. The bank or financial institution sets a Credit Limit and it allows the customer to use the money reserve whenever he or she needs to do so. However, a set minimum amount of the debt must be cleared when the Statement of Account arrives at the end of the month. Otherwise large amounts of interest will accrue on the debt.

When a credit card is used to deposit and withdraw funds the chip and PIN facility is very convenient for the customer. Nowadays most shops and business outlets have machines allowing a customer to pay for goods or services by inserting their credit card into the desktop card machine and keying in their PIN number. This increases the negative balance on the credit card – in other words the customer's debt – but it is a very convenient payment method.

3. Charge Cards

Charge cards are issued by businesses to their regular customers, allowing them a money reserve that is based on the same principle as credit cards. The difference is that the customer is confined to shopping in that store or business when availing of the money reserve. The shop issues the customer with a bill and a minimum amount of the debt must be paid off at the end of the month to avoid large interest charges.

Credit and Charge Cards are very useful if the bills received are managed tightly. They give the customer a sense of security always knowing that money is available if needed (positive cash flow). On the other hand, they can work out to be a debt-generating habit, that is, prone to getting out of control.

4. Cash Availability from Banks or Financial Institutions (Plastic Cards/ATM)

Some people refer to the ATMs (Automatic Teller Machines) jokingly as 'The Hole in the Wall' or 'The Drink Link'. Most are open twenty-four hours a day. This method of using the Plastic Card, keying in a PIN Number (Personal Identification Number) and withdrawing money is, nowadays, the most convenient and common method of withdrawing cash. Cash can also be lodged in this way by using a Lodgment Envelope. During office hours, cash can also be withdrawn using a Withdrawal Docket in the bank or financial institution.

5. Internet/24-hour Banking, Code Cards, ATM/Laser Cards and Cashback

This type of payment method is common nowadays when transacting in business. ATM cardholders can register for 24-hour banking and using a registration number and secret PIN number can access their accounts either online or on the phone instead of having to visit the bank or financial institution.

Options that are available include funds transfer (EFT, discussed in Chapter 3) from one account to another and bill payments. The cardholder has to key in his or her secret PIN number and for security reasons to verify numbers that either appear on a code card or that are part of the PIN number.

The extra facilities available with an ATM card makes it simple and convenient to pay bills and transfer funds using only the computer keyboard or the phone.

There is now a Laser facility on ATM cards that allows cardholders to pay bills in shops, for example the shopping bill at the checkout. Instead of having to go to the ATM machine the customer can simply pay with their ATM debit card (Laser card) and can opt to get cash back with their change. This money is taken straight out of the cardholder's bank account at the checkout. Customers can also pay using Online Debit (also known as PIN Debit) or Offline Debit (also known as Signature Debit)

Businesses are increasingly using these methods to pay their creditors and other overheads like phone and electricity bills.

6. Bank Giro/Credit Transfer

The method used to pay a person to whom you owe money (creditor) by bank transaction (filling in a bank giro form) allowing for the transfer of money direct into the creditor's account. It avoids having to wait for a cheque and the inconvenience of having to get to a bank to lodge it.

7. Bank Draft/Money Order

If you do not have a cheque book, buying a bank draft in the bank will allow you to send money safely by post. The person or firm named on the draft will be paid by lodging it to their own bank account.

8. Postal Order

Postal Orders can be purchased from Post Offices if you do not have a cheque book and you need to pay a smaller sum of money to a creditor. They are a similar type of payment method to bank drafts. The banks, however, handle small as well as larger sums of money.

9. Direct Debit Mandate

The Direct Debit Mandate is under the control of the financial institution that sets it up for the customer. It cannot be cancelled without the agreement of the financial institution. Most mortgages (house loans – long-term loans) are paid off by direct debit. The money is taken out of the bank account that the customer nominates. If the customer defaults on payment, there is a risk that, for example, their house might be repossessed by the bank or financial institution the mortgage is taken out with.

10. Standing Order

A Standing Order is under the control of the customer. The customer can cancel the Standing Order at any time. Short-term and medium-term loans are usually paid off by the customer setting up a Standing Order allowing the institution (for example, the credit union) to take the money that is owed to it out of the customer's bank account.

11. International Bank Transfer

Depositing and withdrawing funds by International Bank Transfer is a more expensive way of transferring funds to foreign bank accounts than by using the online transfer method (with a debit card/code card).

IBAN is the identification number of the bank account that is used for foreign money transactions.

12. What is Western Union?

It is an alternative method of sending a money transfer online, making it possible to send money abroad from Ireland or receive money from Ireland in another country (see Chapter 3).

13. What is Paypal?

Paypal is how individuals and businesses send and receive money online – it is a fast, easy and secure way of making online payments.

For buyers: customers can choose to pay with their credit card, debit card or bank account. They can make secure purchases without revealing their credit card number or financial information.

For sellers: sellers accept credit cards, debit cards, and bank account payments for low transaction fees. It is possible to add Paypal to a customer's website in minutes, no downtime required.

Millions of active online shoppers use this payment method. It is also possible to shop using Paypal on eBay (a type of online auction room) and this makes it possible to trade with thousands of merchants worldwide.

14. *Neteller*

This is a money transfer system that allows transfer between merchants and individuals. It is an online payment service used in particular for gambling transactions. This system of payment is commonly used in the gambling industry in North America, e.g. for poker accounts and accessing and using winnings acquired from gambling in casinos, etc.

15. *Traveller's Cheques*

When people travel abroad they usually bring enough money with them but do not carry it in cash. Instead, they change it into Traveller's Cheques and keep receipts of them in a different location in case they are lost or stolen. They are only accepted by banks for cash. In the foreign country the bank will convert the cheques at the current exchange rate into the foreign country's currency. The adoption of the euro currency in many countries has lessened the need to carry Travellers' Cheques because cash can be withdrawn using Bank Cards at ATM machines in these countries. Bank charges for these services can, however, be expensive and there is also a risk of travellers losing Bank Cards.

16. *Eurocheques* (Eurocheque Card Validation)

The difference between Traveller's Cheques and Eurocheques is that Eurocheques are like regular cheques where the Eurocheque Book holder can write cheques in foreign currency and the amount when reconverted into euros will be taken out of the Eurocheque holder's bank account.

It means that the person writing these cheques has to be absolutely sure of the exchange rate and sure that there are enough funds in his/her account to meet the amounts written on the cheques. The accompanying validation card is always requested by those accepting the cheques as a guarantee that the bank regards the customer as creditworthy and reliable in this regard.

Example 6: Statements of Account and Cheques – Questions and Solutions

A Statement of Account is a document that is sent out by the supplier to inform the debtor (person that owes money) how much money he/she owes or if anything is owed at all. If too much is paid, it will indicate this too. Most businesses send out monthly statements to their debtors.

In the case of Bank Statements, the customer can request weekly Statements of Account and in this case the balance on the account will be shown as well as other bank charges, withdrawals and lodgments.

Statement of Account Example – Question and Solution

PRACTICE QUESTION

Kelly and Sons traded with All Weather Paints in the month of July and received the following documents and made the following payments during the month:

Documents Received:

4/7/XX Invoice Number 1181	€250.20
18/7/XX Invoice Number 1311	€100.80
6/7/XX Credit Note Number 1767	€28
20/7/XX Credit Note Number 1858	€18.50
29/7 XX Invoice Number 1102	€476.68
31/7/XX Debit Note D/N 865	€26.14

Payments made:

2/7 XX Kelly wrote a cheque for €100

• Kelly and Sons had a carry forward balance of €200 from June.

You are required to:

(a) Show the Cheque that was sent by Kelly and Sons on 2/7/XX

(b) Compile the Statement of Account for the month of July

SOLUTION:

(a) Cheque

• Cheque Guarantee Card will usually be requested to back up the cheque and to verify the signature.

(b) Statement of Account

All Weather Paints
Weatherfield
Thurles
Co. Tipperary

Statement

To: Kelly and Sons   **Date:** 2 August XXXX
     Painter and Decorator   **No.** 89
     Randles Park
     Clonmel
     Co. Tipperary

Date	Ref No	Details	Debit €	Credit €	Balance €
	-	-			
1/7/XX	-	C/f	-	-	200.00
2/7/XX	121214356	Cheque	-	100.00	100.00
4/7/XX	1181	Invoice	250.20	-	350.20
6/7/XX	1767	Credit Note	-	28.00	322.20
18/7/XX	1311	Invoice	100.80	-	423.00
20/7/XX	1858	Credit Note	-	18.50	404.50
29/7/XX	1102	Invoice	476.68	-	881.18
31/7/XX	865	Debit Note	26.14	-	907.32

Cheque, Bank Giro Form and Petty Cash Voucher

Cheque

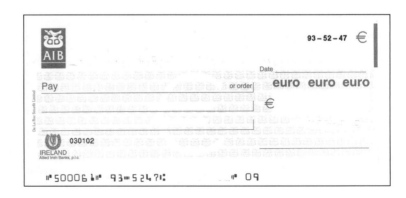

Bank Giro Form

Petty Cash Voucher

Sample Assignment Brief – Business Documents

Suggested Outline for Assignment

Basic layout of pages:

1. Title page.
2. Introduction.
3. Aims, Objectives and Methodology
4. History, Size, Ownership, Products or Services of Organisation (Branches/ National/International)
5. Sketch or Photo of Organisation and/or Logo.
6. Accounts Department: number of staff, how many males and females, and basic functions.

7. Day-to-day routine regarding handling of Business Documents in the Organisation.
8. List of Documents. Include a *List of Actual Documents* included in the project (collected by the learner from a business) with the *definition of each and an analysis of the transactions on each of the documents presented*. (Suggestion: present the documents or photocopies of them back-to-back in poly pockets or a plastic folder.)

These are the documents that should be included in the project:

a. Price List
b. Quotation
c. Purchase Order Form
d. Delivery Docket
e. Invoice – Sales or Purchases (identify whether they are Sales Invoices or Purchase Invoices – ask who is selling to whom or who is buying from whom).
f. Credit Notes – Sales or Purchase Credit Notes (ask: who is sending back damaged goods or was there an overcharge?)
g. Debit Notes (ask: was there an undercharge? Who undercharged whom?)
h. Statement of Account – a list of transactions during (usually) a month
i. Payment Methods – cheque payments or receipts (try to get an example of a cheque or other payment methods used to pay creditors or received from debtors, e.g. online transfer of funds/Internet banking?)

Suggestion: Try to link the order, delivery and invoice with the statement of account where possible.

Note: These headings should be converted into a questionnaire when a learner is compiling primary data, i.e. trying to collect the information and the documents.

The project can also be supported using suitable up-to-date secondary data from sources like the Internet, business leaflets, journals or books and periodicals with particular reference to business documents and transacting in business.

1. Conclusion
2. Bibliography
3. Appendix – include the Questionnaire that was used.

PRACTICE QUESTION 1

Yvonne's Boutique, Harold's Cross Road, Dublin 6 (VAT Number 943126) purchased the following items from Fashion House, Dame Street, Dublin 2 (VAT Number 23165).

10 Handbags @ €25 each
30 Leather Belts @ €15 each (Ref: 62)
28 Hair Clips @ €5 each (Packet number: 101)

Draw up the following documents based on this information:
(a) Purchase Order, no. 231, date 26/4/XX
(b) Delivery Docket, no. 561, date 28/4/XX
(c) Invoice, no. 326, date 28/4/XX

VAT = 21%

(d) Yvonne found that 15 leather belts were scratched and so she returned all 15 of them. You are required to make the appropriate adjustment by compiling the Credit Note no. 846, date 4/5/XX that was sent out.
(e) Draft the Statement Number 922, dated 7/5/XX that Fashion House sent to Yvonne's Boutique.
(f) Draft the Bank of Ireland Cheque dated 10/5/XX that Yvonne's Boutique sends to Fashion House to clear the balance on the account.

Note: In the office the exercise would be to locate and match up the documents.

(b) Write your own account of what you think the Supplier's Office Procedures would have entailed from the moment the Letter of Enquiry was sent. Explore and expand on the ways the Order could have first been received, the Delivery Instructions up to and including when the Invoice was sent out and received by the buyer.

PRACTICE QUESTION 2

(a) Route the following Invoice:

INVOICE

ALL WEATHER PAINTS
Weatherfield
Thurles
Co. Tipperary

Telephone: (0504) 21331
Fax: (0504) 21332
VAT No. IE 1234567 D
Purchase Order Number: 4568
Invoice Number: 1102

Date 10/8/XX

Kelly and Sons
Painters & Decorators
Randles Park
Clonmel
Co. Tipperary

Product Code	Quantity	Description of Product	Price p. unit	VAT 12.5%	VAT 21%
P(IN) 80	5 lt	Interior Vinyl Silk – Rose Colour	€7.50 p. lt		€37.50
P(IN) 110	1 lt	Interior Eggshell (Acrylic)	€8.50 p. lt		€8.50
WSp 12	1 no.	White Spirit (Sm)	€2.00 ea.		€2.00
Br22	5 no.	Paint Brush 6"	€30.00 ea.		€150.00
P(IN) 75 White	10 lt	Interior Matt 1 lt	€7.50 p. lt		€75.00
P(IN) 50 White	10 lt	Interior Gloss 1 lt	€9.00 p. lt		€90.00
P(IN) 80 White	10 lt	Interior Vinyl Silk 1 lt	€7.50 p. lt		€75.00
Total					€438.00
		Less Trade Discount 10%			€43.80
					€394.20
		Add VAT			€82.78
Total Invoice Price					€476.98

PRACTICE QUESTION 3

Jim's Drapery, Mary Street, Cork (VAT Number 43434342 K) purchased the following from Fashion House, Dame Street, Dublin 2 (VAT Number 23165).

35 Handbags @ €25 each
45 Leather belts @ €15 each (ref: 62)
10 Hand and face towel sets @ €25 each set
20 Children's sun caps at €5.50 each
- Trade discount allowed is 15%
- VAT is charged at 21%

You are required to:

(a) Draft the Invoice that Fashion House sent out to Jim's Drapery – Invoice No. 2343, date 23/7/XX.

(b) Fashion House realised on the day after they sent the Invoice that the Purchasing Manager in Jim's Drapery had phoned Fashion House, after the above order was taken, to order an extra 10 children's sun caps. This extra order had not been included in the Invoice.

Based on this information you are required to complete the Debit Note No. 2425 and date it appropriately to rectify the omission.

(c) Given that the following additional documents were sent by Fashion House to Jim's Drapery and the following payments were made by Jim's Drapery in July, compile the July Statement of Account and show the correct balance that is owing.

Documents Received

1/7/XX	Invoice No. 2020	€300.00
2/7/XX	Invoice No. 2031	€400.50
18/7/XX	Invoice No. 2158	€80.50
20/7/XX	Credit Note C/N1255	€30.50

Payments made

| 3/7/XX | Cheque No. 10005 | €400.00 |
| 20/7/XX | Cheque No. 10010 | €100.00 |

The Carry Forward Balance from the previous month was €233.55.

Purchases Book, Sales Book and VAT Returns

Purchase Invoices, Sales Invoices, Credit Notes and Debit Notes are the documents used to compile VAT (Value Added Tax) Returns every two months.

Purchases are divided into

1. Non-resale items – items that are purchased but not sold back to the public, like office furniture or mobile phones, used as part of the daily business routine. Goods that are hired, insurance bills and accountants' invoices are also non-resale items.
2. Resale items – items that are purchased and resold back to the public, such as builder's blocks, because they are going to be used to build a house that will be sold to the public later.

- Make sure to categorise Purchases correctly in this way.

Sometimes small businesses enter their Purchases Returns (Credit Notes) into their Purchases Book together with Purchases, but *write them in red* to denote that they must be subtracted from Purchases. The same applies to VAT on Purchases and Purchases Returns (Credit Notes).

A Self-employed Sales Distributor made the following purchases in March and April XXXX. His VAT Registration Number is IE 5678785 T.

10/3/XX	Purchased €40 worth of diesel from Grange Service Station (VAT included @ 21%).
15/3/XX	Purchased a mobile phone from NCA Mobile Phone Shop which cost €39.00 inclusive of VAT @ 21%.
24/4/XX	Purchased a computer from Filine Technology costing €899.00 inclusive of VAT @ 21%.
25/4/XX	Truck cleaned – a full valet provided by Valetet cost €55.00 inclusive of VAT @ 12.5%. 12.5% VAT is charged because it is a purchase of a service as opposed to a purchase of goods.
20/3/XX	Returned the mobile phone because it was faulty and received a full refund and a Credit Note.
15/4/XX	Purchased bread and confectionery wholesale from Betterbuy Bake to resell to his own customers. The bill was €2,277 inclusive of VAT. There is no VAT on bread. However, there is 21% VAT on confectionery. €130 of the €2,277 was confectionery.

Sometimes only the Selling Price is quoted on the Invoice so it is important to be able to convert back to the figure before VAT and to find the VAT itself. The *quick* way to do this is:

Take €40 divided by 121% = €33.06

(the figure before VAT) also known as the Net Figure.

Take €33.06 multiplied by 21% = €6.94

(the VAT itself).

Take the entry required for 15/4/XX – the following is the breakdown.

€2,277 *minus* €130 = €2,147.

- So €2,147 is the cost of the bread (no VAT)
- €130 divided by 121% = €107.44 (the figure before VAT) and €107.44 multiplied by 21% = €22.56 (the VAT itself)
- Check:

	Bread	**Confectionery**
	€2,147	€107.44
VAT	0	€ 22.56
Total	€2,277	

Note that this entry is recorded under 'Resale' in the next section.

- *Note:* You enter the Invoices into your own books by allocating your own Invoice Reference Number to them in the order that you locate them. Only Invoices, Credit Notes and Debit Notes that are dated in March or April can be included in the March/April VAT Returns.
- (Purchase Invoices received as well as Returns, i.e. Credit Notes received, are entered here in this case. This is not always feasible because the larger the business, the greater the need to have individual Purchases Returns and Sales Returns Books.)

Sample extract from a Sales Distributor's Book (Jim Jones) :

- The self-employed sales distributor made sales in March and April XXXX and the transactions are shown in the Sales Book as follows:

Jim Jones
PURCHASES BOOK

March/April XXXX

Date	Details	Inv/Cn No.	0%	Non-Resale 21%	12.5%	0%	Resale 21%	12.5%	VAT
10/3/XX	Purch Grange Service St	201		33.06					6.94
15/3/XX	Purch NCA Mobile Ph Shop	202		32.23					6.77
24/4/XX	Purch Filine Tech & Computers	203		742.98					156.03
25/4/XX	Purch Valetet	204			48.88				6.11
20/3/XX	*Return NCA Mobile Ph Shop*	*205*		*32.23*					*6.77*
15/4/XX	Purch Betterbuy Bake	206					2147.00	107.44	22.56
Mar/Apr Totals				**776.04**	**48.88**		**2147.00**	**107.44**	**191.64**

Purchases VAT = €191.65

- Check:

	Net	(Selling Prices) VAT	Gross
Non Resale (21%)	776.04	162.97	939.01
Non Resale (12.5%)	48.88	6.11	54.99
Resale (21%)	107.44	22.56	130.00
Resale (12.5%)	0	0	
Total VAT on purchases		191.64	

Sample extract from a Self-employed Sales Distributor's Sales Book:

Sales Book: Jim Jones
March/April XXXX

Date	Details Inv/Dn No.		0%	Net 21%	12.5%	VAT	€ (Gross) Selling Prices
2/3/XX	Franco's	121	32.00	12.00		2.52	46.52
14/3/XX	Betterbuy A/c	122	1172.00		40.42	5.05	1217.47
14/3/XX	Commission	122		182.43		38.31	220.74
20/4/XX	Patricia's Deli	123	30.00	15.00		3.15	48.15
15/3/XX	*Betterby A/c Debit Note*	*124*	*15.00*			*0.00*	*15.00*
	Mar/Apr Totals		**1249.00**	**249.85**		**49.03**	

Summary of March/April VAT Return XXXX – Purchases and Sales

Purchases VAT Figure	€191.64	(Rounded to €192)
Sales VAT Figure	49.03	(Rounded to €49)
VAT Reclaimable (Repayable)	142.61	(Rounded to €143)

- Since the VAT on Purchases is higher than the VAT on Sales, the sales distributor can claim back the difference – €142.61. (Rounded to €143)
- If the VAT on Purchases had been lower than the VAT on Sales, the sales distributor would have had to pay the difference to the Revenue section of government.

A Sample Euro VAT Form:

In all correspondence please quote:

Registration No: IE

Notice No: 02782366-16579P

Period:

Office of the Revenue Commissioners
Collector-Generals Division
Sarsfield House
Francis Street
Limerick

17808 161010 17520 160678 030902VAT3EE

Enquiries: 1890 203070

Payment due by:

VAT 3 RETURN

Please print one figure only in each space using a black or blue ball-point pen.

1. VAT

€ : ENTER WHOLE EUROS ONLY

VAT on sales*   T1   4 9 •00

OFFICE USE ONLY	
AMD A1 ☐	GCD: 014
O/S A2 ☐	UNIT: 101
DRS	CSZ: I

VAT on purchases*   T2   1 9 2 •00

*See notes part 1 overleaf

Net Repayable   OR   Net Payable

T4   1 4 3 •00   T3   —————— •00

(Excess of T2 over T1)   (Excess of T1 over T2)

2. TRADING WITH OTHER EU COUNTRIES

Total goods to other EU countries   Total goods from other EU countries

E1   —————— •00   E2   —————— •00

3. BANK DETAILS FOR REPAYMENTS/REFUNDS

SORT CODE B1   ☐ ☐ ☐   ACCOUNT NUMBER B2   ☐

Only complete if you have not previously advised us of account details or you wish to amend previously submitted details.
Any repayment of VAT will be repaid to the bank or building society account as notified.

I declare that this is a correct return of Value Added Tax for the period specified:–

Signed:– *Jim Jones*   Status:– *Director*   Date:– *19th May xxxx*

PRACTICE QUESTIONS

1. What books are required to be written up in order to do a VAT return?
2. A self-employed bread sales agent, John Ryan, has the following Purchases and Sales for May–June XXXX, VAT Number 48567591K

Purchases (Purchases Invoices and Credit notes)	**Sales** (Sales Invoices)
5/5/XX €40 Trailer Service Station (VAT 21%)	2/5/XX Mary's Deli €500 (VAT 21%)
6/5/XX €980 Computer Literate (VAT 21%)	8/6/XX Superbuy €1,000
	(VAT €800 @ 12.5% €200 @ 0%)
15/6/XX €20 Trailer Service Station (VAT 21%)	10/6/XX Monalisa €550 (VAT 21%)
16/6/XX €1,000 Betterbuys – Bread for resale	20/6/XX Monalisa €550 (VAT 21%)
(VAT 0%)	
17/6/XX €29 Return of Bread to Betterbuy	
(Credit Note) (VAT 0%)	26/6/XX Superbuy €950 (VAT 0%)

All figures above are *inclusive* of the VAT stated

You are required to:

(a) Enter each transaction into the appropriate books and make appropriate pre-calculations.

(b) Complete the VAT Return for John Ryan for the period May–June XXXX.

Note: Be careful to categorise Purchases in Resale/Non-Resale form and do a summary of the return before you enter anything in the VAT return form itself.

Sample Assignment

PART 1 (Kelly & Sons Ltd Question): .

PRICE LIST OF PAINTING AND DECORATING PRODUCTS

ALL WEATHER PAINTS

PRODUCT CODES	DESCRIPTION OF PRODUCTS	VAT	UNIT PRICE per tin, per bottle, each etc.
P(IN) 75	Interior Matt 1 lt tin	B	€7.50
P(IN) 50	Interior Gloss 1 lt tin	B	€9.00
P(IN) 80	Interior Vinyl Silk 1 lt tin	B	€7.50
P(IN) 100	Interior Eggshell (Alkyd) 1 lt tin	B	€11.00
P(IN) 110	Interior Eggshell (Acrylic) 1 lt tin	B	€8.50
P(Ex) 150	Exterior Matt 2.5 lt tin	B	€12.00
P(Ex) 90	Exterior Matt 10 lt tin	B	€37.00
P(Misc) 120	Scrumble Trans Oil Glaze 2.5 lt tin	B	€45.00
Br200	Badger Softener	B	€41.00
Br195	Stencil Brush	B	€1.50
Br90	Sable Writer	B	€7.00
Br12	Paint Brush 1.5" pure bristle	B	€6.00
Br14	Paint brush 2" pure bristle	B	€10.00
Br16	Paint brush 2.5" pure bristle	B	€12.00
Br18	Paint brush 3" pure bristle	B	€15.00
Br20	Paint brush 4" pure bristle	B	€25.00
Br22	Paint brush 6" pure bristle	B	€30.00
Sp110	Sea Sponge (Synthetic)	B	€7.50
Sp120	Marine Natural Sea Sponge (Lge)	B	€40.00
Sp80	Marine Natural Sea Sponge (Sm)	B	€30.00
Pap100	Wall Stripper	B	€250.00
Pap120	Wallpaper Table	B	€15.00
Pap130	Wallpaper Hanging Brush	B	€20.00
Pap133	Seam Roller	B	€4.50
Sc170	Scaffolding 4' h x 3.5' w	B	€70.00
WSp12	White Spirit (Sm)	B	€2.00
WSp14	White Spirit (Lge)	B	€4.75
Ro186	Roller (9")	B	€12.50
Ro120	Roller (6")	B	€6.50
Ro124	Roller Extension Pole	B	€15.00
SERVICE	INTERIOR DESIGNER	A	QUOTE

Large range of paints and wallpaper available   VAT   A = 12.5%

CODES B = 21%

Wallpaper prices from €10 to €150 per roll

Wallpaper borders from €10 to €20 per roll

You are employed as a sales clerk in the offices of All Weather Paints, Weatherfield, Thurles, Co. Tipperary.

On 29 July XXXX you receive an order from Kelly and Sons, Painters & Decorators, Randles Park, Clonmel, Co. Tipperary, for the following:

Code No.	Quantity
P(Ex) 150 Magnolia	12 tins
P(IN) 75 White	10 tins
Br12	8
Br14	8
Br20	4
P(Misc) 120	2

QUESTIONS

1. Enter this information on a Purchase Order Form and for use in your firm.
2. Prepare an Invoice to send to Kelly and Sons, dated 30 July XXXX, Invoice Number 1343 and assume it is posted that day. Apply a 10% Trade Discount and VAT at 21%.
3. On 2 August XXXX Kelly and Sons receive the goods. Draft the Delivery Docket.
4. They discovered that 2 of the items, Code Number Br20, are damaged, as well as finding that 2 tins of the items Code Number P(Ex) 150 Magnolia are Gloss Code P(IN) 50. The damaged items were returned and the other items were simply exchanged. Kelly himself is unhappy with the service on this occasion.
   (i) Draft the Letter of Complaint that he sends to you in All Weather Paints
   (ii) Prepare the document you would send him to rectify the mistake dated 5 August XXXX, Document Number 2454.
5. Prepare the Statement of Account at the end of the month.
6. Prepare the cheque which Kelly and Sons send to pay for the goods on 10 September XXXX.

PART 2 (FRANK'S NEWSAGENT'S QUESTION):

Read the following Purchase Order and also study the corresponding Invoice that follows it.

ORDER FORM

FRANK'S NEWSAGENT'S
Main Street, Monaghan.

Order no: 3335/20

BOOKSTORE SUPPLIES
Main Street, Ennis.

Date: 10 July XXXX

QUANTITY	DESCRIPTION	PRICE €
20	Financial Extracts, Pelican, Byrne and Smyth ISBN 2322	15.50
10	DIY Domestic, Pelican, Lee and Lee ISBN 1451	9.50
5	Painting and Decorating, Folens, Rodgers and O'Rourke ISBN 2828	12.20
12	Feathered Friends, O'Brien Publishers, O'Neill and O'Neill ISBN 2222	6.50

INVOICE

BOOKSTORE SUPPLIES
Main Street, Ennis.
Tel: (0503) 23244
Fax: (0503) 23245
VAT No: 1212435F

Invoice No: 1010
Order No: 3335/20

FRANK'S NEWSAGENT'S
Main Street, Monaghan.

Date: 15 July XXXX

QUANTITY	DESCRIPTION	UNIT COST €	TOTAL €
19	Financial Extracts, Pelican, Byrne and Smyth ISBN 2322	15.00	285.00
10	DIY Domestic, Pelican, Lee and Lee ISBN 1451	9.50	95.00
5	Painting and Decorating, Folens, Rodgers and O'Rourke ISBN 2828	12.20	70.00
12	Feathered Friends, O'Brien Publishers, O'Neill and O'Neill ISBN 2222	6.50	78.00

With reference to Order Number 3335/20 and Invoice Number 1010:

(a) Assume that the prices on the Order form are correct. Note the discrepancies and work out the correct total. Exclude VAT and Discount.

(b) State whether an overcharge or undercharge occurred and name the appropriate document to correct the mistake.

(c) Finish off the incorrect Invoice Number 1010, above, and leave it in its uncorrected form by sub-totalling it, deducting 12% Trade Discount and adding VAT at 21%.

(d) Compile the document that will rectify the mistakes occurring in part (b), above, and deduct 12% Trade Discount and add 21% VAT. (Document Number 1586 dated 17 July XXXX.)

(e) If on 1/7/XX a balance of €212.40 exists on Frank's Newsagent's account and if a further two Invoices and one Credit Note were sent to Frank's newsagent's as follows:

> 22 July XXXX Invoice Number 1888   €345.50
> 23 July XXXX Invoice Number 2898   €100.20
> 25 July XXXX Credit Note Number 1090   €20.20

and if €400 was paid by cheque on 30 July XXXX (cheque number 10058) by Frank's Newsagent's to Blank Documents that can be Duplicated

Blank Documents that can be Duplicated

SAMPLE QUOTATION

No:

Supplier Name:

Customer Name:

Customer Address:

Telephone:

Date:

The following are the items of agreement that we wish to offer you with the view to doing business with you in the near future.

Terms:

- **Prices and the terms of agreement will be reviewed every 6 months and are subject to change. We ensure that we will give you due notice of any such planned changes.**

We hope that the terms that we are offering you are to your satisfaction and we anticipate trading with you soon.

We will be glad at any time to clarify any queries that you might have regarding our product range.

Yours faithfully

_____

Sales Manager

LETTER OF ENQUIRY

Customer Address:

Date:

Supplier Name and Address:

Dear

Following our phone conversation, kindly forward to me a current Price List of your products. I hope to purchase some of them in the near future.

Yours truly

PURCHASE ORDER

No:

Customer Name:
Customer Address:

Telephone: **Date:**
To:

Code Ref	Quantity	Description	Vat Rate (%)	Unit Price

Delivery Instructions: Delivery by   on

Signed: _____
      Purchasing Officer

DELIVERY DOCKET

From:

No:
Date:
Order No:

Goods: **Quantity**   **Description**   **Code No.**

Received the above goods:

Signed: _____

INVOICE

Supplier name and address:

Telephone:
Fax:
VAT No:
Purchase Order No:
Invoice No:
Date:

Customer Name and Address:

Product Code	Q	Description of product	Price p. unit	VAT 12.5%	VAT 21%	Total

Total

Less Trade Discount
Add VAT

Total Invoice Price

Terms of Trade:

CREDIT NOTE   **Credit Note No:**

Supplier Name and Address:

Telephone:
Fax:
VAT No:
Reference Purchase Order Number:
Reference Invoice Number:

Date:

Customer Name and Address:

DATE	Q	DETAILS	PRICE	TOTAL
		Add VAT @ 21%		
		Total Credit given		

DEBIT NOTE   **Debit Note No:**

Supplier Name and Address

Telephone:
Fax:
VAT No:
Reference Purchase Order Number
Reference Invoice Number

Date:

Customer Name and Address:

DATE	Q	DETAILS	PRICE	TOTAL
		Add VAT @ 21%		
		TOTAL		

STATEMENT OF ACCOUNT

Supplier Name and Address

Statement

To:

Date:
No:

Date	Ref No.	Details	Debit €	Credit €	Balance €

7. Retail Administration

'The retail sector is becoming an increasingly professional one with skills in IT, HR and marketing being in constant demand.' *Sunday Tribune* – June 2002

Many multi-national giants have set up shop in Ireland in recent times due to our positive economic performance – stores like Tesco, BHS, Marks & Spencer and Boots to name just a few.

Retail administration emphasises 'Lateral Co-ordination'. Managers need to know how their organisation works and there is a need to integrate many elements across the whole organisation in areas such as marketing, finance and people (i.e. staff).

This understanding, as well as a willingness to compromise, will help managers manage teams, projects and departments, specifically within the retail environment.

Forfas Report on the Structure of Irish Retailing

OVERVIEW OF THE RETAIL SECTOR

Retailing is defined as the means by which goods and services are provided to consumers in exchange for payment. Retailing thus excludes wholesaling and business-to-business selling. Retailing can be segmented into three distinct categories:

* Predominantly Food Stores
* Predominantly Non-Food Stores
* Non-Store Retailing.

The following is a description of the elements of these categories as used in the report.

PREDOMINANTLY FOOD STORES

Hypermarkets

Hypermarkets are very large retail outlets, which are defined by the OECD as over 2,500 sq. metres, but which are typically much bigger. For example, the average size of new hypermarkets in Europe is typically 7,500 sq. metres. Hypermarkets carry a wide range of food and non-food items. Hypermarkets are sometimes referred to as Superstores, though Superstores focus primarily on food. They are normally sited on the periphery of towns and cities.

Supermarkets

In the main, supermarkets are 1,500 to 2,500 sq metres and are on the edge of towns or town centre locations. Supermarkets contain much of the product ranges and customer services of hypermarkets.

Symbol Groups

Symbol Groups are a group of outlets, that are generally independently owned, operating under a symbol name and co-operating to gain purchase cost savings and, in some instances, develop own-label products. Symbol groups are essentially managed or grouped around a wholesaler.

Convenience Stores

Convenience Stores are small stores, such as forecourt shops and small supermarkets, with a wide food and non-food product range. They are often part of a Symbol Group and sometimes offer a range of own-brand products. These stores are characterised by convenient town, city or suburban locations, generally have extended opening hours and are used mainly for 'top-up' shopping.

Category Management

The practice of category management is increasingly used by large-scale retailers and involves developing a category or range of processes including product development, consumer marketing, promotions to maximise the yield from that category.

Category Killers

Category killers exist where large retail outlets offer a specialised product range in substantial depth but not in breadth.

Independent Stores

These include specialists such as greengrocers, bakers, fish shops, delicatessens as well as large general grocery stores such as family-owned Spar, Mace, Supervalu or Londis stores, and are typically owner-managed.

Discounters

These are retail outlets that offer a range of goods while focusing on offering substantial discounts over other retailers. Discounters are referred to as 'hard' or 'soft' depending on the levels of discounts provided. Own-label products and dry goods often feature significantly in these outlets.

PREDOMINANTLY NON-FOOD STORES

Department Stores

Department stores are typically large city centre shops, generally multi-storey, offering a range of clothing, footwear, personal care and household products. Areas within department stores may be franchised to specialist operators and leading brands.

Boutiques

Boutiques are typically small, single outlets specialising in one manufacturer's products, or a specialist range of clothing and other merchandise.

Multiples

Non-food multiples are supermarket size outlets selling mainly clothing and footwear, but occasionally other items, e.g. sports goods. These shops tend to be at the lower end of the clothing market in price terms, whereas department stores are in the middle to upper price ranges.

Factory Outlets

These are outlets selling the products of a factory, typically branded goods such as clothing.

NON-STORE RETAILING

This sector traditionally includes mail order, door-to-door, vending machines and repairs to products. However, the boundary between this sector and store retailing is becoming blurred as store retailers develop into non-store selling via the Internet, telephone selling and TV shopping.

Supply Chain

The supply chain is the sequence of companies or individuals involved in the process by which raw materials are transformed into products and delivered to the retail outlets for consumer markets. Historically, manufacturers delivered their products to individual stores using their own transport, distribution agents or wholesalers, or some combination of these. This results in numerous deliveries to shops by many suppliers which is seen as ineffective and inefficient.

In other countries, where appropriate to market conditions, RDCs (Regional Distribution Centres) and Consolidation Centres have evolved to simplify the distribution system and rationalise deliveries to stores. This aim is to maximise the use of full loads, and optimise the efficiency of the distribution system.

The function of the RDC is to consolidate the products of various suppliers into deliveries for individual stores and thereby minimise the deliveries to individual stores. To improve the efficiencies of RDCs, consolidation centres are used to receive part loads from suppliers and to consolidate supplies into full loads for delivery to RDCs.

A key feature of the food retail sector in Ireland is the current emergence of a centralised distribution structure amongst major retailers.

The OECD define supermarkets as stores ranging in size from 400 sq. metres to 2,499 sq. metres.
www.forfas.com

What are the Retail Planning Guidelines?

The RPGs are guidelines provided by the Government:
1. to guide local authorities when they are preparing development plans and assessing applications for planning permission
2. to guide retailers and developers in formulating their development proposals.

These guidelines were revised in 2005 and now contain new policies regarding large retail warehouses (underpinned by Section 28 of the Planning and Development Act 2000).

In 2005 the government agreed to change the planning laws, clearing the way for furniture stores like the Swedish giant Ikea to open in Ireland. The 6,000 square metre cap (limit) on shop size was removed. This applies only in Dublin and the eight gateway towns that were identified as designated for urban regeneration or redevelopment. This change will not affect grocery shops and only affects those selling durable goods.

Most Ikea stores around Europe are four times bigger than the maximum size previously allowed in Ireland (64,000 square metres). Environment Minister Dick Roche was criticised by many and accused of setting policy to suit one company.

Advantages of the change to the RPGs:
1. more consumer choice
2. greater retail price competition
3. urban regeneration
4. greater direct employment and spin-off services.

Disadvantages:
1. increased risk of traffic congestion
2. danger that smaller retailers may go out of business
3. smaller suppliers may go out of business.

IKEA opened a new store in Belfast in November 2007 and (as part of government urban regeneration policy) will open another in Ballymun, Dublin in 2008.

Critics include ISME (the Irish Small and Medium Enterprises Association) and RGDATA (the organisation representing retail grocers). They said that government policy set a bad precedent for many Irish businesses that invest in urban regeneration.

The Competition Authority believed that the decision was a positive one for Irish consumers' choices and price competition.

More information is available at www.irishspatialstrategy.ie and at www.environ.ie.

What was the Groceries Order (Restrictive Practices) 1987?

This was an order that banned the selling of goods at below their invoice price (i.e. it banned below-cost selling). It was introduced in 1987 to prevent small shops being driven out of business by large supermarket chains.

The ban was lifted in 2005 when the then Minister for Enterprise announced the end to the Groceries Order (Restrictive Practices). At the same time the minister promised to strengthen the Competition Act to stop unfair price discrimination and to ban 'hello money'.

Advantages of lifting the ban:
1. The National Consumer Agency believed that less well off households who spend more on groceries stood to benefit most.
2. Lower prices for consumers.
3. The market is now more in line with the natural laws of competition/demand and supply.

Disadvantages of lifting the ban:
1. The risk of dominance by a small number of large retailers.
2. RGDATA believed that large multiples would engage in pricing gimmicks and practices reintroducing the idea of loss leaders into Irish retailing.
3. FDII (Food and Drink Industry Ireland) were concerned about fair trade and that the Irish food industry and retailers may operate in a regime with dominance in the marketplace and predatory pricing.
4. The ICMSA (the Irish Creamery Milk Suppliers Association) were concerned that aggressive discounting by retailers could be detrimental to farmers and producers.
5. While that order existed it helped shopping competition to thrive and facilitated real competition in the grocery retail sector. Now there is the risk that multiple retailers will use below-cost selling to further increase their profitability and put smaller competitors out of business.

Different Types of Retail Outlet in Ireland

1. A franchise – the purchase of the right to run a business, usually using a group symbol or name and its shop layout and trading method/characteristics. The business support network is available to the franchise to allow for maximum efficiency and porfitability. Example: Garvey's SuperValu, Limerick.

2. Irish multi-generation family concerns – Arnotts, Clearys, Dunnes Stores, Heatons.
3. Multi-national giants (European retail groups) – BHS, Marks & Spencers, Boots, Dixons, Currys.
4. Multiples – the Musgrave Group (started life in 1876 as a family owned shop in Cork run by two Co. Leitrim brothers – it is still a family run concern). Musgrave rapidly expanded its Centra and Supervalu operations in the 1990s, thereby quadrupling its business. Other symbol groups include Londis and Spar. These shops are franchised out by Musgrave and owned by independent operators. Ninety per cent of the stock, however, is sourced from Musgrave.
5. Other Multiples are Tesco and Dunnes Stores.
6. Other Food Retailers/grocery sector – SuperQuinn.

Features of Different Types of Outlet

MULTIPLES

These are large business operations. Some oversee the operations of multiple shops that are franchised out by it, e.g. the Musgrave Group. Multiple shops are shops that have branches throughout a region or a country e.g. Supervalu, Londis, Centra.

The characteristics of multiples are:

1. Similar range of products and prices available in each branch.
2. Similar branch layout and appearance.
3. Central control of purchasing in Head Office.
4. Independent manager and sometimes owner (in the case of franchises) per branch hired by head office.
5. No credit offered to the public.

Advantages of Multiples

1. No bad debts because no credit purchases by public.
2. Bulk buying means trade discounts can be gained and competitive selling prices offered to public.
3. Slow selling products can be transferred to other policy branches where demand is greater.

Disadvantages of Multiples

1. No credit given to customers.
2. Less personal consumer attention.
3. Local managers have less input into decision-making at head office.

Acquisition shopping as it should be

Paul O'Kane

The Background

Brothers Thomas and Stuart Musgrave opened their first shop in Cork in 1876. They set up their business as a partnership in 1887, trading as Musgrave Brothers. Seven years later it became a limited company.

The Church of Ireland brothers has an abhorrence of alcohol. Articles of association prevented the company from buying, selling or manufacturing alcoholic liquor. This was why the Musgrave-owned Metropole Hotel in Cork didn't obtain a bar licence until 1956.

By 1899 the company had a turnover of over £67,000 – almost €8.5m in today's terms. By the mid-1920s Musgrave was almost exclusively a wholesale business and by the 1930s it was selling to retailers all over Munster.

In the early 1950s Jack Musgrave took over the reins. Musgrave obtained the VG franchise for Ireland from the Netherlands in 1958 for a nominal £1. By the 1970s Musgrave narrowed its focus, eliminating sweet manufacturing in 1977 and its tea business in 1972. It began opening massive cash and carries in the 1970s and by 1977 turnover was almost £30m.

In 1979 Musgrave began to change its VG stores into the new 'voluntary multiples' it had developed, SuperValu and Centra. By 1990 Musgrave had turnover of £380m and pre-tax profit of £9.9m. The group grew rapidly in the '90s, moving into Northern Ireland and into Spain in 1994. In 2000 it paid almost stg£90m to German food distributor REWE for an effective 43% holding in Budgens.

Despite being a €3.5bn operation Musgrave remains a family company: Thomas and Stuart's descendants still own 76% of the firm.

It's a long way from tea blending, boiled sweets and small shopkeepers.

The acquisition of the British retailer Budgens will transform the Musgrave group. Adding Budgens to Musgrave will grow the company's annual sales from €2.3bn to €3.5bn at a stroke and the move also sets the pattern for future growth at the company, according to Musgrave group managing director Seamus Scally. Although Musgrave also has a business in Spain, Britain will now be the focus for expansion.

Musgrave has owned a stake in Budgens since August 2000 when it acquired a 28% shareholding in the business and convertible loan stock which gave a total effective holding of 43% for €138m. Ten days ago it agreed to buy the remainder of the business for €275m in a deal that values Budgens at €492m. During Musgrave's two years as a minority shareholder with board representation, Scally

said the Irish company 'saw nothing that discouraged us from taking the remaining stock'.

Musgrave which started life 126 years ago as a family-owned shop in Cork run by two Co. Leitrim brothers, has finally arrived in the British market. In a way the company's huge success in Ireland in recent years has forced it to look east. During the 1990s Musgrave quadrupled its business by rapidly expanding both its Centra and SuperValu operations. These fascias replaced the VG stores that had been operated by Musgrave and its partners.

'We have 22–23% of the retail market in the Republic so the opportunity for significant growth here is fairly limited,' according to Scally. 'We're building a successful business in the North and felt that the British market most suited us.' Last year the company made pre-tax profits of €47m on sales of €2.27bn.

SuperValu and Centra have made Musgrave a 'virtual multiple', as although the group doesn't physically own any shops in Ireland it has a presence throughout the country. The company has used this system to its advantage when dealing with media, government and regulators. Its executives will argue that small shopkeepers who are part of Centra or SuperValu struggle daily against big bad multiples such as Tesco and Dunnes. But in fact Musgrave is a large multiple, albeit one that uses a franchise-like model. The shops are owned by independent operators but typically more than 90% of stock is sourced from Musgrave. It also advises on site selection, store layout, staffing and training.

The so-called independent grocery sector, which includes symbol groups such as Centra, SuperValu, Londis and Spar, now has 45–50% of the Irish market, according to Scally. While the sector has been aided by the expansion of almost all symbol operators, Musgrave has been responsible for most of the growth. During the 1990s, at a time when Musgrave and its 'small grocers' were threatened by a powerful new arrival in the shape of Tesco, the Cork-based group quadrupled its turnover.

Despite talk of the threat from the multiples, SuperValu and Centra have blossomed, due in part to the public's willingness to pay over the odds for convenience. The group hopes to continue its success by building a new type of convenience operation in Britain. 'The convenience sector was not particularly well done in the UK. It's a stg£100bn market but the independent sector has less than 20%.'

Scally said shortly after Musgrave began to research the British market they came across Budgens and were impressed by the quality of

its stores and its track record. 'They [Budgens] are very close to the business and they see opportunities and gaps created by the multiples when they move to large centres.'

Budgens has 245 outlets in the south of England, mostly convenience stores. It has been adding 15 to 20 shops a year and Musgrave hopes to continue the expansion. Unlike its Irish parent, Budgens actually owns most of its stores, although it also has a small franchise operation. Scally said Musgrave had no plans to sell any Budgens stores to franchisees as 'the [Budgens] model was working very well' but added that building the franchise operation would be 'speeded up'.

The acquisition will leave Musgrave with debts of €450m–€500m. Scally said the acquisition would result in a debt to EBITDA ratio of 3.5. 'That could be considered on the high side but in 2000 the ratio was 2.9 and by 2001 it had been reduced to 2.3. There's a very strong cash flow in this business.'

Scally admits that given the debt incurred as a result of the Budgens deal, Musgrave will probably not be in a position to make another large acquisition in the short term. 'All going well, after about five years we would take a big bite again.'

Budgens is a publicly quoted operation but Musgrave, which is committed to remaining private, intends to cancel the listing. There will be some savings from delisting but the deal offers few synergies as Musgrave has no existing British business and Budgens will be run as a separate entity. Scally said there may be benefits in terms of buying as the group would now have sales of €3.5bn in Britain and Ireland.

While the real expansion focus has shifted to Britain, Scally believes there is still room for organic growth in the Republic.

'We're adding Centra stores at the rate of 20 a year and we see that happening for the next five years at least, while SuperValu is growing by about five to six stores a year and that will also continue. That expansion should get us another 1–2% market share.'

But having invested so much in the deal, the real growth story over the next five years has to be Budgens. 'It's growing at 5% on a like for like basis, which is an attractive proposition. But Budgens has only stg£500m of sales in a £100bn market, that's only about half a percent of the market. It's much easier to grow that in percentage terms than it is when you have 15–20% of the market.'

If Musgrave's future is to stay bright, that future has to be British.

Courtesy of the Sunday Tribune

CHARACTERISTICS OF DEPARTMENT STORES, HYPERMARKETS AND SUPERSTORES

A department store consists of a number of shops, each called a department, housed under the one roof. It is a spacious building with specialised shops/departments dealing in hardware, cosmetics, clothing, furniture, toys etc. The department store also offers other services to the consumer such as restaurant facilities, coffee shops, post-office and banking services. Examples are Arnotts, Clearys, Roches Stores.

Hypermarkets are large stores with a large area of square footage, which usually have only one floor and deal in groceries, cosmetics and a large selection of household goods depending on the time of the year. Examples are Dunnes Stores, Cornelscourt, Dublin and Lidl (German).

Superstores are large stores that deal in a very large variety of housewares, clothes, food and in recent times different departments on different floor levels. Many Dunnes Stores outlets would fall into this category.

ADVANTAGES

1. Parking and improved infrastructure, giving the public ease of access and convenience.
2. Bulk buying means that companies get trade discounts. This results in lower and more competitive selling prices which are attractive to the public.
3. A wide range of goods and services are at hand under the one roof, making it easy for the customer.
4. Open display leads to impulse buying, and this is good for sales.

DISADVANTAGES

1. Lack of personal service to public.
2. Large population and catchment area needed for centre to be a success.
3. Goods may become damaged more quickly, due to open display.
4. Goods are generally mass produced and little attention is given to detail. Home-produced goods are less common.

RETAIL CO-OPERATIVES

Some Co-operatives, such as Thurles Co-operative Creamery Limited, have had a retail outlet attached to the Co-op. In this they sell fresh produce as well as a range of household items to the public. Retail Co-operatives like this are listed in the 'Registrar of Friendly Societies' under the section 'Industrial and Provident Societies – Dairy Section'. Other Co-operatives, such as Knitwear Co-ops, can also have shops attached to them. They are listed under the Other Productive Societies section of the same publication.

The Impact of the Size and Type of a Retail Organisation

1. OWNERSHIP

The larger retail organisation usually has an ownership structure consisting of shareholders, are private or public limited companies or, in recent times, are multi-national companies, e.g. Tesco, Boots, Currys, Dixons. Multiples, department stores, hypermarkets and superstores also generally have this type of ownership structure.

The smaller shop/newsagent can be a sole trader or a partnership. Specialised shops are smaller and are usually units in shopping centres, with independent ownership per unit. Franchises benefit from the symbol group name and support network. Consumer confidence helps the business run efficiently.

The larger retail organisations are highly competitive, and have been mostly responsible for putting the smaller corner store, drapery etc. out of business. However, they have provided a larger variety of choice for the consumer, employment for people and modern facilities for greater convenience.

2. PROFIT SHARING

The small retail outlet, shop, newsagent, either claims all profit for himself/herself, if they are a sole trader, or if it is a partnership, profits will be divided in agreed ratios, according to the Deed of Partnership. (Refer to the section on partnerships in Chapter 1.) There is a greater possibility of owners/shareholders making greater profits in larger retail outlets, because investment capabilities are much greater with more investors as well as bulk buying abilities and the ability to avail of large trade discounts. This means that costs per unit sold are minimised and sales are maximised. They also have the added advantages of reputation. Moreover, advertising in the large outlet is cheaper per unit sold. These benefits due to larger size are called Economies of Scale and are the reasons why larger retail outlets can generate greater profits, despite these profits having to be divided out between the shareholders, usually in line with their profit-sharing ratios.

The large retail outlets that are owned by multi-nationals repatriate profits (bring back profits to their own countries) and this is not good for the economy of the country in which the stores are located. There is also the danger that businesses like the British multi-nationals will in time move back to their home country, causing a large loss of jobs in the country in which they have temporarily located. This is why establishing home-based Irish retail businesses, that start off small and have the possibility of becoming larger with time and track-record, is very much encouraged. This will lead to home-based profits and Irish jobs will then be guaranteed.

3. MANAGEMENT

In general, the larger retail outlet has a head office with Chief Executives and Assistant Executives who monitor the activities of the different branches. Area managers are usually allocated certain branches in a part of the country and each branch has a Manager, Assistant Manager and Supervisors in different departmental areas.

The bigger the retail organisation, the more complex the management structure will be. The smaller retail outlet will probably have one manager who is the owner and possibly an Assistant Supervisor who will monitor activities in the shop/newsagent/corner shop when the owner is not present. (See tall and flat organisational charts in Chapter 1.)

4. ADMINISTRATION

The larger retail outlet will find it cost-effective to employ more modern technology to complete jobs more quickly and efficiently. Most administrative activities are likely to be computerised. There will generally be specialised areas that deal with administration, for example personnel department, sales and marketing department, buying and stores, financial and accounting, etc. (Refer to the functions of management in Chapter 1.)

The smaller retail outlet will not be subdivided into departments and therefore the administration of the business will be probably confined to one office with one secretary or clerk in charge of all paperwork. There will be fewer employees and wages and bookkeeping might be done manually rather than by computer.

5. STAFFING

The staff structure of the larger retail outlet will be more complex than the small outlet. The larger outlet is likely to have a taller organisational structure, which means that a greater number of lines of authority exist and there is a greater variety of subordinates. Employees are usually directly answerable to one superior, who may be a supervisor or sub-manager. The large departmental structure leads to many heads of department. The smaller retail outlet has a smaller organisational staff structure, where staff are usually within close spatial proximity, and owner, supervisor, and usually a small number of other employees with one secretary/clerk make up the total staff. (Refer to Chapter 1.)

Factors that Affect the Location of a Retail Outlet

Retail outlets usually take the following factors into account when they decide to locate:

1. *POPULATION AND MARKET SIZE* – The larger the population in the catchment area, the greater the demand for goods.
2. *INFRASTRUCTURE* – The road network and accessibility to transport – rail, bus – will make it convenient for shoppers and will stimulate demand.
3. *PROXIMITY TO BACK-UP SERVICES AND SUPPLIERS* – Reordering, repairs and maintenance services as well as suppliers should be located nearby, otherwise time and transport costs will pose a problem.
4. *PROXIMITY TO SKILLED LABOUR SUPPLY* – Local skilled labour is an advantage, as travelling expenses will not have to be paid to them and punctuality will be ensured in most cases.
5. *EXCESS LAND AREA/SPACE SURROUNDING OUTLET* – This applies more to the larger retail outlet, with the aim of providing car park space for customers, which is a major advantage with regard to convenience for the customer.
6. *PLANNING LAWS* – Planning permission and by-law considerations have to be taken into account when a retailer is considering setting up his/her business.
7. *CONSIDERING THE LOCATION OF THE NEAREST COMPETITOR* – The business should weigh up whether the competitor will have a significantly adverse effect on sales, or whether the business is diverse enough and popular enough to maintain consumer loyalty and not be affected by the competitor's location.
8. *GOVERNMENT LEGISLATION* – Tax incentives, if available, will encourage a business to locate in a particular area.

The Impact of Location on a Retail Outlet

When a retail outlet successfully locates, having taken into account the factors above, they set out with the aim of maximising sales and demand and minimising costs, thereby maximising profits. Successful location can lead to:

1. Higher profits, and plans to expand.
2. Higher demand for labour – employment.
3. Higher wages for employees and greater purchasing power as a result, as well as job satisfaction.
4. Greater usage of technology and computers – modern laser cash registers, credit card facilities.
5. Diversification of products – modification and improved products including branding goods, as well as new techniques to interest the customer and provide incentives to buy, e.g. discount cards, stamps to avail of cheaper holidays or to purchase goods at a cheaper price.
6. Greater specialisation and management efficiencies.
7. More consumer-friendly policy.

An Organisational Chart of a Large Retail Organisation

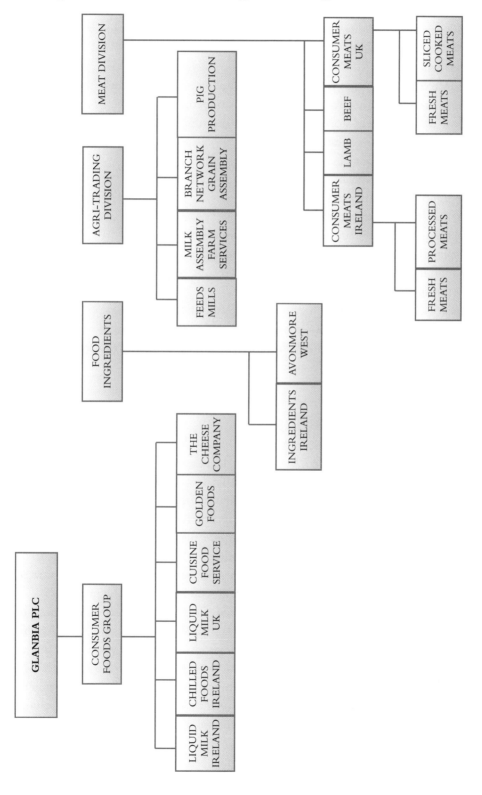

8. Advertising per unit output will be lower as the business grows so more advertising and sales promotion methods might be used.

9. More professional display of goods encouraging impulse buying.

PRACTICE QUESTIONS

1. Define 'Multiples' with reference to retail outlets and explain their characteristics.
2. What are the advantages and disadvantages of being a multiple?
3. How do department stores, hypermarkets and superstores differ?
4. What is a retail co-operative?
5. What are the advantages and disadvantages attached to them?
6. Explain how the size and type of retail outlet can influence:
   (a) the type of ownership required.
   (b) how profits are divided.
   (c) the management organisational structure of the outlet.
7. Explain how the size and type of retail outlet can influence:
   (a) administration procedures.
   (b) staffing levels.
8. What factors influence the location of a retail outlet?
9. What are the implications of good location on a retail outlet?
10. What is EPOS and how do EPOS Systems impact on retailers? (Refer to Chapter 2.)

Legal Aspects of Retailing

THE ESSENTIAL FEATURES OF CONTRACT LAW AS THEY AFFECT THE RETAILER

RGDATA (Retail, Grocery, Dairy and Allied Traders Association) is a representative body for the retail food trade in Ireland. Firms engaged in the retail trade are members of the body. Its aims are to look after the interests of its members and to promote improved efficiency in production and distribution. Its trade journal is available to the public (for a price) and to all members. This gives current trade information and news about trade developments here and abroad. Certain legal services and advice on new or extended premises and layout can be provided.

Other retailers such as bookstores/school suppliers might be members of organisations like the Irish Booksellers Association. Membership of bodies like this keep retailers up to date regarding changes or proposed changes within the area of retailing that concerns them.

A contract is an agreement enforceable by law that retailers, wholesalers, customers and anyone in business must concern themselves with. The following features must exist if a contract is deemed to be valid:

1. OFFER AND ACCEPTANCE

In order to ascertain whether an agreement exists, the offer must be clear, complete and unconditional. The agreement must match the offer exactly and must be communicated to the person who is offered it within a specific time limit in order for it to be legally effective. The offer and acceptance are valid if they are made by word, in writing or by conduct.

- *BY WORD*: In the retail trade, it is very rare that agreements are made orally. An example would be giving goods to a customer who says they will return in an hour's time to pay for them. A better example is the oral agreement that a tenant makes agreeing to pay the required rent to a landlord or landlady.
- *BY CONDUCT*: In the retail trade, a customer in a supermarket or shop who fills their shopping basket with goods is by his or her actions offering to buy the goods. When the checkout assistant accepts the money for the goods, he or she is accepting the offer by actions or conduct.
- *IN WRITING*: When a retailer signs a 'terms of trade' agreement, agreeing to pay the sales agent at the end of every month or when they sign a lease agreement when leasing the business vehicle, the retailer has made payment agreements, the terms of which are outlined in writing.

2. CONSIDERATION

This is the **price** agreed by the parties to the contract. It is the medium of payment whether in the form of goods (barter) or money, a loss or responsibility that is given by one party and subsequently taken by the other party in return for goods or services rendered.

For example Mary offers to purchase Jim's house for €100,000. The €100,000 is the consideration. Even if the house is worth more it is the agreed price that is the consideration. In the retail sector, when the customer indicated his or her intention and offer to purchase by actions and by handing the checkout assistant €100, this is the consideration for the contract. When the checkout assistant takes the money this is the acceptance involved in the contract.

3. CONTRACTUAL CAPACITY

The parties engaging in the agreement must have the capacity to make the contract. The age of majority is 21 years. Anyone entering into a contract with a party below this age is not legally bound to fulfil a contract when it concerns the repayment of money, unless special conditions are attached to it. The contract would be regarded as null and void.

For example in a supermarket, a checkout assistant accepting €5 from a two-year-old child for sweets would not render the transaction valid because of the child's age.

4. *Intention to Create Legal Relations*

The intention of the parties concerned that a legal contract exists must be clear. If you agree to visit a person's house at a particular time on a particular date, this is not a legal contract. 'Intention' alone does not constitute a contract, however.

For example if I go into a supermarket or shop with the intention of buying items and I return home having bought nothing, I am not legally bound to fulfil any contract because the other features of Contract Law have not been adhered to in this case.

5. *Legality of Object*

Some contracts must be in a specific form in writing before they are accepted as being valid. Direct debit mandates and standing orders (discussed in Chapter 2) must be signed before they are accepted. Hire purchase agreements and leases must also be structured in a particular form and signed by the customer of the person entering into the contract.

For example if a retailer wishes to insure his premises against fire and theft he/she must sign a specifically worded insurance form that is issued to him/her by the insurance company with details of what the insurance does and does not cover.

The Implied Conditions that Underlie a Contract for a Sale of Goods under the Sale of Goods and Supply of Services Act 1980

The following conditions are implied in all sale agreements, unless specifically stated:

1. *Merchantable Quality*

It is presumed that all goods for sale are of merchantable quality. This means that if any serious fault exists in the goods, the buyer can take action against the seller for a breach of the implied condition of sale. (Exceptions: a motor vehicle dealer where both parties agree that the vehicle requires repair before use.)

2. *Sale by Sample*

If, for example, a retailer gives a potential customer a sample of the goods on sale, it is reasonable to presume that the goods that will be received by the buyer will correspond (as far as is practicably possible) with the sample. This could be applied to the sale of paint – with colour cards being the sample – or curtains – where sample materials would be provided by the shop assistant.

3. *Sale by Description*

For example, if a firm that fits windows and doors has a brochure with photos and descriptions of the different types of designs available. The buyer receives a door or window that does not fit the original description of the item that he/she agreed to buy. Then the buyer can take action against the seller for breach of the implied condition of sale.

4. FIT FOR PURPOSE

Often when customers are buying, they are relying on the knowledge, expertise and advice of the seller. When a customer informs a seller of the reasons why the goods are required, the implication exists that the seller is verifying that the goods or services are fit for the purpose for which they are going to be used. The buyer can take action against the seller for breach of the implied condition of sale.

5. IMPLIED WARRANTY

When an advertisement for goods or a service appears, and extra conditions are guaranteed with the purchase, such as after sales service, the buyer can take action if these conditions are not honoured.

Another example of a warranty is a guarantee that goods or services will be delivered or provided at the agreed date and time. When a situation occurs where goods are delivered late, the buyer cannot refuse to take them, but he can sue the seller for a decrease in sales and a loss of earnings as a result of the late delivery.

Other Consumer Considerations Relating to the Sale of Goods:

RECOGNITION OF CONSUMER RIGHTS AND REDRESS FOR THE CONSUMER: Statements like 'no liability accepted for faulty goods' CANNOT be publicly displayed and lead to prosecution. Recognition of consumer rights must take precedence.

If the consumer has a reason for complaint he/she must act promptly. Otherwise delays in examining the goods would weaken the case and imply that the fault was caused after the goods were purchased or the service was given.

The Consumer Association of Ireland and Consumer Choice

The Consumer Association of Ireland

The CAI was established in 1966. It investigates complaints regarding consumer goods and services and their conditions of sale. The Association is a non-profit company limited by guarantee.

It is the aim of the CAI to represent and educate Irish consumers within the EU. (It liaises with the Director of Consumer Affairs and other Government bodies, as well as European consumer organisations.) Consumer rights that are represented by the Association include the right to be protected against and compensated for:

1. dishonest advertising or labelling
2. the marketing of unsafe goods and services
3. the marketing of goods and services where prices charged are clearly not in line with expected quality standards.

If the CAI's legal team feel that a particular complaint warrants representation, the consumer can apply for this representation for a set fee.

'CONSUMER CHOICE MAGAZINE' is produced by the Consumer Association and members of the public can subscribe to it to keep themselves aware of consumer issues and changes in legislation regarding consumer rights.

THE BANKS' CUSTOMER SERVICE CHARTER dictates that customers have the right to a prompt, fair and equitable investigation of banking problems and have also a right to redress if the bank is at fault.

Consumer Information Act 1978

Any breach of the conditions of the Act legally entitles the customer to a full refund or some amount of compensation.

The following is *a summary* of the situations in which such entitlements may arise:

1. *misleading information* on products or services and/or a false trade description of same – both producer and retailer would be liable (Act applies to supply, sale, possession and advertising of goods and services)
2. *false claims* about products or services made by, for example, a sales person – reckless claims makes this person liable
3. display products with accessories attached but the price of accessories not included in display price (implied warranty that goods are free from *hidden cost* to other parties)
4. a retailer is responsible under a manufacturer's *guarantee* and a consumer can claim from both
5. *unsolicited goods* – sending goods to people who did not order them and seeking payment. Any person who received such goods may keep them once they have given 30 days' written notice that the goods were not required
6. motor vehicles – usual conditions of purchase apply, once the car is free from defect that might cause danger to the driver, public or passenger. The exceptions are:
   (a) where the buyer is in the motor trade (implied condition does not apply)
   (b) if both parties agree that the vehicle will not be used in the condition it is in.
7. The NCT – National Car Test Certification – guarantees that consumers now have peace of mind when purchasing a used car. The vehicle must meet the requirements laid down by the Department of Transport and is unlikely to be purchased without a recent NCT cert.

SMALL CLAIMS COURT

The Small Claims Court is a consumer service for complainants with claims for damages that amount to a relatively small sum of money. The Small Claims Registrar conducts the proceedings in the District Court. The good or service must have been bought for private use from a business. If the consumer purchases a faulty product and the retailer, having been informed, does nothing, the Small Claims Registrar will try to settle the dispute. If this fails, the parties will be referred to the District Court.

The Role of the Director of Consumer Affairs

The principal functions of the Director of Consumer Affairs are:

- To inform the public of their rights as consumers.
- To conduct investigations under a wide range of consumer protection legislation.
- To prosecute offences as provided for by statute, e.g. breaches of the Consumer Credit Act 1995, false or misleading advertising under the provisions of the Consumer Information Act 1978, food-labelling regulations and general product safety legislation.
- To keep under review practices or proposed practices by business generally which could impact negatively on the rights provided by statute for the consumer.
- To license or authorise moneylenders, pawnbrokers, and mortgage and credit intermediaries as provided for in the Consumer Credit Act 1995.
- To seek High Court Orders in certain circumstances.
- To monitor customer charges by credit institutions and to issue directions in relation to increases in existing charges and charges for new services/products.
- To promote codes of practice.

The structure of the office is mainly divided into:
(a) Consumer Credit Section.
(b) Consumer Protection Section.

(Refer to **www.odca.ie** for more information.)
These functions may be changed or enhanced by the expansion of consumer protection at European Union level – as indicated in the Amsterdam treaty.

PRACTICE QUESTIONS
1. What is RGDATA?
2. List and explain the conditions that must exist for a contract to be valid.
3. What is the Sale of Goods and Supply of Services Act 1980 and what conditions of sale are implied by this Act?

4. What is consumer redress? List three organisations or institutions that consumers can turn to in order to gain redress.
5. Write a note on the Consumer Association of Ireland (CAI).
6. What are the main conditions that underpin the Consumer Information Act 1978?
7. Write a note on the Small Claims Court.
8. What are the main functions of the Director of Consumer Affairs?

Retail Administration

Portfolio of Coursework – Sample Assignment

A CASE STUDY OF AN ORGANISATION

Note: Students should refer to Chapter 1, in particular how students can research organisations, SWOT and PEST analyses before attempting this assignment.

Choose an organisation with which you are familiar or one that will be easy to approach for information and examine a range of the following aspects of the organisation:

- location
- structure (organisational chart)
- ownership
- environmental factors (PEST plus Competition – refer to Chapter 1)
- staffing
- administration
- stock control
- pricing strategy

Note: Any other details given are extra and will earn marks for initiative and originality.

- Work placements can be chosen for analysis.

A Retail Case Study – A School Bookshop

Introduction

This case study aims to explore how a retail outlet, in this case a bookshop/school book supplier, started business and progressed to its current state. Areas of analysis will include the history of the business, its start-up characteristics, advertising, pricing, costs, factors affecting location, safety, health and hygiene procedures and the life cycle of the business. An analysis of its strengths and weaknesses will be carried out. Future opportunities or plans will be enquired into and threats to the business will be pin-pointed. Finally, an analysis of political, economic, social and technological factors that affect the business, or have affected it in the past, will be carried out.

History of the Business

The business was originally established in June 1988. It was located in a first-floor rented unit over a bank in the main street of a small town in Ireland. The owners then decided to relocate at street level in another rented unit on the main street.

The son of the previous owners now owns the shop and has been trading as a sole trader since May 1995. The shop unit in which the business is now located, which was previously a drapery/wool shop, has a larger floor area − 490 square foot approximately.

Set-Up Procedure and Qualifications or Work Experience Necessary to be Successful

Before occupying the unit, it was necessary to invest €15,000 to refurbish it completely. Included in this cost figure was the cost of improvements including ceiling, carpets, walls and lights. The layout of the unit had to be changed completely to make it suitable for a bookshop.

The owner concluded that previous experience of the school retail trade is not absolutely essential for success in retailing. However, some knowledge of the retail trade with regard to books together with appropriate work experience with educational printers, publishers or suppliers like Folens would be an advantage. Experience in receiving orders (types of orders) and previous knowledge of teachers' margins (how many books they might order and under what criteria they order), and publishers' margins would give the entrepreneur wishing to specialise in school supplies (as opposed to more general books) the edge.

Market Research

The daughter of the former owners also takes an active part in the business and undertook the market research. She investigated other bookshops and realised while carrying out this fieldwork that this town was the only town in the region that didn't have a school supplier.

Insurance/Health and Safety Considerations

The business is covered by full Public Liability insurance.

Advertising Before and After Opening

It was estimated that €300 approximately was spent on printing flyers while renovations were being carried out on the unit. These were distributed around the locality. Shortly after opening, an intensive marketing strategy was undertaken by the owners in schools. They provided in-school demonstrations of products, backed up by a catalogue and back-to-school prices quoted for teachers. Most of the arrangements for meeting teachers were made through the principals in the schools and teachers were often invited back to the shop to view the products if time did not allow for it during the day. Long hours after normal trading hours were spent working in order to gain the existing market share.

Expert personal selling techniques and follow-up phone calls, as well as call-in procedures used in order to secure sales, were regarded as key methods of gaining business.

Change in Work Philosophy, Advertising and Target Market

The owners decided to adopt a different work ethos that incorporated a change of emphasis on product range and mix. There was to be more direct selling to schools. The visiting of schools was a major generator of business. Twenty to twenty-five schools are now ordering and buying from the shop whereas two years ago this was not the case.

In more recent times, as well as keeping up the momentum with regard to personal selling, the business has also purchased advertisements in local publications and sports clubs, and has sponsored jerseys for local soccer clubs. The shop holds a January and May Sale, and the January Sale appears to be the most effective.

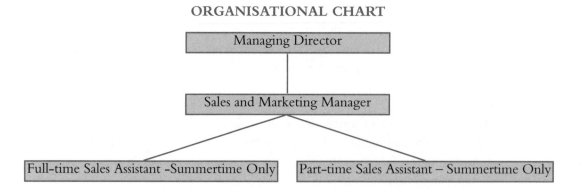

ORGANISATIONAL CHART

Managing Director

Sales and Marketing Manager

Full-time Sales Assistant -Summertime Only

Part-time Sales Assistant – Summertime Only

Functions of Staff

1. MANAGING DIRECTOR

The managing director controls the financial affairs of the business as he is a qualified accountant. He is responsible for the monthly management of accounts. Once a year he submits his tax and VAT returns to be signed off by a firm of accountants. He also takes an active part in the running of the shop and the marketing of products.

2. SALES AND MARKETING MANAGER

The function of the Sales and Marketing Manager is to take charge of the overall marketing of products. She is directly involved in selling to schools, wholesale ordering, dealing with customers, agreeing the end-of-day till balance with opening cash and sales for the day and many other day-to-day routine business dealings.

Ordering is done during the day and in the evening. The efficient suppliers' fax lines are open in the evening and at night after business hours. This facilitates the ordering procedure, particularly at peak trading times of the year.

3. FULL-TIME AND PART-TIME SALES ASSISTANTS

Both of those employees are employed in the peak summertime period only. They are responsible for looking after customer needs, handling cash and other means of payment as well as keeping an account of order requirements. They are also responsible for keeping the shop tidy and in good order.

Business Hours, Type of Stock for Sale, Suppliers and Trading Cycle

Regular business hours are from 9.30am to 6pm Monday to Saturday.

The product and service range consists of:
1. School books (new and second-hand), school stationery and school supplies (arts and crafts).
2. Office and general stationery.
3. Novels and other books (adult, children's, educational materials for younger age groups).
4. Services such as photocopying, faxing and laminating.

The stationery suppliers are Musgraves', Easons, Deales and Morton. The school book and other book suppliers and publishers are: Modern Languages (who have a shop and act as wholesalers), Fallons, Folens, Gill & Macmillan, Educational Company, Celtic Press, AIS, Veritas, Mentor Press, Exemplar Press and Topics Publications.

A large proportion of the annual turnover is generated in the period from 1 June to 30 September. This is mainly due to the demand for school supplies during this time. It is during this time that the demand for the two extra employees occurs every year.

With regard to the life cycle of the business, from 1995 to 1998 has been a 'Growth' stage and the business has not reached its peak as yet – that is, the 'Mature' stage of the life cycle.

October, November and December see a peak in demand for novels in the run-up to Christmas. The Christmas peak generally runs into January when a sale of goods is displayed in the shop front. January is also busy because of the Honours to Pass or vice versa changes in schools and the demand for revision titles and exam papers.

February to May is the off-peak period and this time is used to plan for the forthcoming peak period. If any alterations need to be made to the way the business runs or to its premises, this is the time to make them.

Factors affecting Location

The reasons for the choice of location

1. The town was the only town in the region that did not have a school supplier.
2. The young population meant that a sustained demand for schoolbooks existed in the region.
3. Previous experience in an upstairs location proved that street level was a priority for a retail outlet specialising in schoolbooks and supplies.

The problems with the location

1. It is not close enough to suppliers. (Many suppliers won't deliver due to distance from Dublin.) Costs in terms of time and money are incurred because of delivery problems.
2. There is a shortage of adequate parking along the main street. This is one of the explanations for the stunted growth in retailing along the main street.
3. The lack of passing trade might also be caused by the commercial underdevelopment of the main street.
4. There are threats of future competition because of the relative closeness of the town to busy shopping areas.

Daily and End-of-Day Routine Regarding Cash and Stock Control, as well as General Yearly Stock Control

Every day, the delivery dockets are checked against deliveries and then later checked against order forms and invoices received from the suppliers. When ordering is completed every evening, it is necessary to count the cash. The procedure referred to as 'Agreeing the Till' is undertaken. The control of cash is a priority in a retail outlet.

There are three stock-takes each year, one on 31 May, the second at the end of September/beginning of October, and the third in February/March. Everything in the shop is counted. Then the school order forms are counted and checked against stock.

A minimum stock holding is best in the area of school books because syllabi change yearly and surplus stock would be be impossible to sell into the school year and make a loss.

Pricing Policy

1. The retail outlet has no control over the prices of school books, other general books or novels. The publishers and suppliers have complete control over this. Retail shops, however, get 35% commission on novels and 20% commission on the sale of school books.
2. As regards stationery, the shop can price up from cost higher than the margin set by the suppliers. In this case a 40%–45% mark-up is worthwhile.

Quality and Quality Control

Customers demand that when buying a new book it must look untouched. As near to this as possible applies to second-hand books. School books have to be current and on the book list and in reasonably good condition.

Regarding 'returns' there is often the pretence that the book was bought in the retail outlet whereas in fact a price sticker indicates to the contrary. This is referred to as 'Swop Pretence'.

The customer will dictate the standards regarding quality, and will not buy the book or supply unless it conforms to a certain level of quality.

European Regulations

Novels published in the UK will be priced in both sterling and euro on the price form. Currently there is no VAT on books, however this could change depending on European regulations.

A SWOT Analysis of the Business

Strengths

- Location at street level on a main street.
- Family-run business, therefore security and customer loyalty through family links.
- Only school supplier in the town.
- School loyalty – unwritten guarantee of business.
- Good relationship with banks.

Weaknesses

- Shop layout and size.
- Parking problems.
- Passing trade problem due to underdevelopment of the main street.
- Schoolbook returns are approximately 5%.

- Delivery problems on supplier side, and time and cost of delivering to schools.
- Stock out too often – need to review stocking procedure.

Opportunities
- Expansion will depend on future competition in and near the area.
- Possible further diversification of product and service range.

Threats
- Other similar shops in nearby towns, as well as existing and planned shopping complexes where people can shop for everything including school books.
- The decision to make outlets on the main street residential rather than commercial premises. Passing trade would be virtually non-existent if this happened and would adversely affect the business.

A PEST Analysis of the Business

Political Factors
Family links and good relationships with banks, Chamber of Commerce, clubs that the business sponsored, publishers and authors are factors that positively influence the business.

Economic Factors
- The 'boom' in the economy has meant more houses being built in the area and therefore a larger school-going population which translates into a higher demand for school books and supplies and other book store products and services.
- More finance is readily available from banks and financial institutions and interest rates are relatively low, so the cost of borrowing for renovations is low.
- More money has allowed the business to expand its range of products and services and to diversify.

Social Factors
- The change in the style of selling was part of a new work ethos fuelled by 'the competitive urge'. The success of the marketing strategy that has been employed since 1995 has brought in more customers. Personal selling has achieved the objective of gaining customer confidence as well as convincing them to sample the diverse product and service range that is readily available either in the shop, or which can be ordered in.

Technological Factors
- The business has made use of a new computerised ordering system called 'EROS' which is operated via Eason's Bookshop's modem. The procedure involves

ordering through a bar code or by typing the title or author. The message is sent through via phone link, and provides an efficient and prompt service.

Conclusion

This sample retail case study of a bookshop has highlighted the importance of interpersonal skills and personality in the path to securing future business. Personal selling together with the knowledge that a sustainable market share exists and the youthful ambition to succeed describes adequately the work that was undertaken by the owners. The doubling of turnover since 1995 is evidence of the success of the venture. The diversification of products and services together with the structural improvements that were made to the unit equally contributed to the business's success to date. Finally, despite the weaknesses that were listed, it is encouraging to see how a zestful, refreshing and ambitious marketing strategy can be successful.

PRACTICE QUESTIONS

1. What are the Retail Planning Guidelines?
2. What was the Groceries Order (Restrictive Practices) 1987?
3. What is a Symbol Group?
4. What is a Franchise?
5. Define 'Multiples' with reference to retail outlets and explain their characteristics.
6. What are the advantages and disadvantages of being a Multiple?
7. How do Department Stores, Hypermarkets and Superstores differ?
8. What is a Retail Co-operative? What are the advantages and disadvantages of retail co-operatives?
9. Explain how the size and type of retail outlet can influence:
    a) the type of ownership required
    b) how profits are divided
    c) the management organisational structure of the outlet.
10. Explain how the size and type of retail outlet can influence:
    a) administration procedures
    b) staffing levels.
11. What factors influence the location of a retail outlet?
12. What are the implications of good location for a retail outlet?
13. What is EPOS and how do EPOS systems impact on retailers? (Refer to Chapter 2.)
14. What is RGDATA?
15. List and explain the conditions that must exist for a contract to be valid.
16. What is the Sale of Goods and Supply of Services Act 1980 and what conditions of sale are implied by this Act?
17. What is consumer redress? List three organisations or institutions that consumers can turn to in order to gain redress.

18. Write a note on the Consumer Association of Ireland (CAI).
19. What are the main conditions that underpin the Consumer Information Act 1978?
20. Write a note on the Small Claims Court.
21. What are the main functions of the Director of Consumer Affairs?

8. Sample Exam Papers

Business Administration

Time Allowed: 2 hours

- Answer 10 out of 12 questions in Section A
- Answer two out of three questions in Section B

Section A

- Answer 10 out of 12 questions in this section.

1. List four environmental features that affect an organisation.

2. What are Quality Circles?

3. How does the Formal Organisation differ from the Informal Organisation?

4. List three functions of the Human Resources Department in an organisation.

5. With regard to meetings, what is a motion?

6. Explain the term EPOS.

7. Illustrate, by sketching, the differences between a Component Bar Chart and a Multiple Bar Chart.

8. What is Factoring?

9. In each of the following cases, what document is compiled in order to indicate:
   (a) an undercharge
   (b) a return of goods
   (c) an overcharge
   (d) an omission from an invoice?

10. With regard to Communication, what is the difference between 'Effectiveness' and 'Efficiency'?

11. Who are the Social Partners and what is Collective Bargaining?

12. What is the purpose of a Cash Flow Chart?

Section B

- Answer two out of three questions from this section.

1. (a) Draw the Control Network Diagram and the Gantt Chart.
   (b) Explain how quality control in business is maintained by linking the two illustrations mentioned in (a) to the four most widely used quality control measures.
   (c) Write a note on three quality marks that you are familiar with.

2. (a) Explain the procedures to convert from an Unlimited Partnership to a Private Limited Company.
   (b) What is the purpose of the Deed of Partnership and how is it connected with 'The Partnership Act 1890'?
   (c) What is the difference between the 'Certificate of Incorporation' and the 'Trading Certificate'?

3. (a) Explain the Principles of Insurance.
   (b) Write a note on each of the following:
       i. IBA.
       ii. Premium.
       iii. Comprehensive Insurance.
       iv. Fidelity Guarantee.
       v. Life Assurance.

Business Administration

Time Allowed: 2 Hours

- Answer 10 out of 12 questions in Section A.
- Answer two out of three questions in Section B.

Section A

- Answer 10 out of 12 questions in this section. (Two marks each)

1. List two purposes of the ICTU.

2. List two reasons for differences between a tall and a flat organisational pyramid. Illustrate.

3. List three benefits of a tight credit control policy.

4. With regard to insurance what is the meaning of Indemnity?

5. What is the 'Deed of Partnership?

6. List three Quality Awards.

7. What does a Gantt Chart measure?

8. What is a Certificate of Incorporation?

9. What is the meaning of 'Credit Terms'?

10. Name three common room layout arrangements made before a meeting.

11. What type of organisation is a Credit Union?

12. Give one Irish example each of the following:
    - A non-trading state body.
    - A trading semi-state body.

Section B

   - Answer two questions from this section. (10 marks each)

1. (a) How do price lists differ from quotations?
   (b) Write a note on each of the following:
       i. Terms of trade.
       ii. Discounts given in business.
   (c) Examine the price list given (attached). The following was the order faxed to All Weather Paints from McCarthy & Sons Ltd., Cruises Street, Limerick on 21/1/XX.
       2 PIN 75 purple
       4 PIN 80 white
       6 PIN 110 yellow
       5 Sp 110
       Interior Design Service (from a previous job, to be included in next invoice) €35 net figure. (VAT rates are indicated on the price list.)

Based on the information given:
   i. Compile the Invoice number 2200 sent to McCarthy & Sons Ltd., on 21/1/XX.

    ii. Compile the business document sent to McCarthy & Sons Ltd., document number 511, on 22/1/XX when McCarthy returned five damaged tins of the six paint tins code PIN 110.

    iii. Draft the January Statement of Account dated 31/1/XX, if McCarthy's balance owed to All Weather Paints for January XXXX was €200 and the following additional transactions had taken place in January:

- 4/1/XX Invoice number 2008 – €150 (Received by McCarthy).
- 14/1/XX Cheque Payment number 1000013 made to All Weather paints – €50.
- 18/1/XX Invoice number 2100 – €160.

2. (a) Give one example each of a short-term, medium-term and long-term workforce (workforce) gap.

    (b) Distinguish between the terms 'Job Description' and 'Job Specification'.

    (c) Explain and illustrate Maslow's Pyramid of Hierarchy of Needs.

3. (a) List and briefly explain the six main functions of management.

    (b) Explain the differences between three different types of minutes that are taken at meetings.

    (c) Write a note on the following terms used at meetings:

      i. An Addendum

      ii. A Resolution

      iii. Standing Order

      iv. A Quorum

PRICE LIST OF PAINT PRODUCTS
ALL WEATHER PAINTS

WEATHERFIELD, THURLES, CO. TIPPERARY
VAT NO. 2345678D   **ALL PRICES QUOTED ARE IN EURO**

PRODUCT CODES	DESCRIPTION OF PRODUCTS	VAT	PRICE
P(IN) 75	Interior Matt 1lt	B	7.50
P(IN) 50	Interior Gloss 1lt	B	9.00
P(IN) 80	Interior Vinyl Silk 1lt	B	7.50
P(IN) 100	Interior Eggshell (Alkyd) 1 lt	B	11.00
P(IN) 110	Interior Eggshell (Acrylic) 1 lt	B	8.50
P(Ex)150	Exterior Matt 2.5 lt	B	12.00
P(Ex)90	Exterior Matt 10lt	B	37.00
P(Misc)120	Scrumble Trans Oil Glaze 2.5 lt	B	45.00
Br200	Badger Softener	B	41.00
Br195	Stencil Brush	B	1.50
Br90	Sable Writer	B	7.00
Br12	Paint Brush 1.5 inch, pure bristle	B	6.00
Br14	Paint Brush 2 inch, pure bristle	B	10.00
Br16	Paint Brush 2.5 inch, pure bristle	B	12.00
Br18	Paint Brush 3 inch, pure bristle	B	15.00
Br20	Paint Brush 4 inch, pure bristle	B	25.00
Br22	Paint Brush 6 inch, pure bristle	B	30.00
Sp 110	Sea Sponge (Synthetic)	B	7.50
Sp 120	Marine Natural Sea Sponge (Lge)	B	40.00
Sp80	Marine Natural Sea Sponge (Sml)	B	30.00
Pap100	Wall Stripper	B	250.00
Pap120	Wallpaper Table	B	15.00
Pap130	Wallpaper Hanging Brush	B	20.00
Pap133	Seam Roller	B	4.50
Sc170	Scaffolding 4ft h x 3.5 ft w	B	70.00
WSp 12	White Spirit (Sm)	B	2.00
WSp 14	White Spirit (Lge)	B	4.75
Ro186	Roller (9 Inch)	B	12.50
Ro120	Roller (6 Inch)	B	6.50
Ro124	Roller Extention Poll	B	15.00
SERVICE	INTERIOR DESIGNER	A	QUOTE

Large Range of Paints and Wallpaper available

VAT CODES   A = 12.5%   B = 21%

FETAC Retail Administration Exam, Summer 2006

Answer 4 out of the following 5 structured questions

1. (a) List *6* Functions of Management.
    (b) Explain *4* of these functions and how they might relate to a Retail Organisation.
    (c) List *2* factors that a retailer would take into account when deciding on where to locate.

2. (a) What is a Quality Circle?
    (b) List and explain *4* ways that retailers use to control quality in an effort to maintain quality standards.
    (c) List *3* standard quality marks and in each case indicate who certifies them.

3. (a) What was the Grocery Orders Act?
    (b) Why was it featured in the Media in recent times?
    (c) How will the changes regarding the Act affect
        1. retailers
        2. consumers?

4. Write a short note on *each* of the following:
    (a) The Sale of Goods and Supply of Services Act.
    (b) The Consumer Association of Ireland.
    (c) The Director of Consumer Affairs.
    (d) EPOS.
    (e) Cash flow forecasts.

5. John Rene Men's Fashion Ltd. delivered the following goods to Top Hat Men's Shop Ltd on 5/5/06. (The following figures are selling prices inclusive of VAT @ 21%.)
    15 pairs of Clark's Men's Shoes €428
    5 Louis Copeland Men's Suits €1500
    5 boxes of Men's Assorted Accessories (sunglasses, ties, etc.) €600
    (a) Work back to the figures before VAT was added, i.e the net figures.
    (b) Construct the Invoice (Number 20567) incorporating a 10% trade discount and then add the VAT.
    (c) Distinguish between the use of a Credit Note and a Debit Note.

(d) John Rene Men's Fashion Ltd undercharged Top Hat Men's Shop Ltd by €30 (inclusive of VAT). Draft the appropriate document number 296A, sent on 6/5/06.

(e) On 10/5/06 Top Hat Men's Shop Ltd paid €1000 to John Rene Men's Fashion Ltd and paid off another €400 on 20/5/06. Draft the Statement of Account dated 31/5/06 that John Rene Men's Fashion Ltd sent to Top Hat Men's Shop Ltd, taking into account that the opening balance of €200 existed on 1/5/06.

Retail Administration, Summer 2007

This exam paper contains 5 structured questions.
Candidates must attempt to answer 4 out of 5 questions.

1. (a) What are the RPGs? (5 marks)
   (b) Why have they featured in the media? (5 marks)
   (c) What are the arguments for and against changing the RPGs? (5 marks)

2. (a) What is the role of the Ombudsman? (5 marks)
   (b) Explain 2 main functions of the Director of Consumer Affairs. (4 marks)
   (c) Briefly list and explain the main 3 functions of Management. (6 marks)

3. (a) Write notes on the following:
   • The Sale of Goods Act 1980
   • The effect of Contract Law on the Retailer
   • EPOS systems
   • The difference between a Multiple and a Symbol Group
   • The meaning of a Franchise (15 marks)

4. (a) Carry out a PEST plus C analysis of a Retail outlet of your choice.
   (8 marks)
   (b) What is a SWOT analysis and why would a manager consider it important to carry one out often in a Retail Outlet? (7 marks)

Brian O' Driscoll, Thomond Park, Limerick purchased the following items from Limerick Sports Store, Mulgrave Street, Limerick:

Code	Quantity	Description	Price per unit	VAT
GS	10	Gum Shields	€15	21%
MJ	20	Munster Jerseys	€50	21%
KHS	20	Knee High Socks	€8	21%

Brian avails of a 10% trade discount.

Brian's telephone number is 061 959595, if there are any queries with his order.

Draw up the following documents based on this information:

(a) Purchase Order, number 666, date 10/10/2007   (3 Marks)

(b) Delivery Docket, number 789, date 12/10/2007   (3 Marks)

(c) Invoice, number 484, date 12/10/2007   (5 Marks)

VAT is charged @ 21%.

(d) Brian found that 12 jerseys were ripped so he returned all 12 of them. You are required to make the appropriate adjustment by compiling the Credit Note number 137, date 28/10/2007 that was sent out.   (4 Marks)

Retail Administration

Time allowed: 2 hours.

Please answer four out of the following five questions.

1. Read the following extract and answer the questions that follow it.

Michael Jordan is Managing director of Leoware Ltd., a large multiple which incorporates multiple shops. A department store and hypermarket are located near one of the Limerick multiple shops. This did not seem to affect business, however. Michael believed that a mixture of consumer loyalty and a good marketing strategy were the reasons why the market share had not been affected. The future plan was to diversify and to do so Michael planned to look for either medium-term or long-term sources of finance. Michael planned to make other improvements in the business such as tightening up the credit control policy in the business. This should help profitability and cash flow.

(a) How do multiples, department stores and hypermarkets differ? Give a clear explanation.

(b) In the context of retailing what is the meaning of 'to diversify'?

(c) Distinguish between medium-term and long-term sources of finance. Give two examples of each.

(d) Outline the impact of a business' credit control policy on the profitability of a retail outlet.

2. (a) Define the meaning of 'Trade Union'.

(b) Distinguish between the role of a Trade Union at:
   i. Workplace level.
   ii. Branch level.
   iii. National level.

3. (a) With reference to stock control, what factors will affect a business that wishes to maintain an optimum level of stock? Explain these implications in your own words.

(b) Differentiate between minimum stock and maximum stock and the problems with both.

4. Beauty Depot Supplies Ltd. delivered the following goods to Mary French & Company Ltd., Beauty Salon on 8/8/XX. (The following figures are selling prices inclusive of VAT.)

   10 Boxes Maljay Moisturiser €500
   15 Boxes Disposable Electrolysis Equipment €200
   1 Box Sunbed Bulbs €120

(a) Work back to the figures before VAT was added, i.e. the net figures.

(b) Construct the invoice (number 18564) incorporating a 10% trade discount and then add the VAT at 21%.

(c) Distinguish between the use of a credit note and a debit note.

(d) Beauty Depot Supplies Ltd., undercharged Mary French & Co. by €20 (Figure inclusive of VAT at 21%). Draft the appropriate document that was sent to Mary French & Co. to correct the mistake – document number 35878, sent on 9/8/XX.

(e) On 10/8/XX Mary French & Co. paid €100 to Beauty Depot and paid off another €100 on 20/8/XX. Draft the Statement of Account dated 31/8/XX that Beauty Depot sent to Mary French & Co. taking into account that the opening balance of €50 existed on 1/8/XX.

5. Write notes on the following:

(a) Sale of Goods Act 1980.
(b) Roles of the Irish Ombudsman.
(c) Roles of the Director of Consumer Affairs.
(d) Indemnity (in the context of Insurance).
(e) Control – one of the functions of management.